OXFORD STUDIES IN
CULTURAL ANTHR

### CULTURAL FORMS

This book is published by Oxford University Press thanks to the general editorship of Howard Morphy, University Lecturer in Ethnology at Oxford and Curator at the Pitt Rivers Museum, and Fred Myers, Associate Professor of Anthropology at New York University.

ALSO PUBLISHED BY OXFORD UNIVERSITY PRESS

Organizing Jainism in India and England
*Marcus Banks*

Anthropology, Art, and Aesthetics
*Edited by Jeremy Coote and Anthony Shelton*

Global Migrants, Local Lives: Travel and Transformation
in Rural Bangladesh
*Katy Gardner*

Wrapping in Images: Tattooing in Polynesia
*Alfred Gell*

Contested Hierarchies: A Collaborative Ethnography of Caste in the
Kathmandu Valley, Nepal
*Edited by David N. Gellner and Declan Quigley*

The Female Bridegroom: A Comparative Study of Life-Crisis
Rituals in South India and Sri Lanka
*Anthony Good*

Of Mixed Blood: Kinship and History in Peruvian Amazonia
*Peter Gow*

Wrapping Culture: Politeness, Presentation, and Power in Japan
and other Societies
*Joy Hendry*

The Anthropology of Landscape: Perspectives on Place and Space
*Edited by Eric Hirsch and Michael O'Hanlon*

The Archetypal Actions of Ritual: A Theory of Ritual Illustrated by
the Jain Rite of Worship
*Caroline Humphrey and James Laidlaw*

The People of the Alas Valley: A Study of an Ethnic Group
of Northern Sumatra
*Akifumi Iwabuchi*

Riches and Renunciation: Religion, Economy, and Society Among the Jains
*James Laidlaw*

The Interpretation of Caste
*Declan Quigley*

The Arabesk Debate: Music and Musicians in Modern Turkey
*Martin Stokes*

Inside The Cult: Religious Innovation and Transmission
in Papua New Guinea
*Harvey Whitehouse*

# UNWRAPPING CHRISTMAS

EDITED BY

Daniel Miller

CLARENDON PRESS · OXFORD

*This book has been printed digitally and produced in a standard design in order to ensure its continuing availability*

# OXFORD
UNIVERSITY PRESS

Great Clarendon Street, Oxford OX2 6DP

Oxford University Press is a department of the University of Oxford.
It furthers the University's objective of excellence in research, scholarship,
and education by publishing worldwide in

Oxford New York

Athens Auckland Bangkok Bogotá Buenos Aires Cape Town
Chennai Dar es Salaam Delhi Florence Hong Kong Istanbul Karachi
Kolkata Kuala Lumpur Madrid Melbourne Mexico City Mumbai Nairobi
Paris São Paulo Shanghai Singapore Taipei Tokyo Toronto Warsaw

with associated companies in Berlin Ibadan

Oxford is a registered trade mark of Oxford University Press
in the UK and in certain other countries

Published in the United States
by Oxford University Press Inc., New York

ISBN 0–19–828066–1

For Richard

# CONTENTS

*List of Contributors*                                                          ix

## I. INTRODUCTION

1. Daniel Miller, *A Theory of Christmas*                                         3
2. Claude Lévi-Strauss, *Father Christmas Executed*                             38

## II. CHRISTMAS AND MATERIALISM

3. James Carrier, *The Rituals of Christmas Giving*                             55
4. Russell Belk, *Materialism and the Making of the Modern
   American Christmas*                                                          75
5. Brian Moeran and Lise Skov, *Cinderella Christmas:
   Kitsch, Consumerism, and Youth in Japan*                                    105
6. Daniel Miller, *Christmas against Materialism in Trinidad*                  134

## III. CHRISTMAS AND THE FAMILY

7. Adam Kuper, *The English Christmas and the Family:
   Time out and Alternative Realities*                                         157
8. Mary Searle-Chatterjee, *Christmas Cards and the
   Construction of Social Relations in Britain Today*                          176
9. Barbara Bodenhorn, *Christmas Present: Christmas Public*                    193
10. Orvar Löfgren, *The Great Christmas Quarrel and
    Other Swedish Traditions*                                                  217

*Index*                                                                        235

# LIST OF CONTRIBUTORS

*Russell Belk* is N. Eldon Tanner Professor in the David Eccles School of Business at the University of Utah. Amongst a number of previous appointments he spent 1991–2 teaching at the University of Criova, Romania. He is author and editor of twelve books and monographs and 150 articles and chapters. His work is primarily concerned with the meanings of possessions and materialism.

*Barbara Bodenhorn* is a Fellow and College Lecturer at Pembroke College, University of Cambridge. Her main publications and current researches are concerned with issues of gender, maritime communities, property relations, and anthropologists in the fourth world.

*James Carrier* has taught at the University of Papua New Guinea and as occasional lecturer in Sociology at the University of Virginia. He has published two monographs based on the ethnography of Ponam (Papua New Guinea) and an edited collection on History and Tradition in Melanesia Anthropology. He is currently working on a monograph on gifts and commodities in Western society and an edited collection on Occidentalism.

*Adam Kuper* is Professor of Social Anthropology at Brunel University. He is author of a number of books on the history and theory of anthropology, and on Southern African ethnography, most recently *The Invention of Primitive Society* (London 1988). He was editor of *Current Anthropology* for many years, and was co-editor of *The Social Science Encyclopedia*.

*Claude Lévi-Strauss* is Honorary Professor, Collège de France and the most distinguished anthropologist of his generation.

*Orvar Löfgren* is Professor of European Ethnology at the University of Lund, Sweden. He is the co-author of *Culture Builders: A Historical Anthropology of Middle-Class Life* (Rutgers, 1987), and author of a number of books on Swedish culture. He is currently working on a comparative study of national identities.

*Daniel Miller* is Reader in Anthropology at University College London. He is author and editor of several books including *Material Culture and Mass Consumption* (Blackwell, 1987) and *Modernity: An Ethnographic Approach* (Berg, forthcoming). He is currently writing a book on the relationship between commerce and consumption in Trinidad.

*Brian Moeran* currently occupies the Swire Chair of Japanese at the University of Hong Kong, and is also Professor of Japanese Anthropology at the School of Oriental and African Studies, London. He has published widely on various aspects of Japanese popular culture, and is currently completing a book on a Japanese advertising agency (forthcoming, Routledge).

*Mary Searle-Chatterjee* is a lecturer at Manchester Metropolitan University. Author of *Reversible Sex Roles: The Special Case of the Banaras Sweepers* (Pergamon, 1981). Her most recent publication is 'Religious division and the mythology of the past' in B. Hertel and C. Humes (eds.), *Living Benaras* (SUNY, 1993). She is currently working on the religious ancestry of political activists.

*Lise Skov* is a cultural sociologist from the University of Copenhagen. She is currently doing research on fashion, consumption, and urbanism in Japan, and is planning a study of piracy in the fashion business in Hong Kong.

# PART I

*Introduction*

# 1

# A Theory of Christmas

*Daniel Miller*

## Introduction

A consensus appears to be emerging around the interpretation of the contemporary Anglo-American Christmas which would place this festival firmly within the more general category of phenomenon termed 'the invention of tradition'. This theme is certainly prominent in the most important accounts of the modern Christmas, those by Barnett (1954) on the American Christmas and by Golby and Purdue (1986) and Pimlott (1978) on the British Christmas. In addition, these writers provide useful summaries of the longer historical traditions from which the modern Christmas emerged. Barnett is especially interesting in his account of the opposition to Christmas amongst the Puritan founders of modern America, who went so far as to make the celebration of Christmas illegal during parts of the seventeenth century (as did the British Puritan parliament between 1647 and 1660). Nevertheless they and most subsequent writers on Christmas emphasize the break in the mid-nineteenth century between any previous version of this festival and the Christmas we know today. Amongst the most persuasive evidence for a radical distinction in Britain is that presented by Golby (1981: 14–15) based on a survey of *The Times* newspaper from 1790 to 1836: 'In twenty of the forty-seven years, Christmas is not mentioned at all, and for the remaining twenty-seven years reports are extremely brief and not very informative.' This relative lack of concern for the festival is contrasted with the extraordinary influence of Dickens and especially the tremendous popularity of his *A Christmas Carol*. Barnett credits Dickens and some other authors such as Washington Irving with the development of what he calls the 'carol philosophy', with its emphasis upon sentimentality.

The notion of the invention of tradition seems borne out by the persuasive tenor of Dickensian nostalgia about the festival which clearly purports to be enacting a rite of considerable antiquity. Yet it is only from this point in the mid-nineteenth century that we start to find the crystallization of a range of attributes of the modern Christmas from diverse regional sources into a single homogenized version which has no regional base. This syncretic modern form extracts the Christmas tree from the German tradition, the filling of stockings from the Dutch tradition, the development of Santa Claus mainly from the United States, the British Christmas card, and many other such elements. Folkloristic accounts of Christmas indicate that up to this time the festival is so permeated by specific local elements that it presents a picture of quite spectacular heterogeneity. But in the mid-nineteenth century we see the stripping away of certain customs and the reinforcement of those selected for preservation. For example, mistletoe is enshrined with its associated ritual of kissing, while ivy, equally important in some earlier traditions, diminishes in significance.

The implications of these findings are given still greater significance by the evidence from the subsequent period. It has been argued that once the disparate elements are woven into the modern form this becomes a largely stable concoction with relatively little change occurring over the last century. Despite the tremendous dynamism of popular culture over the twentieth century, it is argued that Christmas has been relatively little altered. Rather each new medium has attempted to appropriate it, as we find with Christmas films or Christmas pop music. The main modern controversy has been whether the most powerful of these new forces, that of commerce, has been so successful in its appropriation as to overturn and then destroy the spirit of Christmas celebrated by Dickens. This question dominated Barnett's analysis and remains the main colloquial debate over Christmas.

Weightman and Humphries provide perhaps the most extreme example of this view, since most of the content of their book is devoted to exemplifying their initial proposition that 'the Christmas ritual which we know today was the "invention" of the relatively well-to-do Victorian middle class, and reflects their preoccupations' (1987: 15). The weight of modern scholarship has defined with increasing precision the period and place we should have to explore if we are to comprehend the causes behind the current scale and specific nature of contemporary Christmas.

Once these now established attributes are in place and increasingly formed in the new images of industrial popular culture, we see the final triumph of the modern Christmas in their global spread. This occurs partly through the influence of American troops in the Second World War, partly through the older influence of British colonialism.

It occurs despite the open resistance from a range of European national traditions which opposed the hegemonic force of the Anglo-American version of the festival. By the 1990s we are faced with the extraordinary phenomenon of a global festival which seems to grow in its accumulated rituals and the extravagance of the homage paid to it, even as all other festivals and comparable events have declined.

This, however, provides the point of departure for this present book and one which serves to separate it from this trend in the analysis of Christmas. The emphasis on the Anglo-American Christmas looks increasingly parochial when we appreciate the nature of contemporary Christmas as a complex amalgam of heterogeneous customs often specific to nations, regions, or even villages, and deriving from both Christian and non-Christian traditions in many parts of the world, together with tendencies towards the formation of 'global' Christmas symbols and customs. This suggests a re-evaluation of even the Anglo-American presumed core from the perspective provided by studies based in various parts of the world which help relativize our assumptions about what constitutes a 'proper' Christmas.

In this collection of essays we are confronted by the extraordinary success of this festival as an international event. The modern triumphant Christmas has conquered not only Christian areas which are quite remote from the secular elements of Christmas popular culture, such as the Iñupiat, but also people of a variety of other religions such as in Japan. Indeed Christmas is today *the* global festival and it is obviously an aim of any comparative appraisal of Christmas, such as this one, to explain why this should have happened and what qualities of Christmas differentiate it from all other festivals.

All the essays included in this volume concentrate on contemporary Christmas, though several include some historical background. All the contributors are either anthropologists or sympathetic (or at least acquainted) with anthropological forms of investigation and analysis. Anthropologists are well known for their orientation towards synchronic study based on detailed observation of current practices amongst social groups, as opposed to explanation by resource to survivals and the folkloristic tradition which would otherwise dominate research into Christmas. Much of the particular character and contribution of this volume comes from its anthropological perspective, which means that most of the contributions make considerable use of direct observation of popular practices. These include representations in the popular media and by commerce, but most especially portraits of the activities

of families within their homes. This adds considerably to our knowledge of the festival since there have been very few previous accounts
based on ethnographic observation. It is noticeable how reliant several
of the chapters are on these precedents for direct observation. Thus
the work on gift-giving as by Caplow (e.g. 1984) and Cheal (1988)
comes up in several chapters, although the material is reinterpreted
in very different ways. All contemporary researchers are in debt to the
excellent bibliography by Samuelson (1982).

It is still possible to identify certain dominant motifs and tendencies
in contemporary Christmas, but these can less convincingly be tied to
a particular regional history. Furthermore no generalizations are likely
to meet the entire range of Christmases now found and anthropologists
would generally prefer to affirm the equal claims to authenticity of all
contemporary versions irrespective of whether they meet some prior
assumption as to the nature of 'proper' Christmas. Most of the subsequent essays do, however, reflect the general literature in identifying
two main focuses of concern—the family and materialism. The
relationship between these two is clearly going to become the pivot of
any more general attempt to account for this festival, since the effect
of this materialism might well be thought to be inimical to the close
domestic atmosphere which otherwise seems to be celebrated. But as
the essays in this volume demonstrate this relationship may be quite
complex. Carrier argues that the consumption of commercial forms
aids rather than hinders the creation of intimate social relations, while
other chapters, e.g. Löfgren's, question the closeness of family which
is central to the image of the 'proper' Christmas.

There are a number of additional well-established characteristics
which might be explored. Christmas appears to be a 'twin peaked
festival', which exists within a relationship to a second festival, either
New Year's Day, or in some cases carnival. There is also an uneasy
relationship between the emphasis on the ritualization of what otherwise would be seen as secular popular culture and the official sanction
of religion, under whose auspices the celebration is legitimated (or
condemned). It is these and other generalizations which would have
to form the basis for a theory of Christmas, but this introduction
also seeks to acknowledge the equal status of that which cannot be
encompassed by such a theory.

I do not want to dismiss the study by social scientists of the modern
'invented' Christmas, which has been perhaps the most productive
approach to the topic in recent decades, but it is not the approach

which I intend to take in this introduction. This is because I believe the value of studying Christmas at the present time lies in its potential contribution to a number of larger theoretical issues. Rather than repudiating particular traditions of analysis the intention is to utilize but also transcend several. This means taking from the newly established Christmases around the world, but also paying attention to much longer trajectories of European Christmas than the 'invention of tradition' school of thought would allow.

The inspiration for such an attempt comes in some measure from the first chapter in this collection, that by Lévi-Strauss. Any generalization about the discipline of anthropology which left as distinguished an authority as Lévi-Strauss out on a limb could not easily be accepted, and in his essay Lévi-Strauss has carefully articulated the more synchronic and comparative study of Christmas with a clear respect for the findings of folkloristics and historical studies. Indeed one can see clear lines being drawn between the implications of that structuralism, of which Lévi-Strauss is the key pioneer, and the earlier tradition of anthropological enquiry associated with the work of Frazer in *The Golden Bough*. By combining the essays in this collection it is possible to follow Lévi-Strauss's lead in attempting to analyse the festival through comparative anthropology rather than as invented tradition.

It is also Lévi-Strauss who provides the imperative towards locating some kind of 'deep structure' to the festival which suggests that an understanding of this event might provide a lead into still wider questions about the fundamental nature of sociality. Within this larger project of anthropology there is room for a search for what might be termed the foundations of Christmas before returning in the remaining chapters, including my own on Trinidad, to focus upon the narrower task of accounting for the triumphant form of the modern Christmas. The obvious place to start such a search for foundations would seem to be the origins of the festival in the late Roman empire.

## Christmas before Christmas

I first felt persuaded that the evidence of earlier periods should be considered as more than just a background for examining the modern Christmas when I encountered the following quotation from Miles's (1912) volume, *Christmas in Ritual and Tradition*. Miles is quoting (via an intermediary source) from Libanius, a non-Christian philosopher of rhetoric at Constantinople, Nicomedia, and Antioch, who was writing in the second half of the fourth century, the time in which Christmas is first established. The description is of the festival of the Kalends which, as we shall see, is one of the three festivals that Christmas in some sense replaces:

The festival of the Kalends, is celebrated everywhere as far as the limits of the Roman Empire extend ... Everywhere may be seen carousals and well-laden tables; luxurious abundance is found in the houses of the rich, but also in the houses of the poor better food than usual is put upon the table. The impulse to spend seizes everyone. He who the whole year through has taken pleasure in saving and piling up his pence, becomes suddenly extravagant. He who erstwhile was accustomed and preferred to live poorly, now at this feast enjoys himself as much as his means will allow.... People are not only generous towards themselves, but also towards their fellow-men. A stream of presents pours itself out on all sides ... The highroads and footpaths are covered with whole processions of laden men and beasts ... As the thousand flowers which burst forth everywhere are the adornment of Spring, so are the thousand presents poured out on all sides, the decorations of the Kalends feast. It may justly be said that it is the fairest time of the year.... The Kalends festival banishes all that is connected with toil, and allows men to give themselves up to undisturbed enjoyment. From the minds of young people it removes two kinds of dread: the dread of the schoolmaster and the dread of the stern pedagogue. The slave also it allows, as far as possible, to breathe the air of freedom ... Another great quality of the festival is that it teaches men not to hold too fast to their money, but to part with it and let it pass into other hands. (Miles 1912: 168–9)

The importance of this quotation is much enhanced by the evidence presented in the next three pages of Miles's work. Miles first notes how 'The church's denunciations of pagan festal practices in the winter season are mainly directed against the Kalends celebrations and show into how many regions the keeping of the feast had spread' (ibid. 169). He quotes a source who collected forty such denunciations dated from between the fourth and eleventh centuries, which suggests that a direct relationship between Christmas and the Kalends is acknowledged for nearly a millennium. Quoting one such denunciation in full he mentions additional practices, such as masquerading, which we now identify more with carnival, but also the feasting, drinking, and the giving of presents still associated with Christmas.

The origins of Christmas are, however, more complex than given in the description of the Kalends alone. The Kalends, at least in earlier Roman times, is much less important than the Saturnalia, which was celebrated from 17 December for five days. This is noted by Scullard

(1981: 205–7) as the most popular Roman festival in republican times. In this festival we see many elements repeated in medieval and later Christmas and carnival celebrations, including not only the general jollity but also such specific elements as the choosing of a mock king to preside over the revels and the giving of presents. Scullard even mentions the wearing of soft (felt rather than paper!) hats. More detailed analysis of this festival and the later evolution of carnival have given rise to a debate on one of the major characteristics which will require discussion, that is the inversion of ordinary social life. In both the Saturnalia and Kalends we find the master feasting the slave and, as Libanius makes clear, this is merely the most extreme example of a sense of inversion from ordinary norms.

The second area of resonance lies precisely in the relationship between these two Roman festivals. As is the case today this was clearly a twin peaked festival with the Kalends (or previously the Compitalia) in a sense repeating in the New Year a similar form of jollity to Saturnalia, including the gambling, feasting, and so forth. A third area of obvious similarity is found in the stress by Libanius on present-giving, lavishness, and the spending of money generally. As Miles notes, Libanius, the moralist and celebrant of what he saw as traditional Roman values including thrift, seems to see nothing to condemn on this particular occasion in behaviour which he acknowledges is the very opposite of such virtues. On the other hand many previous moralists have condemned what they saw as the noise and excesses of Saturnalia. The gift-giving and lavishness that Libanius describes is viewed by others as part of a general rise of crass materialism amongst the Roman élite in particular, and as such a threat to traditional values.

The parallels, and a further clue to their explanation, may be extended if we consider the third pre-Christian festival connected to Christmas. This is the celebration of the Dies Natalis Invicti on 25 December. Miles notes that it is this festival which seems to be deliberately replaced in order to provide a calendrical fixity to Christmas, but then suggests that there is no importance to be attached to it. In this case, however, the formidable scholar of Christmas may have missed something, which is borne out by a subsequent monograph on the cult which surrounded this particular event. The Dies Natalis Invicti, celebrated with chariot racing and decorations of branches and small trees, is part of a cult called Deus Sol Invictus. Halsberghe (1972) traces the development of this cult from its origins in Syria (and possibly before that in pre-Jewish Canaanite practices). It is taken to

Rome originally in the more Syrian form of Sol Invictus Elagabal in 219. It briefly dominates Roman worship until the murder of the supporting emperor in 222. The cult spreads, however, and is then re-established in a more 'Roman' form by the emperor Aurelian, to be proclaimed the dominant religion of the Roman state in 274. The cult continues in its importance thereafter. Halsberghe notes that 'It was during the rule of Constantine the Great (306–37) that the cult of Deus Sol Invictus reached extraordinary heights, so that his reign was even spoken of as a Sun Emperorship' (ibid. 167).

Constantine was, of course, also responsible for the subsequent promotion of Christianity, which was to replace such cults. With this background information we are better able to appreciate the grounds for a decision that took place between the years 354 and 360 to establish the festival of Christmas on the date of 25 December, which later on successfully replaced in the West an earlier tradition in the East that focused on the Epiphany of 6 January. It was not merely that this was the date given in the Julian calendar for the winter solstice, but it meant replacing a key festival of a cult that was probably the main rival to Christianity in its earliest phase. This title of 'main rival' is more usually accredited to the worship of Mithra. Many remains of this latter cult are found by archaeologists in provinces such as Britain, largely because of its association with the Roman army, and in this respect it is unlike that of Deus Sol Invictus, of which we retain much less evidence. The two were clearly related, as the cult of the sun god (despite its polytheistic origins) had by then also become a form of monotheism derived from Syrian origins, and may have shared the Mithraic and Christian concerns with a redeemer and the afterlife. Unlike its two rivals, however, the cult of Deus Sol Invictus, from its earliest introduction to the Roman empire, enjoyed a much closer relationship to the state and the presence and image of the emperor, which gave it considerable political appeal.

There is, however, another characteristic of this cult which is perhaps its most important legacy for the consideration of Christmas. As Halsberghe notes, 'The phenomenon of religious syncretism had certainly been in evidence for a long time before it attained its dominant position in the religious life of the 3rd and 4th centuries. The cult of Deus Sol Invictus, influenced as it was by neo-Platonism, is one of the clearest examples of this phenomenon known to us' (ibid. p. x). It is evident that this cult, which gradually incorporated Roman forms of worship into what was originally a Middle Eastern form, is itself an important parallel religious phenomenon to the impact of Christianity, but most especially to that process which allowed Christianity to adopt and adapt elements of the earlier Roman religion. Indeed from the perspective of recent scholarship on the emergence of Christianity under Constantine (e.g. Barnes 1981), Christianity itself is seen to be marked by considerable continuity of syncretic formation.

Although in the next section I will consider the core concern which Christmas appears to add to its pre-Christian precursors, it is evident that there are many attributes which parallel what has been supposed as the unprecedented in the modern Christmas. As well as that syncretism represented by the formation of religious cults, we see an equally important syncretism between that which is sanctioned by religion and that which seems to emerge from popular culture. As in the Saturnalia, this may be viewed indulgently or with some suspicion by 'purist' and aristocratic writers. In the structure of these festivals we also see the marked importance of rituals of inversion, of feasting, a crucial relationship between lavishness and the domestic sphere, and a twin peaked structure to the festivities. We have the sense of rituals accruing to the performance of the festival but also the sense of the exuberance and the transcending of ordinary life. Apart from this we have that gamut of specific traditions from the use of evergreens to the wearing of hats which have so exercised the concerns of folklorists studying the subsequent two millennia.

We therefore have two periods in which we can observe the juxtaposition of a number of features. The implications are yet to be determined. It might be simply as argued by some folklorists, that there is direct continuity of features which while submerged for a period manage to emerge again under favourable conditions. Alternatively we may have two periods which coincidentally possess the circumstance of a fear of being modern or at least of fragmentation but also homogenization of the world. Before attempting to resolve such different approaches we have first to examine the impact of the development of Christmas itself.

## Christmas and the Family: Embodiment or Inversion?

All interpretations of Christmas acknowledge the central image of the family in its celebrations. Indeed its very birth as a festival could be argued to be another 'invention of tradition' since it has often been remarked that there is very little attention paid in the original Gospels to the events which are given such emphasis in Christmas celebrations (none at all in the earliest Gospel). Despite this we find the emergence of a festival that takes as its heart the relationship of parents to child, constantly reflected in the domestic focus found in the celebration of Christmas and in the importance, as a number of the essays in this collection stress, of the family as an idiom for wider sociality.

This seems to represent the single most important contribution of Christmas itself to the further development of that festive tradition which preceded its creation. Although much of the literature, including the quotation from Libanius, dwells upon the importance of the domestic sphere and its incorporation of wider social groups, there is nothing which echoes the specific devotion to the nuclear family at the moment of the birth of a child. There is no particular suggestion that the relationships of the nuclear family are the focus of any of the three festivals which preceded Christmas. Only in the new festival is the trinity of mother and father devoted to the birth of their child the unambiguous centrepiece.

The invention of Christmas itself clearly alters the relationship between the festivals and the family. In a sense this gives Christianity quite an odd role. On the one hand Christianity seems to be constantly vilified by contemporary non-Christian Romans because it does not fulfil the central religious axiom of the Roman period, which is to be true to one's own traditions. Christianity was seen not only as threatening to the rites of Rome, but as repudiating even its own regional origins in its rejection of Judaism, which for a while made it something of a pariah cult. On the other hand I have noted how writers such as Libanius seem to have reflected a strong tradition in Roman scholarship to concern itself with the failure of contemporary families to live up to traditions associated with the norms and life-styles of the 'ancients', which might be identified with the stern figures of republican Rome or the Greeks before them. In a sense then Christianity, despite its origins outside the establishment, could at least be incorporated by some such as Constantine as a re-establishment of traditional virtues. In this case an ideology legitimated by a belief in the centrality of the family during the early Roman Republic is made to fit a transformation in the late Roman Empire consisting of a refocusing upon the family which is thereafter most fully objectified in the festival of Christmas.

In many ways it would be much easier to appreciate this birth of Christmas if we were to refer to it as an Italian rather than a Roman festival. This is because the literature on the Roman family has tended to have a rather dry and legalistic bias in the tradition of classicists. By contrast, if we think of Christmas as originally an Italian festival then it would immediately find resonance with many long-established colloquial views and stereotypes of Italian society and its family-centredness.

A similar point emerges in a reading of Marina Warner (1976) on the evolution of the worship of the Virgin Mary, a cult which seems to have first emerged at the same period as Christmas. The cult of Mary also exhibits considerable continuity with pre-Christian religions, from which base it grows to incorporate the considerable emphasis upon the figure of the mother and virgin in Italian society in history. Italy here stands for a more general Mediterranean and then Catholic tradition, but with Italy as seeming most conspicuously to embody the specific relation of the nuclear family in a form in which one sees literal devotion of its members to each other. It comes as no surprise that it is Italy (more specifically St Francis of Assisi) that is credited with the invention of the crib out of the various Christmas paraphernalia which survive until today. Warner indicates that this is part of a larger role taken by the Franciscans in developing the sense of the domestic family with the feminine image of humility and innocence (ibid. 179–91).

This leaves us, however, with an uncomfortable break between the portrayal of the Roman and the Italian family. One solution would be to argue that there is a rapid and radical transformation between the two. The strongest argument for such a change and one which would fit precisely with the birth of Christmas comes from Goody's (1983) book on the development of the family and marriage in Europe. Goody argues that 'key features of the kinship system have undergone a sudden change from the former "Mediterranean pattern" to a new "European one" or in Guichard's terms, from the oriental to the occidental' (1983: 39). Goody argues that the instrument of these changes was Christianity; not the original Christianity, but that which became the faith as a result of taking over the state and the establishment (ibid. 85). It is at this period of the mid to late fourth century, precisely the time when Christmas was invented, that we find the narrowing down to the modern ideology of the nuclear family, through the suppression of a much wider range of strategies for securing direct inheritance. Wider networks established through adoption, wet nursing, and concubinage, as well as the widening of forbidden degrees of marriage, all come into play at this time. Goody explains such changes in terms of the desire of the Church to secure those inheritances which resulted in a massive shift of land and goods to itself. The emphasis was placed upon the Church as natural inheritor in those families where the now narrower possibilities of direct inheritance to a son were not realized. Goody's thesis has certainly been challenged, and the effect of the Church is clearly controversial. Nor does Goody address the necessity for an equally massive shift in sentiment and emotional attachment which could literally forge the Italian family out of the Roman. Some of these changes in relation to the child in particular may have been exaggerated (Garnsey 1991), but there remains an overall picture of a long-term shift at least in the ideology and probably in the balance of affectivity in the Italian family (Kertzer and Saller 1991: 15–17). The sources are stronger on shifts in legality than in sentiment, although one striking piece of evidence emerges from a systematic study of funerary inscriptions, which shows a marked increase in the emphasis upon children as compared to pre- and non-Christian families (Shaw 1991). More generally it may be the fact that Christianity's emergence as a dominant religion from popular practice, in contrast to state cults such as Deus Sol Invictus, led to a focus on the family of ordinary people's experience. By contrast, in the earlier period, the debates about imperial legislation suggest a much narrower concern for the impact of the state upon practices amongst élite families only.

Out of these controversies, the key finding, for present purposes, is merely the direct correspondence in time between the birth of the festival and a major shift in the norms and practices of family life, which led to the foundation of the idealization of the nuclear family that has continued in Western Europe ever since. This suggests that the foundation of Christmas is one of a number of strategies by which the early Church transformed the patterns of kinship and associated sentimental attachments which together make up our sense of the family. What we can attest to is the crucial role played by Christmas ever since in the objectification of the family as the *locus* of a powerful sentimentality and devotion.

At this point a further strong parallel may be noted between the fourth century and the twentieth century relevant to the larger relationship between Christmas and the family. The collection contains two essays based upon the study of the family and Christmas in contemporary Britain. Both Kuper and Searle-Chatterjee provide considerable evidence to suggest that the family remains the pivotal point around which British Christmas rituals are organized. Both recognize the intense concentration on rituals that incorporate the immediate family, but in circumstances which make for clear links with royal families, divine families, and a more general devotion to the family as idiom for wider sociality.

Having established this role for Christmas they then provide rather different interpretations of this phenomenon. Kuper is concerned (following Pimlott 1978 and others) to understand why we should have this, if anything, growing emphasis on a family which is clearly regarded otherwise as in decline. He rejects the idea that the festival is merely nostalgia for a lost form. Instead he argues that Christmas constructs, almost as a formal structure, an alternative reality of a world in which the family retains its central presence and by extension those values which are associated with this core of our sociality. This enactment of another world is recognized to be in the tradition of those, including Lévi-Strauss in his chapter, who perceive a continuity with the inversion themes of the original Saturnalia.

By contrast, Searle-Chatterjee, while noting the same set of beliefs about the family as lost core, argues that Christmas could also be an embodiment rather than an inversion. If we follow much of the recent sociological literature on the contemporary British family, this suggests that with growing life expectancy we may today have rather more experience of its extended form than a century ago, and for working-class households at least there is a continuing reliance on networks of kindred. If this is the case then what is astonishing is the degree to which this sociological reality is denied in ordinary life where loss of family is constantly asserted. From this perspective Christmas may be the one time when the actual importance of the family is valorized and given its due. The strains of Christmas come here from a confrontation with our circumstance, which we normally prefer to avoid, rather than from a discrepancy from the experience of daily life.

I suspect most readers of these two chapters will tend to echo my own impression that they are both 'right'. The descriptive details and the analysis which emerge from them both seem resonant as they are informed by considerable recent scholarship on the experience of the contemporary English Christmas. It seems incumbent upon us, therefore, to devise an analytical perspective which can encompass both views. This point seems confirmed by the second contrastive pair of essays that make up this section of the book. The content of Löfgren's chapter echoes both Searle-Chatterjee's constructivism and Kuper's idealized rituals. Löfgren views them simultaneously in order to focus on the anxiety, tension, and quarrelling which arise from the problems of reconciling these two.

In many ways this argument over inversion as against embodiment could be repeated for the fourth century. The nature of the Roman 'familia' remains contentious, but Rawson (1986: 1) notes that partly this is because there exists a tradition of scholarship that sees the family as in decline or degeneration towards the later period, which reflects the writings of upper-class Romans of that time. Whatever the actual social relations pertaining for most families, the dominant class had, since the days of the republic, a tendency to see themselves as having lost traditional close family ties. The legalistic account which notes the relative detachment of the mother from the inherited line, seems matched by a more sociological concern with the actual falling apart of the family into its individual components. From this perspective the festivals of Saturnalia and Kalends may well be viewed as an inversion of ordinary life—an alternate reality.

The writings on the Roman family during this period suggest that the ties between members of the family and their commitment to some larger sense of the family as transgenerational project appear either loose or under threat. The considerable concern of emperors such as Augustus and Constantine to enact legislation which is supposed to enforce a renewed commitment to the traditions of the domestic sphere seem to demonstrate the official recognition of this theme. But the same writings suggest that the Roman upper-class family, at least, can only properly be understood as a larger unit including its often numerically more important slave component (e.g. Bradley 1990: 90, 164). Several of the 'functions' which we today associate with the notion of the 'domestic' or the 'family' were then mainly left in the hands of the slave. Relations between mother and child were often much more attenuated than the close relations of child and nurse, though there are many examples of affective parent–child relations, especially amongst those such as Augustus who were intending themselves to be viewed as exemplary (Dixon 1988: 104–67). The impression is that although clearly excluded by any more legalistic perspective, the slave seems integral to any attempt to view the actual experience of domestic life and its associated sentiments.

The one event most commonly used to demonstrate the inversion aspect of the pre-Christmas Roman festivals (both Saturnalia and Kalends) is the feasting of slaves by their masters together with the public acknowledgement of the master and slave gambling and enjoying their leisure together. In terms of the accepted relations between these two, and the formal hierarchy, the use of the word 'inversion' is entirely appropriate. But viewed from another perspective these festivals may be seen as the only time of the year when the domestic sphere is actually recognized for what in practice it is, a larger form in which the slave is integral to the core functions of social reproduction. It is as though there is another family not described by any formal term, which is valorized and given its due solely at this period. Once again we have an alternative reality which is simultaneously an embodiment.

As might be anticipated the varieties of contemporary Christmas also provide other social articulations than are encompassed by this particular debate. One chapter which seems to stand out as exceptional is the account by Bodenhorn of Iñupiaq practice. Here there is virtually no acknowledgement of the family *per se* during the Christmas celebrations. This absence is significant, since as Bodenhorn argues there seems to be almost a studious avoidance of this element of social organization and a desire to dissolve it into images of a larger sociality. Christmas is used in this case to prevent a 'breakdown' of society into mere family, or in so far as this has already occurred to use the occasion to assert an ideology of traditional communal form. Bodenhorn notes that the atmosphere which pervades this variety of Christmas is in marked contrast to precisely the kinds of tensions over the objectification of the family described by Löfgren. If Bodenhorn demonstrates 'resistance' then Moeran and Skov point out the possibilities of creative appropriation with respect to Japan. Here the festival is also a social celebration, but given the prior existence of other festivals directed to the family and home, Christmas has been appropriated for the idealization of a new social formation—the 'dating' of young couples. Here the focus is clearly outside the home environment, and Christmas seems to be employed with the enthusiastic support of commerce to provide a guide to the normative if dynamic form this new social activity should take. These chapters demonstrate that we cannot predict how the social foundations of one version of Christmas may be transformed when the festival is re-established in a new context, where the domestic family may not be the primary concern of Christmas. This should not, however, prevent us from attempting to analyse comparatively the relationship to the family in the many cases where this seems to have been or have become central to the celebration of Christmas.

## Christmas and Materialism

The evidence from the Roman period, and in particular the quotation from Libanius, puts us on our guard against what is probably the most common colloquial account of the dynamics of contemporary Christmas. According to this account Christmas was once indeed the pure festival of close family togetherness, but its heart has been lost in the relentless exploitation of its possibilities by a combination of individual materialism and capitalist profit-taking. The chapters in this volume suggest that this has become in effect a global cliché about Christmas. Libanius's portrait of a thousand presents pouring out like flowers in spring in the fourth century AD may, however, make us hesitate about accounting for this phenomenon as merely the outcome of recent capitalist imperatives.

The two chapters which address the issue of materialism most directly are those concerning the history of the relationship between Christmas and materialism in the United States. This is especially apt, first because the same relationship is the central theme to Barnett's study of the American Christmas and secondly because this association of materialism and Christmas is often viewed elsewhere as part and parcel of a global 'Americanization' of popular culture, which has promoted materialism under the umbrella of other forms and values. Although each is well aware of the evidence presented by the other, Belk and Carrier have obligingly focused upon the two ends of the spectrum of opinions as to the nature of this relationship.

Both chapters demonstrate the weaknesses in the colloquial argument by providing such a wealth of material on the intimacy of the connection between materialism and Christmas as to dispose of any notion that the modern Christmas could ever exist outside this relationship. Belk shows capitalism as active in the development and promotion of Christmas from its very rebirth in the mid-nineteenth century, but especially since the 1920s. Belk in this and previous papers (1987, 1989) indicates how many key Christmas elements were invented for specific marketing purposes. In this he echoes the earlier work of Barnett, who provides, for example, the case of Rudolph the Red-Nosed Reindeer devised as a highly successful marketing gimmick by an advertising executive in 1939 (1954: 108–14).

By contrast, Carrier focuses on the consumption rather than the production of Christmas. Using well-established anthropological models of the gift and the evidence of recent sociologists working on

Christmas gifting, he argues for the role of Christmas in taking from the anonymity of the commodity and transforming it into the sociality of gift exchange. Dickens is the key figure here. Belk, Carrier, and Kuper all also follow Barnett and Pimlott in reflecting upon the enormous popularity and power of the images devised by Dickens in *A Christmas Carol* and other writings in creating the modern Christmas. On first reading the evidence would seem to support the point made by Carrier and Miller with regard to Christmas as an anti-materialist festival. Dickens was certainly celebratory of an affluent, expansive, even hedonistic Christmas (see Carrier on the images of feasting), but this is always constructed as an image against two alternatives. One is poverty, that lack of resources which prevented participation, and surely no major British writer has ever been as eloquent in the rendition of the unremitting misery of contemporary British poverty and as condemnatory of those who refused to recognize this. But the second enemy of Christmas is of course Scrooge, the miser and skinflint who knows all about accumulation but has lost the spirit which turns money back into sociality and morality, in other words has lost the spirit of Christmas.

This view would make Christmas a case-study of what Miller (1987: 178–217) argued is an increasingly common role for mass consumption, the negation of the abstract nature of the commodity through rituals of appropriation by which social groups (in this case particularly the family) are created. Dickens and his readers created a Christmas whose prime concern was precisely the central problem of the new materialism—how in a world of increasing commodification was one to enjoy the benefits of an escape from poverty but not be lost in the reification and asocial abstractions of goods as commodities. The 'spirit' of Christmas provided the answer. Indeed this would account for the timing of this reinvention of Christmas and its subsequent importance as a contemporary festival. The contradiction of materialism was particularly evident for the specific group that Dickens wrote for. This was a middle class whose new importance at that time was the first sign of what has since emerged as the most powerful class fraction in global terms. Christmas provided the means by which this class could enjoy the benefits of their new wealth while believing that they could still turn their base coin back into the golden-hearted spirit of Christmas sociality.

This rendering of the effect of Dickens must, however, be set against the ability of Belk to use the same source to argue for Christmas as a front for the promotion of hedonistic materialism and behind this capitalist profitability. In examining the evolution of Santa Claus as the 'deity' of materialism we see a figure that has come a long way since the time of Dickens. Belk's abundant evidence and argument for Christmas as an embodiment of capitalist values seems just as convincing as Carrier or Miller on the attempt to 'tame' capitalism or ameliorate its negative consequences for society. Once again we seem to require a model which transcends any simple 'for' and 'against' portrayal of what is clearly an intense and intimate relationship to materialism. A central image in Dickens's portraits of Christmas is the domestic sphere—the coldness of Scrooge's home versus the warmth of Cratchit's. It has commonly been found by anthropologists that money, and more particularly expenditure, are not just powerful metaphors, but may be central to the very concept of the home. An excellent example of this is a recent analysis of the meaning of the term 'house' amongst peasants in Colombia (Gudeman and Rivera 1990). The centrality of thrift as an idiom of retention and the perception of the health of the house in terms of abundance and increase will be familiar also to observers of peasant households elsewhere (e.g. Du Boulay 1974 for Greece).

Where the domestic sphere is represented by its ability to retain through thrift then the enemy is clearly lavishness as the clear precursor to what we today identify as the antisocial potential of materialism. The same Libanius, echoing earlier Roman moralists, can be harshly condemnatory of the lack of proper values which lavishness at other times is seen as reflecting. Yet as noted above, he does not appear to condemn, but actually to celebrate, the extravagance, feasting, and present-giving represented by the pre-Christmas festival. The first element which would account for this is clearly argued by Carrier. It is the 'taming' of commodities by incorporating them into the sociality of the home as gifts, thus transforming the potential threat into the means of social construction. But beyond this there is this emphasis on the feasting of the outside world, the incorporation of the world into pseudo-family relations, the opening up of the domestic through an expansive outer-directed lavishness. It is as though once the bastion of the domestic is secure it is ready to take on the much larger forces of the outside world which otherwise would threaten it. This view provides the basis for much of my chapter on Trinidad, where we see the centripetal incorporation of ever-wider layers of Trinidadian society within the domestic sphere in the hospitality extended by the home during the weeks following Christmas. In some cases there is more a sense of the abundance of the thrifty home flowing outwards in order to incorporate dangerous forces.

This may not always occur quite so literally. Löfgren's Swedish festival seems a very private affair, of a form which is increasingly common elsewhere in the United States and Western Europe. Here feasting is limited to family members. The linkage remains, however, through the symbolic connections that make the family not only an idiom for the larger (e.g. divine) family, but also a systematic microcosm. The belief is that one's family rituals are a reflection on the normative order of all other families who carry out these rites in the same way at the same time. This may in part account for the considerable concern Löfgren documents in getting Christmas right.

Lavishness is then both the inversion of the home as thrift but also the embodiment of the home as the idiom for a wider sociality. This may be analogous to the argument by Lévi-Strauss which focuses upon the feasting of the dead (often symbolized in the form of children) and other dangerous outsiders as a key ritual element in the festival. Here the thrifty house is placating with abundance the envy and greed in this world (and the other). Through the combination of Belk and Carrier's papers we gain the sense of sociality playing dangerously with the devil (or Santa Claus?) as commodity fetish. This is also reflected in the centrality of this act of shopping, which, even if enjoyed at other times, on this occasion seems almost to deaden the senses and crush our individuality, while also seeming essential to the resurrection of the family and wider sociality. As understood by Libanius this ritual immersion in lavishness and materialism has to be understood as a moral act.

The rituals of intensive shopping may be contextualized by analogy with Lévi-Strauss's comments on the feasting of the dead. It is materialism itself which, as Simmel and others have argued, is always understood as potentially the death as well as the medium of social life. Statements in most of the chapters reflect this sense around Christmas of materialism as social death. It is therefore this larger sense of materialism which has to be objectified then placated and then re-socialized or brought back as the living in the form of a gift. From this perspective the appropriation of commodities noted by Carrier and Miller becomes in effect a moment within a larger annual ritual act. There are parallel tensions made manifest in recent attempts to control Halloween rituals in the United States (Belk forthcoming).

There is one further significant contribution of Christmas to under-standing the place of consumerism within modernity. This is reflected in the evidence within these essays for Christmas as a site of what may be called 'creative consumerism'. The most evident example is Japan, where Moeran and Skov document a national dialogue articu-lated through advertising and the media which is pitched at the level of deciding what Christmas goods should be about and how they should be marketed. As such, capitalist commodity culture becomes a kind of language through which a national discussion takes place as to the future form of culture (compare Wilk 1990). In this case materi-alism is not a 'problem' which Christmas may be 'for' or 'against'. On the contrary it is the new possibilities and strategies of juxtaposition by both commerce and consumers which utilize what the authors call 'kitsch' to constitute new social and material possibilities.

In Sweden, by contrast, creative consumption is manifest at the domestic level. New traditions constantly emerge, and form part of what Löfgren calls a 'lust for ritual'. Such differences may emerge in the attitude to the objects as gifts. In Sweden there is a concern to include home-made gifts and decorations, precisely because anxiety arises over the articulation with folk culture, while Carrier argues that these must be eschewed in the United States since here it is anxiety over the articulation with commercial popular culture, i.e. the over-coming of materialism, which is of greatest concern. In all these cases, however, it is the diversity of modern goods and media images, whether Searle-Chatterjee's Christmas cards or Belk's annual Christmas films, and the struggle over what symbolic value these should have which seem to have become the main battleground for the conflicts over what Christmas should properly be. As Moeran and Skov note, when this reaches the extreme integration between commerce and Christ-mas found in Japan consumerism and culture become essentially synonymous.

## Christmas as the Festival of the Local and the Global

Creative consumerism has increasingly become the main instrument for achieving one of the most often observed attributes of Christmas and the other factor which forms the focus for several chapters in this volume. Christmas appears as historically the best example out of the Christian liturgy of a syncretic festival, and one which today has man-aged to conquer the globe well beyond the reach of its original religious base. These two observations could hardly be coincidental. It seems likely that the same properties of syncretism have enabled Christmas today to establish its global reach and its local significance. Christmas is a festival beloved of folklorists, it is they who have provided by far the richest literature on the festival. It seems that at whatever date and region we encounter the festival it has accreted to itself a wealth of local rites and customs often of considerable specificity. If a given region of Europe has no other memorable and 'quaint' traditions it would seem at least to have some Christmas 'mumming' house visiting or special foods in association. Admittedly this may not be for the 25 December festival, since Christmas seems to be dispersed amongst a wide range of feasts and saints' days from November to New Year's Day, but there is a recognizable commonality to these winter festivities. Today if there remains some possibility of the larger community of a village or suburb having a sense of itself as such then this is the festival in which the original villagers combine with the newly settled commuters and recently retired to show their devotion to the local community as pseudo-family. Here they will sing Christmas carols, but be delighted also to sing a version or tune that is remembered as specific to this region.

In this respect Christmas differs at least in degree from other religiously sanctioned festivals to make it appear as the quintessential local occasion. Miles (1912) is very good at separating out the Christian elements from the pagan elements, but also makes clear the artificial nature of this exercise since in parallel with Warner (1976) on the formation of the cult of the Virgin Mary it was based upon very specific elements extracted out of a most unpromising foundation in the Christian Gospels. Amongst the best evidence for this is the radical rejection of Christmas by more fundamentalist Christian groups wishing to return to the true faith.

If it were not that we invent a conceptual gulf between 'authentic' folklore and 'inauthentic' popular culture, we would probably credit considerable continuity between these works on regional customs and the volume of recent studies on the emergence of the modern Christmas, which shows the same capacity to develop rituals of popular culture, from Santa Claus in his department store grottoes, to the speeches of queens and presidents, to office parties. In both cases we find an uneasy but marked relationship between the legitimacy of formal religion and the actual popular practices, which usually have a tenuous religious justification at best. In many respects we see a classic form of syncretism in which a wide range of local elements take form under the umbrella of some more general image of which they are all in some sense 'versions'. Once again the classical antecedents could hardly be more evident. The writings of Halsberghe on the cult of Sol Invictus as the high point of classical syncretism, the specific replacement of these and other Roman celebrations by Christmas as a deliberate attempt to secure Christianity through syncretism where simple replacement seemed impossible to secure: these dominate the birth of Christmas.

This ability of Christmas to appropriate, that is to secure its identity almost irrespective of the content of the rites which take place in its name, is reflected once again in the several chapters in this volume exploring Christmas in regions far from its original heartland in Christian Europe. Moeran and Skov's paper on Japan and Bodenhorn on the Iñupiat provide portrayals of the most exotic 'Christmas' in this regard, but my own chapter also notes the manner in which Christmas has become if anything more important to Hindu and Muslim peoples of Trinidad than to Christians. At the limits Christmas may be merely a façade for quite heterogeneous events. Bodenhorn's description of Christmas amongst the Iñupiat suggests that this has indeed become a key winter festival with a variety of associated celebrations. But there is no attempt to include the specific forms of Christmas that have become established in the global form, rather there is a focusing upon dance, song, and rituals explicitly linked to Iñupiat customs which aim to focus the festival on the celebration of 'local' forms. In stark contrast are those cases where it is the familiar Christmas rites that remain while the title changes. Lane (1981: 137–8) notes that in the Soviet Union Christmas was abolished, but Lenin created the 'New Year's Celebration', which included lighting up a tree, giving presents to children, sending out cards, and the figure of Grandfather Frost.

As the festival starts to penetrate into areas such as South Asia, China, and the Muslim world it seems that potentially at least we have the makings of the first truly global festival as popular culture (though we are admittedly a long way from such a state at present). In many respects the case-study of Christmas provides the vanguard for the now fashionable studies which come under the term 'local' and 'global'. It demonstrates more securely than any theoretical argument the weaknesses of approaches which posit global homogenization against local heterogeneity. In this case we see clearly that the ability of this festival to become potentially the very epitome of globalization derives from the very same quality of easy syncretism which makes Christmas in each and every place the triumph of localism, the protector and legitimation for specific regional and particular customs and traditions. As Löfgren points out for Sweden this is the festival *par excellence* where the arguments emerge from the strong sense that 'we' have always done it this way, even though the rite in question may be watching Walt Disney cartoons.

Once again it is noteworthy how fully the modern consciousness of this local–global condition is reflected in the fourth century AD. The relationship which today is labelled that of the 'local' and the 'global' would have seemed quite familiar to this period of the Roman Empire, which certainly had pretensions to the global at least in relation to the equivalent concept of civilization. The meaning of the core term 'Roman' had obviously been expanding during the building up of the republic and then the empire. But in this century it is likely that there was a considerable jolt to the given sense of Roman identity. It was not merely that increasing numbers of recruits from far-flung corners were settling in and adding to the heterogeneity of the core. There was also the increasing influence of cults such as Sol, Mithra, and Christianity, which together amounted to a syncretism fusing traditional Roman forms with Eastern traditions. Most of all there was the impact of the foundation of Constantinople as a result of which the empire itself no longer had an unambiguous centre at its original point. For the Romans of the fourth century, as for us in the twentieth, the legacy of an expansion of empire/colonialism meant this simultaneity in the sense of the world becoming one place, but that one place fragmenting into heterogeneity. The attraction of syncretic strategies which resolve these tensions, partly by denying them, is evident and provides the backdrop to the foundation of this festival which remains a high point of syncretism thereafter. We can see the same process operating in the contemporary world, as in Trinidad, which takes a festival condemned as an unwarranted importation of 'tropical snowscapes' and makes from it the prime instrument for creating the specific and distinct sense of being Trinidadian.

Christmas is then the festival *par excellence* of both the local and the global, but this simultaneity in the sense of expansion and localism is itself in turn a key attribute of the more general sense of modernity. Indeed this same Janus-faced structure seems also to encompass the temporality of Christmas, and thereby to implicate the festival in the response to the contradictions of living with a sense of modernity.

Christmas is today, as it has always been, a dynamic festival highly responsive to the changes in its external conditions and simultaneously perhaps the best example of a nostalgic festival which seeks to deny time in its embodiment of rites as they have always been. It is this temporal component to the larger contradictions of Christmas that comes to prominence in Löfgren's Swedish families who cannot but impose the Christmas they are engaged in upon a backdrop of Christmas past. I do not wish to deny that Christmas today is essentially a modern festival to be understood in relation to modernity, but as the extended comparison with the fourth century AD has attempted to demonstrate, this is not the first time this has been the case.

## The Structure and Dynamics of Christmas

In the above account three major attributes of Christmas have been considered: its relationship to the family, to materialism, and to syncretism. In each case the relationship to Christmas seemed to exhibit contradictory features. The festival manages to be both inversion and embodiment with respect to family values. Similarly it seems the most extravagant promotion of commodity values and yet the instrument which negates them as gift. It also manages to be both the most local and most global of religious festivals. This sense of contradiction seems to pervade, as ambivalence, the experience of the festival today. We are used to thinking of Christmas as the time for both joy and suicides, of materialism and also its repudiation, of family togetherness and family quarrelling.

At this point the evidence for such contradictions may be placed against the material on the internal structure and dynamics of the festival. I noted at the beginning of this introduction that the festival may be regarded as commonly having 'twin peaks'. In the Roman pre-Christmas traditions this is clear in that the period of the Saturnalia and the Kalends seem in some sense a whole but with two periods of more intensive celebration. Similarly in the contemporary English Christmas there seems to be some relationship with New Year's Eve, which as Kuper points out, seems to repeat but then close off the festival. A point made by Moeran and Skov is that Christmas in Japan as in other areas has to establish itself against pre-existing festivals and indeed in this case this appears to be accomplished again through the development of a 'twin peaked' relationship with the Japanese New Year. In many areas and historical periods, however, this dualism within a single festival seems to be replaced by two apparently independent festivals, those of Christmas and carnival. It should be clear, however, looking at the historical trajectory, that there is an important relationship between these, and certainly common origins. Indeed many writings on carnival which generally ignore its relationship to other festivals may thereby have failed to perceive key relational components.

It may help at this stage if we take advantage of those historical periods which do see a radical break between the two festivals, since they may enable us to examine in turn the two tendencies otherwise conflated within the single event. While Christmas has attracted mainly folklore and historical works, carnival is a favourite topic of theorists and social scientists more generally, and it is here that the topic of inversion receives its fullest treatment. Many analyses treat carnival inversion in relatively simple terms, usually celebrating it for its objectification of some radical political alternative (Gilmore 1975 and to an extent Le Roy Ladurie 1981), or arguing that it provides cathartic support for a dominant ideology (DaMatta 1977, Eco 1984). More recently the analysis of carnival has itself emphasized contradictions within its structure, especially since the influential article by Cohen (1982) on the Notting Hill Gate Carnival.

Although Cohen demonstrates the importance of ambivalence in practice to the 'success' of carnival, the main attempt to account for it as integral remains the work of Bakhtin (1968) on Rabelais. This deals with that part of the medieval period in which by and large the pre-Puritan Church actively sanctioned a series of inversion forms, including the ridiculing of priests and serious religion. Bakhtin argues that this was in large measure because they recognized that laughter as a particular form of truth and mockery could also be a valid approach to the mysteries of the divine. Most especially it becomes a victory over fear and awe, as the terrifying is recognized as the merely grotesque (ibid. 91). As the attacks on the popular culture of early Christmas, noted by Miles, make clear there are strong continuities between the Roman festivals and elements of Christmas inversion found in the election of the mock king and the boy bishop. Bakhtin helps us to comprehend the contemporary elements of inversion as not merely destructive of orders but productive of perspectives, as constitutive instruments, not merely radical alternatives. His approach is invaluable in resolving what up to now have seemed like contradictory readings of the event. We can still see today feasting, lavishness, and disreputable behaviour as key points in the formation of the sense of the family and the home.

It is much less common to find instances of Christmas which are so 'purified' of their carnivalesque elements as to make clear the other side to this Christmas structure. Contemporary Christmas in Western Europe may come close to this, however. In Britain there remains the cross-dressing and burlesque of the pantomime (Cinderella's passage from domestic to palace has been the traditionally most popular— Pimlott 1978: 155). Going to see a pantomime remains one of the near to obligatory events of Christmas, but this is shunted off from the main festivities, which retain only the element of drinking and possible impropriety around the Christmas meal. Instead we have a considerable emphasis on the 'serious' element of re-establishing the domestic, the sentimentality and nostalgia of family life, and the continuity of home and tradition. A similar situation exists with regard to Trinidad, where the clear separation of Christmas from carnival means that we find a Christmas which is perhaps closer to the Dickensian image than anything experienced in British popular culture. Here we find an intense domesticity in the virtual devotion to the home and the larger project of descent continuity, in almost total opposition to the event-centred, street-based festivities of carnival.

The West Indian case is helpful in indicating the importance of dynamism to the structure of the festival. The original celebration of Christmas by West Indian slaves has been the subject of a detailed study whose conclusion is mirrored in the title of a recent book *The Black Saturnalia* (Dirks 1987). This was the period of licensed mockery, inversion, and quite commonly open revolt against oppression. In some West Indian islands Christmas retains elements of this original inversion form. In others, however, including Trinidad, we see the emergence of first a dualism and then a clear split between the celebration of carnival and Christmas. Most recently we find that Christmas has been finally denuded of virtually all carnivalesque elements to become an unambiguously domestic festival.

This two-century period in the West Indies seems thereby to replicate something of a two-millennium trajectory in Europe. Prior to the invention of Christmas we see a single form of festival in the Saturnalia/Kalends with the gifting and feasting closely integrated into the inversion/embodiment aspects. The festivities which related to Deus Sol Invictus seem to have had a more serious form establishing a central if syncretic cult focus. Christmas then follows by solidifying this serious and religious element and adding to it the unambiguous focus of attention in the image of the family. The historical sources suggest, however, that Christmas for all but a few is quickly integrated into a continuity with the bacchanalic elements of the surrounding festivities as popular culture. Thereafter we find the development of carnival as an independent legacy of Saturnalia and a Christmas which sometimes seems to retain the sense of inversion and bacchanal while at other times developing into a more purist celebration of the domestic as serious and nostalgic or religious ritual. What this historical survey should tell us is that what is created in Christmas and carnivalesque celebration may be, even when apparently distinct and different, actually closely related and perhaps even the same.

## Interpretation

Bakhtin's work suggests that the subject of such festivities should first be understood at the level of cosmology, and its effects on society should be seen first in cosmological terms. Indeed the interpretation of this festival I wish to propose is that it is primarily concerned with the distance between the moral and normative order objectified in the domestic and family setting and the moral and normative order which is understood as pertaining to the larger universe within which we live, which itself, although vast, is also expected to share certain social, affective, and 'human' properties. The birth of Christmas is itself an attempt to anthropomorphize the divinity in the form of the domestic family unit, and I would argue that we can interpret much of the associated ritual as an attempt to bring 'home' cosmological principles. This, it may be noted, is hardly a novel perspective inasmuch as anthropological perspectives on religion have since Durkheim been dominated by the relationship between cosmology and society.

Christmas is then the festival of the family as microcosm. The relationship may be drawn between 'ideal' royal and divine families, but also possible is the application of 'family' to wider social groups such as the local community at Christmas. All of this establishes the family as the primary unit of sociality. Once established the idiom is used to encompass an ever wider sense of potential sociality until it becomes an emblem of cosmological notions of the universe as religion or 'humankind' objectified as the 'spirit' of Christmas. Christmas in Japan does not conform to these generalizations about the family, partly because, as Moeran and Skov make clear, prior festivals occupy this niche. The instructive exception is Christmas amongst the Iñupiat. As Bodenhorn notes, the celebration seems to reverse many of the generalizations I am making, but this may be precisely because the implications of the category of family itself are reversed. In this case there remains at the level of ideology a powerful integration between a wider cosmology and a wider sociality. The principle image of society includes all members of the Iñupiat as well as the whales with whom they are in a continual cycle of exchange. The emergence of a strong nuclear family represents not a microcosm but, quite the contrary, a 'modern' threat to sociality. Christmas here is a political strategy attempting to use the possibilities of this festival to deny a threat which actually is very present.

The historical festival of Christmas has worked in two directions, often at the same time. There is the carnivalesque element, which is centrifugal, throwing us out into the burlesque of the streets, over-coming our awe of the outside world, conquering it in mockery and music. Where this is the sole strategy we cannot talk about Christmas but only pure carnival. The other side, which sometimes becomes the sole element of Christmas, is the centripetal process, which first stabilizes around the most basic unit of sociality and then gradually extends towards some sense of the divine for those with religious beliefs or an equivalent larger morality for the secular celebrants. For the most secular the family itself may be the sole repository of those feelings of general 'goodwill' and social obligation which stand as larger moral and social imperatives. Amongst the Iñupiat we have the opposite process, where first it is the widest image of society that is secured and the emphasis is then turned inwards to dissolve smaller social units and networks into the larger whole.

The most important instruments for achieving these goals have his-torically been materialism and syncretism. Syncretism is perhaps the more obvious as the creation of linkages between the local and the global. Universalistic religious images and mass media rituals such as Christmas carol singing and shopping become also localized within the specificity of their relationship to the home. Christmas may be everywhere but the only true Christmas is within one's own home. In some cases the home 'captures' the world through the creation of wider relationships as by feasting or through gifts. The minimal units of sociality are constructed, such as the Christmas card relationship, noted by Searle-Chatterjee, where for twenty years the only communi-cation between two households is the annual exchange of these tokens.

This is done with the understanding that such cards keep alive the potential for intimacy if circumstances should ever change to allow it. In many cases the local custom becomes a token of what is thought to happen throughout the world at Christmas time. Thereby the actual expansion of Christmas across the globe becomes itself an instrument in accomplishing that sense of Christmas as the festival of the microcosm. The more people believe that their celebration is a token of a global action, a rite being repeated by millions across the world, the more Christmas is felt to establish a relationship between the celebrant and the world at large.

The place of materialism is less obvious but increasingly important. The tension between the gift as 'local' and commodity as 'global' form and the way in which Christmas attempts a reconciliation between them emerges from the combined papers of Belk and Carrier on the American Christmas. The two possibilities they explore seem to be if anything extended once one looks at Christmas elsewhere. Carrier's point about the appropriation of commodities is a still better description of what is happening in Trinidad than in the United States, while Belk's point about the ability of Christmas to express aspects of capitalism seems to be taken to a still finer pitch in Japan than in the United States. The context for this lies in an 'updating' of the conclusions of Lévi-Strauss's paper, where it has become clear that the very image of social death that is placated is increasingly occupied by the spectre of antisocial and crass materialism, which thereby may have become in many instances the dominant concern of Christmas today. It is the 'spirit' of Christmas which is expected to transmute the image of fetishized commodities as the death of authentic social life into the very instrument for this crucial vision of pure sociality.

In Japan the paraphernalia associated with Christmas coalesce as 'manuals for consumerism'. These provide mechanisms by which people are instructed to construct a very specific social form (though as couples rather than as families) out of the myriad object arrays cascading from Japanese and international capitalism. As such Japan exemplifies a larger point made in all four chapters which asserts that whether Christmas is used to express the imperatives of capitalism or to transform these into sociality it is the goods themselves and the symbolism granted to them that is a central instrument in accomplishing this expressive purpose.

To account for the wide variety of Christmases as actually celebrated and the varied relationship between Christmas and carnival obviously no single interpretation will suffice. Nevertheless I will suggest a linkage between various related factors in order to account for certain tendencies that may be generalized over several (but certainly not all) regions and histories. The underlying factor is the sense of distance which a society feels exists between itself and the larger world inhabited as cosmology. In many periods and regions there may not be any strong sense of distance. In such cases where there may indeed be only a weak or indeed no notion of society, the cosmological task of what has become Christmas is achieved as a structural motif. Here the creation of the festival image is a temporary externalization for reincorporation. It may be compared with the Frazerian motif noted in Lévi-Strauss's paper of an externalizing figurehead of society being killed and then renewed. The more recent manifestation is in carnival, when the order of the world is overturned in an almost abstract logical form through Lords of Misrule and so forth, as part of renewal. In such periods cosmology is close to hand and religion is strong, as in the original Saturnalia of the Roman republic or in the Rabelaisian images of medieval Christianity. Gifting may be less prominent, and religions less syncretic. The emphasis is less on the home and more on the public sphere and the streets. Indeed the distance to the domestic sphere is not so great and one has more a sense of the household spilling onto the street. The overall message is life affirmation.

The second version comes during periods when a community has a strong sense of itself as a 'society' and sees this as under threat. Here we may find a much stronger desire to objectify a solid sense of the social. The starting-point in the objectification of sociality is commonly some immediate form such as the house or family. There is a desire to re-establish and retain this highly localized image. This then sets up a problem of distance between this strong sense of retention and enclosure (e.g. as thrift) and the universalistic sources of morality which are supposed to justify the moral community. Typically in such cases we find that once the family and home is secured it becomes incorporative through gifting, feasting, the exchange of cards, and other such strategies. The bright lights within the home illuminate and gradually dispel the dark cold and austere outside, making it bow to the sociality within. From this base it reaches out with the aim of incorporating some larger humanity in a divine or global sphere. In the contemporary Christmas it is often not a wider social group so much as materialism itself which must be placated and reincorporated. The syncretic imperative is very strong, with the local rites being understood as versions or embodiments of much larger even eschatological concerns. It is society rather than life *per se* which is affirmed.

These are only proposed as ideal types in the cultural logic of Christmas. There are certainly comparative anthropological approaches as, for example, in the work of Victor Turner, Hilda Kuper, and Max Gluckman on African ritual, but the specific articulations argued here may pertain largely to this European trajectory until the quite recent 'global' expansion. If the relationships posited are correct it may be that several of the elements of the fourth-century Christmas, such as the emphasis on gifting, would not have been as prominent in the earlier Saturnalia of the Roman republic, which did not possess the same sense of modernity and threat. Similarly in the contemporary Christmas there may be an element of this distinction in the contrasts Löfgren and Searle-Chatterjee note between the dominant middle-class modern form and a working-class version which refuses the sentimentality and anxious ritualism by which the family is painfully constructed. Christmas amongst the Iñupiat seems to be striving towards the first version of Christmas, a festival which integrates sociality with cosmology and does not use gifting but emphasizes public celebration.

Any given instance may only exhibit some of these aspects. Quite commonly they are separated off, as when we see Christmas opposed to carnival; in other instances we see them as tensions and contradictions inhabiting the same events and often causing much quarrelling and dispute as a result. In some cases, as in the chapter by Moeran and Skov, the festival is stretched through syncretism beyond the point at which this general model has any use as an interpretive tool. In other cases, as implied by Belk with regard to materialism or those who see carnival as the force behind insurrection, the 'means' overcome the original 'ends', at least with regard to their social and political effects. Perhaps most interesting are cases such as portrayed by Bodenhorn where this process of Christmas as private microcosm can be seen as being actively resisted, but in a manner which seems to acknowledge that this tendency is emerging through the appropriation of Christmas.

In conclusion, the work on the 'invention of tradition' as a description of the formation of the contemporary Christmas would seem to need complementing by an attempt to account for its extant features. This implies an explanation of these traits in relation to the experience of modernity. At first glance this would seem to render the analysis of contemporary Christmas rather an isolated case incommensurable with earlier periods. The theory espoused in this introduction denies this. Instead we can contrast the manner of Christmas celebration between two states of society, one of which not only tends to characterize several established features of contemporary Christmas, but perhaps surprisingly also seems apt for the period when Christmas was first 'invented'. This is because it was quite as open to the Romans, as to us today, to see themselves as both the vanguard relative to others and also as those who have lost the inheritance of their forebears, which seem two of the central conditions of being modern. We do not want to project some sort of *déjà vu* implying that Romans of this period sensed a forthcoming 'decline and fall' (to the extent that historians still regard this phrase as appropriate), but the writings of the fourth century AD have a strong sense of rapid change and transformation away from established customs associated with the 'ancients'.

The Romans clearly possessed a parallel sense of modernity, as found in the deliberate archaism in the sculpture and decorations at Pompeii and in the emphasis upon the 'ancients' in much of their writings. Later on there is a constant harking back to republican times or at least the original empire of the Augustan age. As noted above, Christmas is for the Romans, despite its newness, also in some sense a return to a concern with traditional values in which the future lies in the domestic and its inheritance through the child. The concern with comparing the present with the time of the ancients and of potential fragmentation within the contemporary world is highly reminiscent of our own self-appraisal and suggests an analogy with many of the main characteristics we have come to regard as amounting to a perception of ourselves as belonging to 'modern' or perhaps even 'post-modern' societies. This is why the extended comparison with the pre-Christmas festivals of ancient Rome would seem most apt. It allows us to interpret the varieties of contemporary Christmas in relation to the condition of modernity, but at the same time makes modernity itself a precedented and comparative condition that does not determine one particular version of such festivals.

Anthropology as a comparative and generalizing discipline founded in the close observation of specific instances but then transcending these in order to attempt wider interpretations of the nature of sociality still retains a vital role in the understanding of contemporary phenomena. In this case the comparisons are both between different social contexts and historical periods. It is through such an approach that the specific features which seem to unify what otherwise might appear a disparate and contingent festival can be recognized. We should not be misled by the capacity of Christmas to attract to itself those local and specific rites which exercise the close attention of folklore studies and regional historians. It is this same syncretic tendency which enables the festival to achieve that bridge between domestic ritual and a sense of global and cosmological scale. Academic analysis should therefore strive to achieve the same effect as Christmas itself. That is to recognize that the apparently parochial and local rites are actually significant materials for understanding the articulation between key components of contemporary life—religious and secular moralities, the role of contemporary families, and the threat posed by the sheer scale of materialism.

### Note

I could not possibly have written this introduction without the assistance of Lyn Foxhall. The majority of the points I have made with regard to the fourth century AD emerged from conversations with her or books she lent me. I am also grateful for criticisms of an earlier version by various contributors to this book as well as Bruce Kapferer and Buck Schieffelin.

### References

BAKHTIN, M. (1968). *Rabelais and his World*, trans. H. Iwolsky. Cambridge, Mass.: MIT Press.

BARNES, T. (1981). *Constantine and Eusebius*. Cambridge, Mass.: Harvard University Press.

BARNETT, J. (1954). *The American Christmas: A Study of National Culture*. New York: Macmillan.

BARTH, F. (1987). *Cosmologies in the Making*. Cambridge: Cambridge University Press.

BELK, R. (1987). 'A Child's Christmas in America: Santa Claus as Deity, Consumption as Religion', *Journal of American Culture*, 10/1: 87–100.

—— (1989). 'Materialism and the Modern U.S. Christmas', in E. Hirschman (ed.), *Interpretive Consumer Research*. Provo, Ut.: Association for Consumer Research: 115–35.

—— (forthcoming). 'Carnival, Control and Corporate Culture in Contemporary Halloween Celebrations', in J. Santino (ed.), *Halloween*. Knoxville, Tenn.: University of Tennessee Press.

BRADLEY, R. (1990). *Discovering the Roman Family*. Oxford: Oxford University Press.

CAPLOW, T. (1984). 'Rule Enforcement without Visible Means: Christmas Gift Giving in Middletown', *American Journal of Sociology*, 89/6: 1306–23.

CHEAL, D. (1988). *The Gift Economy*. London: Routledge.

COHEN, A. (1982). 'A Polyethnic London Carnival as a Contested Cultural Performance', *Ethnic and Racial Studies*, 5: 23–42.

DAMATTA, R. (1977). 'Constraint and License: A Preliminary Study of Two Brazilian National Rituals', in S. Moore and B. Meyerhoff (eds.), *Secular Rituals*. Assen: Van Gorcum: 244–64.

DIRKS, R. (1987). *The Black Saturnalia*. Gainsville, Fla.: University of Florida Press.

DIXON, S. (1988). *The Roman Mother*. London: Croom Helm.

DU BOULAY, J. (1974). *Portrait of a Greek Mountain Village*. Oxford: Oxford University Press.

ECO, U. (1984). 'The Frames of Comic Freedom', in U. Eco, V. Ivanov, and M. Rector (eds.), *Carnival*. The Hague: Mouton: 1–9.

GARNSEY, P. (1991). 'Child Rearing in Ancient Italy', in D. Kertzer and R. Saller (eds.), *The Family in Italy*. New Haven, Conn.: Yale University Press.

GILMORE, D. (1975). 'Carnival in Fvenmayor', *Journal of Anthropological Research*, 31: 331–49.

GOLBY, J. (1981). 'A History of Christmas', in *Popular Culture: Themes and Issues*. Milton Keynes: Open University Press: Block 1, Units 1/2.

—— and PURDUE, A. (1986). *The Making of the Modern Christmas*. London: Batsford.

GOODY, J. (1983). *The Development of the Family and Marriage in Europe*. Cambridge: Cambridge University Press.

GUDEMAN, S., and RIVERA, A. (1990). *Conversations in Colombia*. Cambridge: Cambridge University Press.

HALSBERGHE, G. (1972). *The Cult of Sol Invictus*. Leiden: E. J. Brill.

JONES, A. (1964). *The Later Roman Empire 284–602*. Oxford: Basil Blackwell.

KERTZER, D., and SALLER, R. (1991) (eds.). *The Family in Italy*. New Haven, Conn.: Yale University Press.

LACEY, W. (1986). 'Patria Potestas', in B. Rawson (ed.), *The Family in Ancient Rome*. London: Croom Helm.

LANE, C. (1981). *The Rites of Rulers*. Cambridge: Cambridge University Press.

LE ROY LADURIE, E. (1981). *Carnival in Romans*. Harmondsworth: Penguin.

LIBANIUS (1977). *Selected Works*. Cambridge, Mass.: Harvard University Press.

MILES, C. (1912). *Christmas in Ritual and Tradition, Christian and Pagan*. London: T. Fisher Unwin.

MILLER, D. (1987). *Material Culture and Mass Consumption*. Oxford: Basil Blackwell.

—— (Berg, forthcoming). *Modernity: An Ethnographic Approach*.

PIMLOTT, J. (1978). *The Englishman's Christmas*. Hassocks: Harvester Press.

RAWSON, B. (1986). 'The Roman Family', in B. Rawson (ed.), *The Family in Ancient Rome*. London: Croom Helm: 1–57.

SAMUELSON, S. (1982). *Christmas: An Annotated Bibliography*. New York: Garland Publishing Inc.

SCULLARD, H. (1981). *Festivals and Ceremonies of the Roman Republic*. London: Thames & Hudson.

SHAW, B. (1991). 'The Cultural Meaning of Death: Age and Gender in the Roman Family', in D. Kertzer and R. Saller (eds.), *The Family in Italy*. New Haven, Conn.: Yale University Press: 66–90.

WARNER, M. (1976). *Alone of All her Sex*. London: Weidenfeld & Nicolson.

WEIGHTMAN, G., and HUMPHRIES, S. (1987). *Christmas Past*. London: Sidgwick & Jackson.

WILK, R. (1990). 'Consumer Goods as a Dialogue about Development', *Culture and History*, 7: 79–100.

# 2

# Father Christmas Executed

## *Claude Lévi-Strauss*

Christmas of 1951 in France was marked by a controversy—of great interest to press and public alike—that gave the generally festive atmosphere an unusual note of bitterness. A number of the clergy had for several months expressed disapproval of the increasing importance given by both families and the business sector to the figure of Father Christmas. They denounced a disturbing 'paganization' of the Nativity that was diverting public spirit from the true Christian meaning of Christmas to the profit of a myth devoid of religious value. Attacks spread just before Christmas; with more discretion, but just as much conviction, the Protestant Church chimed in with the Catholic Church. A number of articles and letters in the press bore witness to a keen public interest in the affair and showed general hostility to the Church's position. It came to a head on Christmas Eve with a demonstration that a reporter from *France-soir* described as follows:

### SUNDAY SCHOOL CHILDREN WITNESS FATHER CHRISTMAS BURNT IN DIJON CATHEDRAL PRECINCT

#### Dijon, 24 December

Father Christmas was hanged yesterday afternoon from the railings of Dijon Cathedral and burnt publicly in the precinct. This spectacular execution took place in the presence of several hundred Sunday school children. It was a decision made with the agreement of the clergy who had condemned Father Christmas as a usurper and heretic. He was accused of 'paganizing' the Christmas festival and installing himself like a cuckoo in the nest, claiming more and more space for himself. Above all he was blamed for infiltrating all the state schools from which the crib has been scrupulously banished.

On Sunday, at three o'clock in the afternoon, the unfortunate fellow with the white beard, scapegoated like so many innocents before him, was executed by his accusers. They set fire to his beard and he vanished into smoke.

At the time of the execution a communiqué was issued to the following effect:

'Representing all Christian homes of the parish keen to struggle against lies, 250 children assembled in front of the main door of Dijon Cathedral and burned Father Christmas.

'It wasn't intended as an attraction, but as a symbolic gesture. Father Christmas has been sacrificed. In truth, the lies about him cannot arouse religious feeling in a child and are in no way a means of education. Others may say and write what they want about Father Christmas, but the fact is he is only the counterweight of a modern-day Mr Bogeyman.

'For Christians the festivity of Christmas must remain the annual celebration of the birth of the Saviour.'

Father Christmas's execution in the Cathedral precinct got a mixed response from the public and provoked lively commentaries even from Catholics.

The affair has divided the town into two camps.

Dijon awaits the resurrection of Father Christmas, assassinated yesterday in the cathedral precinct. He will arise this evening at six o'clock in the Town Hall. An official communiqué announced that, as every year, the children of Dijon are invited to Liberation Square where Father Christmas will speak to them from the floodlit roof of the Town Hall.

Canon Kir, deputy-mayor of Dijon, will not take part in this delicate affair.

The same day, the torture of Father Christmas became front-page news. Not one newspaper missed an article on it, some—like *France-soir*, which has the highest circulation of all French papers—even went so far as to make it the subject of an editorial. There was general disapproval towards the attitude of the Dijon clergy. It would seem that the religious authorities were right to withdraw from the battle, or at least to keep silent. Yet they are apparently divided on the issue. The tone of most of the articles was one of tactful sentimentality: it's so nice to believe in Father Christmas, it doesn't harm anyone, the children get such satisfaction from it and store up such delicious memories for their adulthood, etc.

They are, in fact, begging the question. It is not a matter of rationalizing why children like Father Christmas, but rather, why adults invented him in the first place. Widespread reaction to the issue, however, clearly suggests a rift between public opinion and the Church. The incident is important, despite its apparent pettiness; since the war there has been a growing reconciliation in France between a largely non-believing public and the Church: the presence of a political party as distinctly denominational as the MRP[1] on government committees is proof of this. The anti-clerical faction was well aware of the unexpected opportunity offered to them: they are the ones in Dijon and elsewhere who are acting as protectors of the threatened Father Christmas. Father Christmas, symbol of irreligion—what a paradox! For in this case everything is happening as if it were the Church adopting an avidly critical attitude on honesty and truth, while the rationalists act as guardians of superstition. This apparent role reversal is enough to suggest that the whole naïve business is about something much more profound. We are in fact witnessing an important example of a very rapid shift of customs and beliefs both in France and elsewhere. It is not every day that an anthropologist gets the chance to observe in his own society the sudden growth of a rite, even a cult; to research its causes and study its impact on other forms of religious life; and, finally, to understand how both mental and social transformations relate to the seemingly superficial issue on which the Church, so experienced in these matters, has in fact been right to point out a deeper significance.

In the past few years the celebration of Christmas has expanded in a way unknown since before the war. This development, both in form and content, is undoubtedly the direct result of the influence and prestige of the USA. Thus we have simultaneously witnessed the appearance of large illuminated and decorated Christmas trees at crossroads and along motorways; decorated wrapping paper for Christmas presents; illustrated Christmas cards and the custom of displaying them on the mantelpiece during the fateful week; pleas for contributions from the Salvation Army with their great begging bowls on squares and streets; and finally, people dressed up as Father Christmas listening to the requests of children in department stores. All these customs which just a few years ago seemed so puerile and weird to French visitors in the USA, showing clear evidence of a basic incompatibility of mentality between the two cultures, have been introduced to, and spread through, France with an ease that offers food for thought to cultural historians.

In this case we are witnessing a huge process of diffusion, similar to remote examples of ancient technological innovations in fire-lighting or boat-building techniques. Yet it is both easier and more difficult to analyse events that are happening before our very eyes in our own society. It is easier because ongoing experience is protected in all its moments and nuances. Yet it is harder because it is on such rare occasions that we can see the extreme complexity of even the most subtle social transformations; and because the obvious explanations of events in which we ourselves are involved are very different from the real causes.

Thus it would be too easy to explain the development of the celebration of Christmas in France simply in terms of influence from the USA. This alone is inadequate. Consider briefly the obvious explanations along these lines: there are more Americans in France celebrating Christmas according to their own customs; the cinema, 'digests' and American novels, articles in the national press have all introduced American customs that are backed up with American economic and military power. It is even possible that the Marshall Plan, directly or indirectly, may have encouraged the import of various products linked to the rites of Christmas. But none of that is enough to explain the phenomenon. Customs imported from the USA influence strata of the population that do not realize their origin. Thousands of workers for whom communist influence would discredit anything marked *made in USA*, are adopting them as readily as others. In addition to simple diffusion we need to recall the important process first identified by Kroeber called *stimulus diffusion*, whereby an imported practice is not assimilated but acts as a catalyst. In other words, its mere presence stimulates the appearance of a similar practice which had already existed in a nascent state in the secondary environment. To illustrate this with an example from our subject: a paper manufacturer goes to the USA, at the invitation of American colleagues or a member of an economic mission, and notices that they make special wrapping paper for Christmas. He borrows the idea: that is an example of diffusion. A Parisian housewife goes to her local paper shop to buy some wrapping paper and notices some paper on display that she finds more attractive than the sort she usually buys. She is not aware of American customs, but the paper pleases her aesthetically and expresses an existing emotional state which previously lacked expression. In using it, she is not directly borrowing a foreign custom (as the paper manufacturer was), but the behaviour, as soon as it catches on, stimulates the spread of an identical custom.

Second, it should be remembered that before the war the celebration of Christmas was on the increase both in France and the rest of Europe. Though this is most obviously linked to a general rise in the standard of living, there are also more subtle causes. Christmas as we know it is essentially a modern festival in spite of its archaic characteristics. The use of mistletoe is not a direct survival from druid times. Rather, it seems to have come back in fashion in the Middle Ages.

The Christmas tree is only mentioned for the first time in some seventeenth-century German texts. It appears in England in the eighteenth century and not in France until the nineteenth century. Littré hardly seemed to know of it at all, or only in a form quite different from the one we know.[2] As he says: 'in some countries a branch of pine or holly, decorated in different ways, covered with sweets and toys for the children, makes up the festival'. The variety of names given to the person who distributes the children's toys—Father Christmas, Saint Nicholas, Santa Claus—shows that it is a result of a process of convergence and not an ancient prototype preserved everywhere intact.

Yet the contemporary development is not an invention either: it is an old celebration pieced together with various fragments which have not quite been forgotten. If, for Littré, the Christmas tree seems an almost exotic institution, Cheruel notes, significantly, in his *Historic Dictionary of French Institutions, Customs and Practices* (in the author's opinion, a revision of the Dictionary of National Antiquities of Sainte Palaye, 1697–1781): 'Christmas . . . was for several centuries and *up until recently* (author's emphasis) an occasion for family festivities'. There follows a description of eighteenth-century Christmas festivities which seem to bear no resemblance to ours. So the importance of our ritual has already fluctuated through the course of history; it has had its ups and downs. The American version is just its most recent form.

Let it be said in passing that these brief indicators are enough to show how in problems of this sort we must beware of overly easy explanations by an automatic appeal to 'relics' and 'survivals'. If in prehistoric times there had never been a cult of tree worship that continued in a variety of folklore customs, modern Europe would no doubt not have invented the Christmas tree. Yet—as shown above—it is also a recent invention. None the less, this invention was not born from nothing. Other medieval practices testify to this perfectly: the yule log (turned into cakes in Paris) made from a log big enough to burn through the night; Christmas candles, large enough to achieve the same result; the decoration of buildings (a custom in existence since the Roman Saturnalia, which we will return to) with green branches of ivy, holly, pine. Finally, and with no relation to Christmas, stories of the Round Table refer to a supernatural tree all covered in lights. In this context the Christmas tree seems to be a syncretic response, that is to say, it focuses on one object previously scattered attributes of others: magic tree, fire, long-lasting light, enduring greenness. Conversely, Father Christmas is, in his actual form, a modern invention. Even more recent is the belief (which makes Denmark run a special postal service to answer the letters from children all over the world) that he lives in Greenland, a Danish possession, and travels in a sleigh harnessed to reindeer. Some say this aspect of the legend arose during the last war because of American troops stationed in Iceland and Greenland. And yet the reindeer are not there by chance, for English texts from the Renaissance mention the display of antlers during Christmas dances long before any belief in Father Christmas, much less the development of his legend.

Very old elements are thus shuffled and reshuffled, others are introduced, original formulas perpetuate, transform, or revive old customs. There is nothing specifically new in what might be called (no pun intended) the rebirth of Christmas. Then why does it arouse such emotion and why is Father Christmas the focus for hostility from some?

Father Christmas is dressed in scarlet: he is a king. His white beard, his furs and his boots, the sleigh in which he travels evoke winter. He is called 'Father' and he is an old man, thus he incarnates the benevolent form of the authority of the ancients. That is quite clear, yet in what category can he be placed from the point of view of religious typology? He is not a mythic being, for there is no myth that accounts for his origin or his function. Nor is he a legendary figure, as there is no semi-historical account attached to him. In fact, this supernatural and immutable being, eternally fixed in form and defined by an exclusive function and a periodic return, belongs more properly to the family of the gods. Moreover, children pay him homage at certain times of the year with letters and prayers; he rewards the good and punishes the wicked. He is the deity of an age group of our society, an age group that is in fact defined by belief in Father Christmas. The only difference between Father Christmas and a true deity is that adults do not believe in him, although they encourage their children to do so and maintain this belief with a great number of tricks.

Father Christmas thus first of all expresses the difference in status between little children on the one hand, and adolescents and adults on the other. In this sense he is linked to a vast array of beliefs and practices which anthropologists have studied in many societies to try and understand rites of passage and initiation. There are, in fact, few societies where, in one way or another, children (and at times also women) are not excluded from the company of men through ignorance of certain mysteries or their belief—carefully fostered—in some illusion that the adults keep secret until an opportune moment, thus sanctioning the addition of the younger generation to the adult world. At times these rites bear a surprising resemblance to those considered here. For example, there is a startling analogy between Father Christmas and the *katchina* of the Indians of the south-west United States. These costumed and masked beings are gods and ancestors become incarnate who return periodically to visit their village and dance. They also come to punish or reward children, who do not recognize their elders in their traditional disguise. Father Christmas certainly belongs to the same family as now long-forgotten associates: Croquemitaine, Père Fouettard, etc. Significantly, the same educational trends which today forbid appeal to these punitive 'katchina' have succeeded in exalting the benevolent character of Father Christmas instead of—as the development of rationalism would have us suppose—dismissing him in a similar way. Education is in this sense not so rational as it might seem, for Father Christmas is no more 'rational' than Père Fouettard—the Church is right about this. Rather, what we are witnessing is a shift of myth and it is this that needs explaining.

Initiation rites and myths have a practical function in human societies: they help the elders to keep the younger generation in order and disciplined. All through the year we tell children Father Christmas is coming, to remind them that his generosity is in proportion to their good behaviour. Giving presents only at certain times is a useful way of disciplining children's demands, reducing to a brief period the time when they really have the *right* to demand presents. This simple explanation alone is enough to challenge the tenets of utilitarian explanations. For where do children get rights in the first place, and how is it these rights are imposed so imperiously on adults that they are obliged to work out an expensive and complex ritual in order to satisfy them? It can be seen straight away that belief in Father Christmas is not just a *hoax* imposed by adults on children for fun; it is, to a large extent, the result of a very onerous *transaction* between the two generations. He is part of a complete ritual, like the evergreens—pine, holly, ivy, mistletoe—with which we decorate our homes. Today a simple luxury, in some regions they were once the object of an *exchange* between two social groups. On Christmas Eve in England up until the end of the eighteenth century women used to go *gooding*, that is, begging from house to house and offering evergreen branches in return. We find children in the same bargaining position and it is worth noting here that when they beg on Saint Nicholas's Eve, children sometimes dress up as women—women, children: in both cases, the uninitiated.

Now, there is a very important aspect of initiation rituals which has not always been given adequate attention but which clarifies their nature far better than the utilitarian models discussed above. Consider the example of the katchina ritual of the Pueblo Indians mentioned earlier. If children are kept in the dark about the human nature of the people incarnating the katchina, is this simply to get them to fear, respect, and behave well? Of course, but that is only a secondary function of the ritual. There is another explanation which the myth of origin clarifies perfectly. This myth explains that the katchina are souls of the first native children who were dramatically drowned in a river at the time of the ancestral migrations. So the katchina are simultaneously proof of death and evidence of life after death. Moreover, when the Indians' ancestors finally settled in their village, the myth relates how the katchina used to come every year to visit them and, when they left, took away the children. The Indians, desperate at losing their off-spring, made a deal with the katchina that they would stay in the other world in exchange for promising to honour them every year with masked dances. If the children are excluded from the secret of the katchina it is not primarily to intimidate them. I would say just the opposite: it's because they *are* the katchina. They are kept out of the mystery because they represent the reality with which the mystery constitutes a kind of compromise. Their place is elsewhere—not with the masks and the living, but with the gods and the dead—with the gods who are the dead. And the dead are the children.

Arguably this interpretation can be extended to all initiation rites and even to all occasions when society is divided into two groups. 'Non-initiation' is not just a state of deprivation defined in terms of ignorance, illusion, or other negative connotations. There is a positive aspect to the relationship between initiates and non-initiates. It is a complementary relationship between two groups where one represents the dead and the other the living. Moreover, even during the course of a ritual the roles are often reversed, for the duality engenders a reciprocity of perspectives which, like a reflection in a mirror, can be endlessly repeated. If the uninitiated are the dead, they are also the super-initiated. And if, as also often happens, it is the initiates who personify the spirits of the dead to scare the novices, it will be their responsibility at a later stage of the ritual to disperse them and warn of their return. Without pushing the argument too much further, it should still be pointed out that, to the extent that rituals and beliefs linked to Father Christmas relate to a sociology of initiation (and that is beyond doubt), it reveals that beyond the conflict between children and adults lies a deeper dispute between the living and the dead.

I reached this conclusion by a synchronic analysis of the function of certain rituals and the content of myths that give rise to them. Yet a diachronic analysis would have produced the same result. For historians of religion and folklorists both generally agree that the distant origin of Father Christmas is to be found in the Abbé de Liesse, *Abbas Stultorum*, Abbé de la Malgouverné, a replica of the English Lord of Misrule, all characters who rule for a set period as kings of Christmas and who are all heirs of the King of the Roman Saturnalia. Now the Saturnalia was the festival of the *larvae*, those who died a violent death or were left unburied. The aged Saturn, devourer of his children, is the prototype for a number of similar figures: Father Christmas, benefactor of children; the Scandinavian Julebok, horned demon from the underworld who brings presents to the children; Saint Nicholas, who revives them and inundates them with presents; finally, the katchina, prematurely dead children who renounce their role as child murderers to become dispensers of punishments and presents. It should be added that, like the katchina, the ancient prototype of Saturn is a god of germination. In fact, the contemporary character of Santa Claus or Father Christmas is a result of a syncretic fusion of several different characters: Abbé de Liesse, child-bishop elected by Saint Nicholas; Saint Nicholas himself from whose festival beliefs in stockings, shoes, and chimneys originated. The Abbé de Liesse reigned on 25 December, Saint Nicholas on 6 December, the child-bishops were elected on Holy Innocents Day, i.e. 28 December. The Scandinavian Jul was celebrated in December. This leads us straight back to the *libertas decembris* of which Horace speaks and which du Tillot cited as early as the eighteenth century linking Christmas with the Saturnalia.

Explanations in terms of survivals are always inadequate. Customs neither disappear nor survive without a reason. When they do survive, the reason is less likely to be found in the vagaries of history than in the permanence of a function which analysing the present allows us to discover. The reason for giving so much prominence in this discussion to the Pueblo Indians is precisely because there is a lack of any conceivable historical link between their institutions and ours (with the exception of some late Spanish influence in the seventeenth century). This demonstrates that with the Christmas rituals we are witness not just to historical relics but to forms of thought and behaviour which illustrate the most general conditions of social life. The Saturnalia and the medieval celebration of Christmas do not contain the ultimate explanation for an otherwise inexplicable ritual devoid of meaning, but they do provide useful comparative material for making sense of the survival of institutions.

It is not surprising that non-Christian aspects of Christmas resemble the Saturnalia, as there are good reasons to suppose the Church fixed the date of the Nativity on 25 December (instead of March or January) to substitute its commemoration for the pagan festival that originally began on 17 December, but which at the end of the empire spread out over seven days, i.e. until the 24th. In fact, from antiquity up until the Middle Ages the 'festivals of December' show similar characteristics. First, the decoration of buildings with evergreens; next, the exchange, or giving to children, of gifts; gaiety and feasting; and finally, fraternization between rich and poor, masters and servants.

Looking more closely at the facts, certain structural analogies become strikingly evident. Like the Roman Saturnalia, medieval Christmas had two syncretic and opposite traits. It was first of all a gathering and a communion: distinction between class and status was temporarily abolished. Slaves and servants sat next to masters, and these became their servants. Richly stocked tables were open to everybody. There was cross-dressing. Yet at the same time the social group split into two. Youth formed itself into an autonomous group, elected a sovereign, the Abbot of Youth or, as in Scotland, *Abbot of Unreason*, and, as the title suggests, they indulged in outlandish behaviour taking the form of abuse directed at the rest of the population and which we know, up until the Renaissance, took extreme forms: blasphemy, theft, rape, and even murder. During both Christmas and the Saturnalia society functions according to a double rhythm of *heightened solidarity* and *exaggerated antagonism* and these two aspects act together in balanced opposition. The character of the Abbé de Liesse acts as a kind of mediator between the two extremes. He is recognized and even enthroned by the regular authorities. His mission is to demand excess while at the same time containing it within certain limits. What connection is there between this character and his function, and the character and function of Father Christmas, his distant descendant?

At this point it is important to distinguish between the historical and the structural points of view. Historically, as we have already seen, the Father Christmas of Western Europe, with his partiality for chimneys and stockings, is purely and simply a result of a recent shift from the festival of Saint Nicholas which has been assimilated to the celebration of Christmas, three weeks later. This explains how the young abbot has become an old man, though only in part, for the transformations are more systematic than historical accidents and calendar dates might suggest. A real person has become a mythical person. A figure of youth, symbolizing antagonism to adults, has changed into a symbol of maturity which is favourably disposed towards youth. The Lord of Misrule has taken charge of sanctioning good behaviour. Instead of open adolescent aggression to parents, we now have parents hiding behind false beards to gratify their children with kindness. The imaginary mediator replaces the real mediator, while at the same time as he changes his nature he begins to function in the opposite way.

There is no point in discussing points which are not essential to the debate and which risk confusing the issue. 'Youth' has largely disappeared as an age group from contemporary society (although there have been several attempts in recent years to revive it, it is too early to know what the result will be). So far as Christmas is concerned, a ritual that once affected three groups of protagonists—little children, youth, and adults—now only affects two: adults and children. The 'madness' of Christmas has thus largely gone; it has been displaced and at the same time toned down and only survives in adult groups during the Réveillon at nightclubs and, on the night of Saint Sylvester, at Times Square. But let us consider the role of children instead.

In the Middle Ages children did not wait patiently for their toys to come down the chimney. Variously disguised they gathered in groups which were known as 'guisarts' and went from house to house singing and offering their good wishes, in return for fruit and cakes. Significantly, they invoked death to back up their demands. Thus in eighteenth-century Scotland they sang this verse:

> Rise up, good wife, and be no' swier [lazy]
> To deal your bread as long's you're here;
> The time will come when you'll be dead,
> And neither want nor meal nor bread.

(Brand 1900: 243)

Even without this valuable piece of information and the no less significant one of disguises that change the actors into ghosts or spirits, there are still others concerning children's quests. It is known that these are not limited to Christmas (see on this point Varagnac 1948: 92, 122, and *passim*). They go on during the whole critical time of autumn when night threatens day just as the dead menace the living. Christmas quests begin several weeks before the Nativity—usually three, thus establishing a link between the similar quests of Saint Nicholas (which also use disguises), when dead children come to life, and the even more clearly defined initial quest of the season, that of Hallow-Even, which was turned into All Saints' Eve by ecclesiastical decision. Even today in Anglo-Saxon countries, children dressed up as ghosts and skeletons hassle adults unless they reward them with small presents. The progress of autumn from its beginning until the solstice, which marks the salvation of light and of life, is accompanied, in terms of rituals, by a dialectical process of which the principal stages are as follows: the return of the dead; their threatening and persecuting behaviour; the establishment of a *modus vivendi* with the living made up of an exchange of services and presents; finally, the triumph of life when, at Christmas, the dead laden with presents leave the living in peace until the next autumn. It is revealing that up until the last century the Latin Catholic countries put most emphasis on Saint Nicholas, in other words, the most *restrained* version, while the Anglo-Saxon countries willingly split it into the two extreme and antithetical forms of Halloween, when children play the part of the dead to make demands on adults, and Christmas, when adults indulge children in celebration of their vitality.

As a result of this, apparently contradictory aspects of the Christmas rites become clear: for three months the visit of the dead among the living becomes more and more persistent and tyrannical. Thus on the day of their departure it becomes permissible to entertain them and give them a last chance *to raise hell*. But who can personify the dead in a society of the living if not those who, one way or another, are incompletely incorporated into the group, who, that is, share the *otherness* which symbolizes the supreme dualism: that of the dead and the living? Therefore it should come as no surprise that foreigners, slaves, and children become the main beneficiaries of the festival. Inferior political or social status becomes equated with age difference. There is in fact a great deal of evidence, especially from Scandinavia and the Slav countries, that the real essence of the Réveillon is a meal offered to the dead, where the guests play the part of the dead, as the children play that of the angels, and the angels themselves, the dead. It is thus not surprising that Christmas and New Year (its double) should be festivals for present-giving. The festival of the dead is basically the festival of the others, while the fact of being other is the nearest image we can get of death.

This brings us back to the two questions posed at the beginning of the essay. Why did the figure of Father Christmas develop, and why has the Church been worried about its development?

It has been shown that Father Christmas is the heir to, as well as the opposite of, the Abbé de Liesse. This transformation primarily indicates an improvement in our relationships with death. We no longer find it necessary to settle our debts with death and allow it periodic transgression of order and laws. The relationship is now dominated by a slightly disdainful spirit of goodwill. We can allow ourselves to be generous, because this now consists of nothing more than offering presents or toys—that is, symbols. Yet this weakening of the relationship between the living and the dead has not been made at the expense of the character who embodies it. On the contrary, it could even be said to have improved. This contradiction would be inexplicable if it were not that another attitude towards death seems to be gaining sway in our society. It is no longer the traditional fear of spirits and ghosts that prevails, but instead a dread of everything death represents, both in itself and in life: degeneration, desiccation, and deprivation. We should reflect on the tender care we take of Father Christmas, the precautions and sacrifices we make to keep his prestige intact for the children. Is it not that, deep within us, there is a small desire to believe in boundless generosity, kindness without ulterior motives, a brief interlude during which all fear, envy, and bitterness are suspended? No doubt we cannot fully share the illusion, but sharing with others at least gives us a chance to warm our hearts by the flame that burns in young souls. The belief that we help to perpetuate in our children that their toys come from 'out there' gives us an alibi for our own secret desire to offer them to those 'out there' under the pretext of giving them to the children. In this way, Christmas presents remain a true sacrifice to the sweetness of life, which consists first and foremost of not dying.

Salomon Reinach once wrote with much insight that the main difference between ancient and modern religions was that 'pagans prayed to the dead, while Christians prayed for the dead' (Reinach

1905: i. 319). No doubt it is a long way from the prayer to the dead to this muddled prayer we increasingly offer each year to little children —traditional incarnations of the dead—in order that they consent, by believing in Father Christmas, to help us believe in life. We have disentangled the threads that testify to a continuity between these two manifestations of the same reality. The Church was certainly not wrong to denounce the belief in Father Christmas, one of the most solid bastions and active centres of paganism in modern humanity. It remains to be seen if modern humanity can defend its right to be pagan. One final remark: it is a long way from the King of the Saturnalia to Father Christmas. Along the way an essential trait—maybe the most ancient—of the first seems to have been definitely lost. For, as Frazer showed, the King of the Saturnalia was himself the heir of an ancient prototype who, having enjoyed a month of unbridled excess, was solemnly sacrificed on the altar of God. Thanks to the *auto-da-fé* of Dijon we have the reconstructed hero in full. The paradox of this unusual episode is that in wanting to put an end to Father Christmas, the clergymen of Dijon have only restored in all his glory, after an eclipse of several thousand years, a ritual figure they had intended to destroy.

### Editor's notes

The Editor would like to thank Diana Gittins for her translation of this article and Prof. Lévi-Strauss for his permission to have the article translated and included in this collection. The French original appeared as: 'Le Père Noël supplicié' in *Les Temps modernes* 77 (March 1952), 1572–90.

1 MRP is a reference to the Mouvement Républicain et Populaire, a left-wing Catholic political party of the period.
2 The reference is to the entry 'Noël' in E. Littré, *Dictionnaire de la langue française* (Paris: Hachette, 1876), iii. 732.

### References

BRAND, J. (1900). *Observations of Popular Antiquities*. New edn., London.
REINACH, S. (1905). 'L'Origine des prières pour les morts', in *Cultes, mythes, religions*. Paris.
VARAGNAC, A. (1948). *Civilisation traditionelle et genres de vie*. Paris.

# PART II

*Christmas and Materialism*

# 3

# The Rituals of Christmas Giving

## James G. Carrier

The arguments I make in this chapter echo those made by others in this collection. They revolve around the idea that the materialism associated with Christmas is much more complex than it appears at first glance. I pursue this by placing Christmas in the broader context of gift exchange. Certainly gifts are material objects. However, equally certainly they are more than neutral utilities, for they express and recreate a range of social values.

Complaints about the materialism of American Christmas spring from this dual nature of the gifts given. (While my main focus will be on American Christmas, the points I make should apply more generally.) The thing given at Christmas is a material object, usually a commodity bought in a crowded, garishly decorated store. But it is also a vehicle of affection that expresses private sentiment within a relationship that is personal and probably familial. Complaints about materialism typically point out that we pay too much attention to the vehicle and too little to the sentiments and relationships it is supposed to express. Thus, these complaints are one way of expressing a tension within the thing that is given. On the one hand it is a commodity purchased for money in an impersonal transaction, and on the other it is a gift given to express affection in a personal relationship (see Carrier 1990a).

Perhaps the most useful treatment of the distinction between gifts and commodities springs from Marcel Mauss's *The Gift* (1990), as his basic ideas have been elaborated by C. A. Gregory (1980, 1982) and Jonathan Parry (1986). I want to sketch briefly the main threads of this approach.

A basic Maussian point is that social relations can be located along a continuum defined by a pair of polar opposites. At one pole are gift relations. In these, people are linked to each other and to the things around them in enduring ways. These links are the basis of people's identities (Mauss 1985) and they define people's obligations to each other. At the other pole are commodity relations. In these, people are not linked in any enduring ways to the people and things that surround them. Instead, they are isolated individuals whose identities spring from internal sources and whose relations with others are governed by personal will rather than interpersonal identity and obligation.

From the Maussian perspective, gift relations are characterized by the transaction of inalienable objects, 'never completely detached from those carrying out the exchange' (1990: 33). I call such objects 'possessions', to denote the relationship of identity between possessor and object. Thus, giving a possession is not merely giving a material object, it is as well the giving of something identified with the giver. In 1844, Ralph Waldo Emerson (1983: 94) expressed in striking form the point that gifts must be possessions that bear the identity of the giver:

The only gift is a portion of thyself. Thou must bleed for me. Therefore the poet brings his poem; the shepherd, his lamb; the farmer, corn; the miner, a gem; the sailor, coral and shells; the painter, his picture; the girl, a handkerchief of her own sewing. This is right and pleasing, . . . when a man's biography is conveyed in a gift.

In modern capitalist societies, the fact that the gift should be a possession creates problems. This is because the objects people confront in such societies overwhelmingly are impersonal commodities. And because these objects are impersonal, they do not make good gifts. Again, Emerson (1983: 94) expresses this forcefully: 'it is a cold, lifeless business when you go to the shops to buy me something, which does not represent your life and talent'. The distinction between gift and commodity finds expression in people's understandings of the distinction between home and the world of work and the economy more generally (see Schneider 1980). Home is the world of durable and affectionate relationships, where things are done for love. On the other hand, work is a world of fleeting relationships and self-interest, where things are done for money. (For qualifications to this starkly drawn contrast, see Carrier 1992.)

## Christmas Giving

Because Christmas is a ceremony of affection and stability, its celebration should be most pronounced in the realm of the nuclear family (Bennett 1981; Caplow, Bahr, and Chadwick 1983: 188–92). Festivities in general and affectionate giving in particular will be more intense within the family than outside it. Further, compared to giving outside the family, giving within the family will be more concerned with the expression of sentiment and less concerned with the reciprocation of equivalents, the sort of exchange suited to commodity transactions. The evidence bears out this prediction. Giving and other key features of Christmas are centred on the immediate family. For instance, in his study of Middletown Christmas, Theodore Caplow (1984: 1308–9) found that having a Christmas tree was not ubiquitous. Instead, it was the norm for married couples with children, but rare among the unmarried and the childless. Likewise, the vast majority of presents went to those within the nuclear family rather than elsewhere (ibid. table 2). Thus, people gave presents to their fathers, mothers, children, children's spouses in over 90 per cent of cases, regardless of whether the relative lived in Middletown or was distant from it. However, gifts to relatives outside the core family were less common and more conditional. For grandparents and grandchildren, people gave presents in over 90 per cent of the cases where those relatives were within fifty miles of Middletown, but in only half to three-quarters of the cases where those relatives were more distant. For collaterals—siblings, siblings' spouses, siblings' children, and parents' siblings—giving was less frequent yet. Regardless of where these relatives lived, less than a third of Middletown residents gave them presents. In other words, at least in modern Middletown, Christmas is not simply a time of home and family, it is almost exclusively so.

Lack of concern for reciprocity also is most pronounced in giving between parents and children in the household. Caplow found that parents and young children exchange gifts unequally 'in both quantity and value. Respondents gave 946 gifts to persons under 18 and received 145 in return; 84 of these were of substantial value and six of the return gifts were' (Caplow 1984: 1316). While gifts within the core family are given without the expectation of equivalent return, Caplow found a growing concern for reciprocation with the realm of collaterals and their spouses. Not only were gifts to those relatives less frequent, but it is in gifts to them that there appears 'active concern that the gifts exchanged be of approximately equal value' (1984: 1316).

David Cheal studied gift-giving in Winnipeg and found a similar break between gifts to core family members and to collaterals. Children received the largest Christmas gift from about 30 per cent of Cheal's subjects, spouses accounted for another 30 per cent, and parents 15 per cent. All other sorts of recipients were below 10 per cent (Cheal 1986: table 6). Similarly, J. Bussey and his colleagues (1967: 10) found that over three-quarters of their Bradford respondents gave their

largest gifts to spouses or children. And although there is little demographic data in this report, it seems that not all respondents were
married or had children, suggesting that three-quarters is an under-
estimate for those who did in fact have a spouse and child.[1] Finally,
Adrian Ryans (1977), studying how people buy gifts, found an analogous distinction between gifts intended for those within the household
and for those without. Those buying gifts for people within the household were likely to spend more time considering what to buy and were
less likely to have fixed in advance an approximate amount of money
they were prepared to spend (Heeler *et al.* 1979 demonstrate a similar
pattern). This suggests that gifts to fellow household members were
more likely to reflect the giver's understanding of the needs and desires
of the recipient, and were less likely to be concerned with reciprocation.

When we move beyond the circle of kin, the nature of giving changes
once more. In Middletown, at least, the concern with reciprocation
disappears, reflecting a degree of disengagement from the relationships
involved. These include gifts at club meetings and office parties, where
'each recipient gives and receives some small gift, but there is no direct
exchange between giver and receiver', gifts such as those from pupil
to teacher or patient to physician, and gifts to those who provide
services, such as letter carriers, garbage collectors, and apartment
house doormen (Caplow 1984: 1316). Though they occur around
Christmas, a better term for such gifts would be tips or, more accurately if more archaically, *douceurs*, a sort of gift that 'keeps the wheels
greased. It's a recognition of good service, and hope that the service
will continue' (quoted in Streitfeld 1987).

Thus it is that transactions within the core family are most likely to
conform to the model of affectionate Christmas giving. And it is in
these relationships that the objects transacted most need to be
expressions of the transactors and their relationships. As we move
away from this core the nature of the relationship changes, and with it
the nature of transactions and of what is transacted. As the relationship
becomes more distant, transactions become less the expression of
affection and more the calculated concern for tit-for-tat or the for-
mulaic and relatively alienated giving that marks relationships that are
fairly impersonal or utilitarian. The office-party gift is hardly spontaneous; the *douceur* is almost coerced. Paralleling this, the gifts given
are less personal and more stereotyped. The office-party gift is more
impersonal than the family gift because it reflects impersonal office

relations rather than mutual affection. The annual *douceur* to the door-man is the most impersonal object of all, money.

The use of money as a gift is intriguing, because people usually see it as anonymous. It is almost impossible to identify money with the transactor or give it a social history, so that it appears to be indifferent to the social relationships in which it is given. Cheal, in his Winnipeg study, found an informant who explained this nicely: 'Money is kind of cold. It's spent usually on nothing in particular, and when it's gone the memory's gone' (1987: 165). Even so, people do give money. Appropriately, its use as a gift is ambiguous. In Christmas *douceurs* it is given by superiors to inferiors, but not equals, in impersonal relations (Caplow 1982: 386). However, money can be given from parents to children, though not from children to parents, but usually only on birthdays (Bussey *et al.* 1967: 57). In Middletown, only 5 per cent of Christmas gifts were of money, over 90 per cent of them between people of different generations (Caplow 1984: 1315). Money is also given outside the household in the guise of help for major purchases or for setting up a new household (e.g. Bell 1969: 92–3; Cheal 1988: ch. 7). Thus, it would appear that money is undesirable in close relationships outside that between parents and children unless it is likely to be memorialized in a durable object.

## Christmas Gifts and Commodities

I have argued that Americans see the family as the place of gift relations. Yet their understanding of and experience with the objects that are commonly available for use as gifts means that those objects are inappropriate. Simply, these objects are unsuited to what people want them to mean and to be, for they bear no human identity or being. They are manufactured in the world of work and express only the impersonal desire for profit by the company that made them and the impersonal acting out of work roles, lightly adopted and in return for money, by the unknown people who produced them. Likewise, they are impersonal when people first confront them in stores or adver-tisements. This does not mean that such objects have no social mean-ing. The objects one has help identify the sort of person one is (see e.g. Baudrillard 1981; Bourdieu 1984). But this social meaning is impersonal in that it refers to abstract categories of sorts of people, rather than to specific individuals and their relationships.

Americans deal with this contradiction in different ways. One technique is expressed in the saying, 'It's the thought that counts.' This reasserts the importance of the sentiment and relationship that the gift embodies, relative to the material embodiment itself.[2] Perhaps associated with this is the notion that gifts should not really be very useful. By having gifts be frivolous, luxurious, or otherwise special, they are distinguished from the concern for ordinary utilities that lead people to purchase commodities more routinely (analogous points are in Belk 1989).[3]

Also, practices of the presentation and treatment of gifts help to overlay their commodity identity with sentiment and festivity. Once again, Caplow's study of Middletown is illuminating. Among the unspoken rules about Christmas that he describes, there is one that produces 'exceedingly high' conformity, the Wrapping Rule: 'Christmas gifts must be wrapped before they are presented' (Caplow 1984: 1310). Wrapping overlays the commodity with sentiment and the giver's identity, as Lévi-Strauss (1969: 56) argues. The ubiquitous Christmas wrapping is complemented by unspoken rules about display, particularly display that is memorialized in Christmas photographs. Caplow says:

the pile of wrapped gifts was photographed; and individual participants were photographed opening a gift, ideally at the moment of 'surprise'. Although the pile of wrapped gifts is almost invariably photographed, a heap of unwrapped gifts is not a suitable subject for the Christmas photographer (1984: 1311).

The heap of loot is too obviously a pile of commodities rather than gifts. (In asserting that wrapping reflects the contradiction between gifts and commodities, I am not arguing that this is the only reason to wrap presents.)

Although it bears only obliquely on my main point here, it is worth noting that wrapping in Middletown was dominated by women (Caplow 1984: 1311), as was a range of Christmas practices. Their importance is appropriate, given the general primacy in industrial capitalist societies of women in defining and maintaining the sorts of relations that Christmas gifts reflect (e.g. Adams 1968: 30; Firth 1956: 40–1). However, there is evidence that in less developed countries like Mexico, men have a greater role in making important decisions about Christmas activities (Jolibert and Fernandez-Moreno 1982).

Caplow provides only one class of exception to the Wrapping Rule: 'Difficult-to-wrap Christmas gifts, like a pony or a piano, are wrapped symbolically by adding a ribbon or bow or card and are hidden until presentation' (Caplow 1984: 1310). In other words, awkward gifts are wrapped less than others. However, Caplow does not mention another class of items that is also relatively unwrapped: gifts made by the giver, especially foodstuffs. At least in cultural imagery, home-made jams and sweet breads are wrapped simply. (They also are the province of women, further pointing out the cultural links among women, familial relations, and gift transactions.) The breads are wrapped in aluminium foil with a simple card. This foil is less than wrapping because it is not wrapping paper, because it is considered necessary to keep the food fresh, because it is associated strongly with the kitchen. The jam is likely to have only a bow and a card. These are not hard to wrap, they just do not need wrapping. And they do not need wrapping because they have the personal identity that commodities do not.

## Christmas Shopping and Christmas Giving

I said that Christmas gifts within the family need to be possessions. However, Americans routinely give purchased commodities, which are culturally inappropriate. Why do they do so? To begin to answer this, it is necessary to consider Christmas shopping.

Christmas shopping and the cultural responses to it are important for understanding American Christmas. After all, people do not just casually go and buy the odd item. Instead, they shop for Christmas presents intensely. As Caplow notes for Middletown, Christmas 'mobilizes almost the entire population for several weeks, accounts for about 4% of its total annual expenditure, and takes precedence over ordinary forms of work and leisure' (Caplow 1984: 1306–7; see also Davis 1972). The impact of this expenditure is particularly marked in the area of retail sales. One economist (quoted in· Mayer 1987) estimated that about a third of all retail sales come in November and December and are accounted for by Christmas, twice what would be expected if retail sales occurred evenly throughout the year. In other words, a sixth of all retail sales is brought about by Christmas shopping and related activities.

All this activity does not pass without comment. Americans commonly see Christmas shopping as an onerous task. People regale each other with stories about how hard it is and they resolve to start earlier next year. Further, complaints about the materialism of Christmas frequently are complaints about commercialism.[4] Stores put up their decorations earlier and earlier, the advertising, the Christmas sales, and the need to buy more and more drown out the familial values that were supposed to exist in the Christmases of our youth and before. The title of a column in the *Washington Post* is apt: 'Christmas Run Amok: Our Gift-Giving has Gotten Out of Hand' (Raspberry 1988). Further, the majority of Americans are practising Christians, and the materialistic, commercial air of Christmas conflicts with important religious values bearing on the birth of Christ in particular and the glorification of material wealth more generally (cf. Belk 1987; Caplow, Bahr, and Chadwick 1983: 182–3).

In the face of this bother and complaint, why do Americans, even devout Christians, spend so much effort in Christmas shopping? Why not give home-made gifts? Indeed, why give presents at all? Why not give a Christmas card instead? It is true that the giving of purchased gifts reflects a number of motives, ranging from displays of affluence to a desire to shower a loved-one with lovely things. However, these more commonly recognized motives do not explain the intensity of Christmas shopping and people's ambivalence toward it.

An additional, and important, reason to buy and give lies below the surface. This reason becomes more apparent if we expand 'Christmas' to include the arduous shopping that goes with the activities that the word normally denotes. This expanded view sees shopping as an integral part of Christmas, rather than as an unfortunate commercial accretion on a real ritual and familial core.

To understand this expanded view, it is necessary to return to the distinction between gifts and commodities. While the mass of the objects that confront Americans are commodities, they do not remain in this impersonal state. Instead, people routinely appropriate their purchases. They convert them into possessions, objects that bear a distinct personal identity and embody distinct social relations and so are suitable for use within the household. For example, people often 'break in', alter, or otherwise physically transform what they buy, further stamping it with the identity of the owner (see Beaglehole 1932: 142; Csikszentmihalyi and Rochberg-Halton 1981: 108; Miller 1988). This process is exemplified in family cooking. Here, a person converts a collection of raw materials purchased as commodities into a meal that expresses and embodies the relationships that unite family members.

Appropriation can take less visible and more symbolic forms. One of the more important of these is shopping. While shopping serves a range of purposes, it has as a fundamental feature the exercise of choice in selecting what is bought. In the exercise of this choice, the shopper appropriates commodities at least partially, transforms them from a part of the indifferent mass of objects in the store to the special things that the shopper selects, things that thereby reflect the shopper and the social relations in which the shopper is located (see Carrier 1990*b*; Miller 1987: 190).

Shopping is a mundane activity that occupies people throughout the year. Christmas shopping is a heightened version of this activity. The volume of items to be purchased, the range of social relations that are taken into consideration and the intensity of those social relations all are greater than normal. The heightening of sociality at Christmas heightens the importance of the giving and the gifts, and this is reflected in the common feeling that Christmas shopping is especially hard work. In a sense, then, Christmas shopping is an annual ritual through which we convert commodities into gifts. Performing this ritual demonstrates that we can celebrate and recreate personal relations with the anonymous objects available to us, just as it strengthens and reassures us as we undertake the more mundane appropriation of everyday life during the rest of the year.

This is what makes shopping an integral part of Christmas. It is a mistake to construe Christmas in isolation, to see it only as a celebration and recreation of family and friendship. Rather, it is a celebration and recreation that needs to be seen in its socio-economic context. Americans see family and friendship as surrounded by the impersonal world 'out there', the world of work and alienated commodities. It is the Christmas shopping that proves to them that they can create a sphere of familial love in the face of a world of money. Shopping is a key part of Christmas.

With this enlarged view of Christmas some things that had been anomalous begin to make sense. For instance, it begins to make sense that people complain about the hard work of shopping. The sense of hard work, together with complaints about growing commercialization, help affirm that the impersonality of the commercial world does contradict family relations, and that people are, at this heightened time of the year, really able to wrest family values from recalcitrant raw materials. It is work, it has to be hard work, but they can do it. Equally, this enlarged view helps make sense of the status of home-made objects. Though they are possessions, they are not satisfactory as presents. In Middletown, for instance, less than 2 per cent of gifts were home-made, mostly by young children (Caplow 1982: 386). The home-made gift is unsatisfactory because it denies the ritual of Christmas shopping. Finally, this view suggests that children give few gifts partly because they do not normally undertake the daily round of shopping, transforming, and giving objects. The ritual of Christmas shopping is, therefore, inappropriate to them, and the few gifts they give are usually only markers of family relationships.

The argument I have laid out about American Christmas relies on common cultural conceptions of the sort of relations proper to family and economy, and the place of objects in each of those realms. But precisely because it relies on common cultural conceptions it is limited in important ways. Though probably everyone in America knows these conceptions, there is no reason to assume that everyone responds to them in the same way. First of all, while the relatively poor may confront the same problem of appropriation as those who are wealthier, they may very well be more likely than others to see in Christmas presents the sheer ability to buy (see Miller's discussion in this collection of house redecorating in Trinidad). Their gifts would likely carry a strong message of economic security, a message more muted, though hardly absent, among the wealthier. Second, my model would be less likely to reflect the position of those whose experience with objects and with the economic sphere more generally departs from the common cultural assumption of alienation. Those who produce and transact in relatively personal and less alienated relations may feel less need to celebrate their ability to appropriate commodities.

My reference to the variability of people's experience of alienation raises perhaps the most important qualification to my argument, a historical one. That is, my model should apply only to those societies in which family and economy, and the sorts of relations proper to each, are separated sharply. I turn to that issue now.

### *The Spirit of Christmas Past*

Drawing on Mauss, Jonathan Parry argues that a historical process underlies the importance of the affectionate giving that I have said is stressed in American Christmas. A concern with such giving 'is most likely to develop in state societies with an advanced division of labour and a significant commercial sector' (Parry 1986: 467). This is because the means of subsistence are no longer regulated by family or kinship groups. One consequence of this differentiation of economy and society is that household relations and gifts become not only distinct from but the inversion of market relations and transactions: 'altruistic, moral and loaded with emotion' (1986: 466). Parry's point is reflected in the history of American Christmas, for its modern form emerged at the same time as industrial capitalism.

The history of Christmas is described sufficiently by Daniel Miller in his Introduction and by other contributors to this volume that I need only sketch the pertinent parts of it. I will begin by considering end-of-year festivities (which took place at New Year rather than at Christmas) in England, the cultural ancestor of America, before the end of the eighteenth century. Although there is substantial variation across time and space it is possible to draw out two important themes that differentiate these festivities sharply from the modern American Christmas. The first is that gifts moved outside the family in hierarchical structures. The second is that gifts were generally of food, often given as feasting (see generally Golby and Purdue 1986: ch. 2).

For much of the English population, year-end was marked, if it was marked at all, by a feast, in which subordinates gave foodstuffs to their superiors, such as the local gentry, who prepared and served the meal. While feasting was important for those higher up the social scale, presents also were important. These appear to have moved in clear hierarchical patterns, with the net flow upward. They culminated in a standard gift from nobles to the monarch: a purse of £20 or the equivalent in plate at the end of the sixteenth century (Davis 1966: 131). Other practices also stressed hierarchies. The Lord of Misrule, the Boy Bishop, and Boy Abbot—in which humble people, especially children, were selected to act important borough and ecclesiastical roles—stressed the importance of hierarchy by inverting it (Jones 1978: 303–6). Also, Boxing Day presents from burghers to borough employees and menials, from merchants to their more substantial customers (Davis 1966: 209), and from householders to servants and merchants (Hervey 1845: 184; Hood 1991: 241–2) celebrated hierarchical relations outside the household. While these are general themes, it is also true that there were sporadic attempts to suppress seasonal festivities, especially in northern Europe following the Reformation. The main objections were that the festivities were idolatrous and bacchanalian (Golby and Purdue 1986: 35; Jones 1978: 305–6, 321).

This state of affairs existed in what became the United States. Puritan New Englanders suppressed Christmas, while Southerners followed the pattern of seasonal feasting (Richards 1971: 56). Generally, however, and in contrast to the English pattern, seasonal celebration occurred in urban rather than rural areas (Golby and Purdue 1986: 37). New York was exceptional in its celebration of St Nicholas, precursor to Santa Claus, from the 1770s. This celebration symbolized anti-British sentiment, advocates specifically linking it to the customs of the earlier Dutch settlers, including the figure of St Nicholas (Jones 1978: 338–9). However, the saint only slowly became recognizable as Santa Claus bringing presents to children. Until the 1820s in New York he was likely to bring little more than seasonal sweets. This is illustrated by a poem addressed to St Nicholas published in the New York *Spectator* in 1810 (Jones 1978: 346–7). In its sixty-nine words, it asks him to bring oranges, almonds, raisins, waffles, doughnuts, crullers, oley-cooks, and cookies, ending: 'Or if in your hurry one thing you mislay, I Let that be the Rod—and oh! keep it away.' By the 1820s, children in New York City, the seat of industrial and commercial capital in the United States, were likely to be getting toys as well as sweets. However, festivities were still held indifferently on Christmas and New Year's Eve, and they centred on adult conviviality (Jones 1978: 350–1).

In sum, by the end of the first quarter of the nineteenth century there were no marked signs of modern Christmas in the United States. Seasonal customs varied and frequently entailed feasting. Gifts to children were only beginning to appear, predominantly in New York City. The next forty years, until 1865 (the end of the American Civil War), marked the clear emergence of industrial capitalism in the United States. During this period, production and circulation increasingly moved out of the household and into an independent commercial sphere (e.g. Clark 1979). A concomitant was a growing sense of the household as a realm of domestic affection distinct from the outside world (Matthews 1987). And appropriately, it is during this period that the family and its relationships became the subject of seasonal celebration.

A number of factors shaped the emerging Christmas. An important one was a growing German influence in the United States (and in England as well, embodied in Prince Albert), which led to the introduction of elements of German end-of-year festivities, most notably the Christmas tree (Richards 1971: 97–102). Also influential was Charles Dickens's *A Christmas Carol*, which appeared in the United States in 1843. It was wildly popular, and Dickens read from the work on long

American tours, where many people reported being strongly affected by the sentiments he expressed.

Because *A Christmas Carol* was so important at the time, and because often it is said to mark the onset of the modern Christmas (e.g. Belk 1989: 118), it is worth devoting some attention to it. Doing so will show that if indeed it did mark the onset of modern Christmas, it did so only obliquely. Modern understandings of the work as a Christmas tale tend to focus on Tiny Tim and Bob Cratchit, who embody modern values of familial affection. However, the book contains strong elements of the older themes of feasting and hierarchy.

*A Christmas Carol* clearly revolves around hierarchical relations outside the household. For instance, when the Ghost of Christmas Past takes him to revisit the Fezziwig Christmas ball, Scrooge explains why the ball was so important to Fezziwig's employees:

He has the power to render us happy or unhappy; to make our service light or burdensome; a pleasure or a toil. Say that his power lies in words and looks; in things so slight and insignificant that it is impossible to add and count 'em up—what then? The happiness he gives is quite as great as if it cost a fortune. (Dickens 1918: 70)

More striking, perhaps, are the words of Scrooge's nephew on the meaning of Christmas. He says that it is the only time of the year 'when men and women seem by one consent to open their shut-up hearts freely, and to think of people below them as if they really were fellow-passengers to the grave, and not another race of creatures bound on other journeys' (Dickens 1918: 14). This hierarchical element has not disappeared from Christmas, which is still a season marked with charity and concern for the poor. However, this element is clearly a secondary concern in the modern Christmas (Belk 1987: 95).

Likewise, the older theme of feasting is strong in the book. Consider the description of a room prepared for the Ghost of Christmas Present:

Heaped up on the floor, to form a kind of throne, were turkeys, geese, game, poultry, brawn, great joints of meat, suckling-pigs, long wreaths of sausages, mince-pies, plum-puddings, barrels of oysters, red-hot chestnuts, cherry-cheeked apples, juicy oranges, luscious pears, immense twelfth-cakes, and seething bowls of punch, that made the chamber dim with their delicious steam. (Dickens 1918: 94)

Such sybaritic imagery is reflected in English representations of Father Christmas at the time (see Golby and Purdue 1986: figs. 3.40, 3.41).

Food to the point of sensual, even erotic, excess appears frequently in the book, as when Scrooge is led around to see people spending Christmas:

The poulterers' shops were still half open, and the fruiterers' were radiant in their glory. There were great, round, pot-bellied baskets of chestnuts, shaped like the waistcoats of jolly old gentlemen, lolling at the doors, and tumbling out into the street in their apoplectic opulence. There were ruddy, brown-faced broad-girthed Spanish Onions, shining in the fatness of their growth like Spanish Friars; and winking from their shelves in wanton slyness at the girls as they went by, and glanced demurely at the hung-up mistletoe. There were pears and apples, clustered high in blooming pyramids; there were bunches of grapes, made, in the shopkeepers benevolence, to dangle from conspicuous hooks, that people's mouths might water gratis as they passed; there were piles of filberts, mossy and brown, recalling, in their fragrance, ancient walks among the woods, and pleasant shufflings ankle deep through withered leaves; there were Norfolk Biffins, squab, and swarthy, setting off the yellow of the oranges and lemons, and, in the great compactness of their juicy persons, urgently entreating and beseeching to be carried home in paper bags and eaten after dinner. (Dickens 1918: 99–100)

These passages demonstrate that the old themes of feasting and public, hierarchical relations were alive and apparently influential in the 1840s in the United States. The most that can be said is that Dickens marked, not the onset of the modern Christmas, but something more modest, the onset of a transition.

Even so, the transition appears fairly rapid. For instance, fairly quickly Christmas Day became a public holiday in the United States —as it did in Britain in 1834, even though some workers preferred New Year (Golby and Purdue 1986: 76). The first state to declare it a holiday did so in 1836; in 1855 even Puritan Massachusetts declared it a public holiday; between 1845 and 1865 twenty-eight states did so (Golby and Purdue 1986: 76). And in 1865 it was declared a national holiday (Jones 1978: 354). Further, it was during the Civil War that the modern image of Santa appeared, from drawings by Thomas Nast published in *Harper's Weekly* (see Belk 1987). The first of these appeared in 1862 ('Christmas in Camp') and 1863 ('A Christmas Furlough'). Both included Santa Claus and presents, and the latter included the family and a Christmas tree (Jones 1978: 354).

The cultural influences that I have described were significant because they attracted attention and helped shape modern Christmas symbolism. But it is important to remember that the attraction was not Christmas itself, but a particular construction of a festival that celebrated relations within the family that are distinct from relations in the outside world. Evidence that it is this complex and markedly capitalist-industrial imagery that was popular is found in the emergence of a related American celebration, Thanksgiving.

Like Christmas, Thanksgiving is a festival whose history is much shallower than is commonly assumed. Again like Christmas, Thanksgiving emerged by the end of the Civil War. Prior to the 1860s there had been thanksgiving days in the United States. However, these were distinctly religious, declared whenever an event had occurred that called for national prayer and the giving of thanks to God. Prior to the Civil War, the last day of thanksgiving was during the War of 1812 with Britain (Sickel 1940: 30). However, in the 1860s Thanksgiving Day became established as an annual holiday not associated with any particular event. During the Civil War it was linked closely to the Union effort, as is clear in Abraham Lincoln's 1864 proclamation, which enjoined

all loyal and law abiding people, to assemble at their usual places of worship or wherever they may be: To confess and to repent of their manifold sins; to implore compassion and forgiveness, of the Almighty, that the existing Rebellion may be suppressed and the supremacy of the Constitution and the Laws of the United States may be established throughout all the states; that we as a people may not be destroyed. (Quoted in Sickel 1940: 34)

By the end of that war, however, it had become an anodyne national holiday, fixed at the last Thursday in November, as is illustrated by the beginning of Andrew Johnson's proclamation of 1867, 'In conformity with a recent custom that may now be regarded as established on National consent and approval . . .' (in Sickel 1940: 40). Quickly it became particularly identified as a family event, 'a reunion of families sanctified and chastened by tender memories and associations; and let the social intercourse of friends, with pleasant reminiscence, renew the ties of affection and strengthen the bonds of kindly feeling' (Grover Cleveland, in Sickel 1940: 40). The emergence of Thanksgiving that I have sketched is an event parallel with the emergence of modern Christmas, both oriented towards a celebration of family relationships in a world increasingly dominated by commodities.

## Conclusions

The points that I have made in this chapter echo points made by other contributors to this collection. Modern American Christmas has strong elements of materialism and commercialism, as people remind themselves frequently during the season. Further, Belk certainly is correct when he says in this volume that the commercial drive for more profits has underlain many American Christmas symbols. However, just as it would be wrong to see the profit drive as the cause of the popularity, rather than the genesis, of 'Rudolph the Red-Nosed Reindeer', so it would be wrong to see those commercial elements as unfortunate adjuncts to a ritual the heart of which is really home and family, the joy of giving. Home, family, and giving do lie at the heart of Christmas. But the reason they do so is not some primeval urge to gather around the hearth. Instead, they lie at the heart of Christmas because they are distinctive. And one of the things that Americans celebrate is the very distinctiveness: not home and family, but a form of life that is different from the world outside.

Consequently, there is not just one ritual of Christmas giving, the transaction of presents within the family. There is another ritual of Christmas giving as well, the activities of Christmas shopping. It is in the performance of these two rituals that Americans can satisfy themselves that, once again, they have made a family in a world of money. This production need not flow smoothly, for Christmas is often a time of tension as people try to juggle complex social relations and obligations. But whether it goes smoothly or not, it goes at last, and for most people the season, at least in reflection, passes reasonably well.

In this way, American Christmas can be seen as lying between and linking two social realms that loom large in people's consciousness, that of the family and that of the economy. The season, with its complex of meanings and practices, reflects and heightens the opposition between these two realms. At the same time, people show themselves that they can transcend that opposition and reaffirm the strength and importance of the family in an impersonal world.

## Notes

As always, I want to thank Achsah Carrier for her help and encouragement. I thank also Eric Hirsch and Jonathan Parry for what I learned in discussions with them, and Daniel Miller for encouraging me to work out these ideas.

1 Russell Belk (1979: table 2), studying adults in Philadelphia, found a very different pattern: the main recipient was 'friend' (33% of cases) and there

was no difference between 'child/child-in-law' and 'sibling/sibling-in-law' (12%). However, Belk asked people to describe any three gifts given over the past year, so the results may be not typical patterns but gifts that were memorable because unusual.

2 Of course, people do attend to the object. Is the gift useful? Does it cost too little? Too much? (See Cheal 1987.) These considerations have too calculating an air, and though people may indulge in them in private, they are inappropriate in public at times of high ceremony like Christmas.

3 This belief that gifts should not be utilitarian is part of what led Garner and Wagner (1988) to exclude gifts between household members from their analysis of the economics of gift-giving for the US Department of Labor. They feared that such gifts would be too utilitarian really to count.

4 Such complaints are neither new nor distinctly American. *The Times* complained about commercialization in its leader of Christmas Day 1912 (Golby and Purdue 1986: 10). There was much public complaint in the United States when, during the Depression, Franklin Roosevelt moved Thanksgiving one week earlier in November, to extend the period of Christmas shopping (Sickel 1940: 87–8).

## References

ADAMS, BERT (1968). *Kinship in an Urban Setting*. Chicago: Markham.

BAUDRILLARD, JEAN (1981). *For a Critique of the Political Economy of the Sign*. St Louis: Telos Press.

BEAGLEHOLE, ERNEST (1932). *Property: A Study in Social Psychology*. London: George Allen & Unwin.

BELK, RUSSELL W. (1979). 'Gift-Giving Behavior', in Jagdish E. Sheth (ed.), *Research in Marketing*, vol. ii. Greenwich, Conn.: JAI Press: 95–126.

—— (1987). 'A Child's Christmas in America: Santa Claus as Deity, Consumption as Religion', *Journal of American Culture*, 10/1: 87–100.

—— (1989). 'Materialism and the Modern U.S. Christmas', in Elizabeth C. Hirschman (ed.), *Interpretive Consumer Research*. Provo, Ut.: Association for Consumer Research: 115–35.

BELL, COLIN R. (1969). *Middle Class Families*. London: Routledge & Kegan Paul.

BENNETT, TONY (1981). 'Christmas and Ideology', in *Popular Culture: Themes and Issues*. Milton Keynes: Open University Press: Block 1, Units 1/2: 47–73.

BOURDIEU, PIERRE (1984). *Distinction: A Social Critique of the Judgement of Taste*. London: Routledge & Kegan Paul.

BUSSEY, J., BANKS, S., DARRINGTON, C., DRISCOLL, D., GOULDING, D., LOWES, B., PHILLIPS, R., and TURNER, J. (1967). 'Patterns of Gift

Giving: Including a Questionnaire Survey of Bradford Households'. B.Sc. (Hons.) thesis, University of Bradford.

CAPLOW, THEODORE (1982). 'Christmas Gifts and Kin Networks', *American Sociological Review*, 47: 383–92.

——— (1984). 'Rule Enforcement without Visible Means: Christmas Gift Giving in Middletown', *American Journal of Sociology*, 89/6: 1306–23.

——— BAHR, HOWARD M., and CHADWICK, BRUCE A. (1983). *All Faithful People: Change and Continuity in Middletown's Religion*. Minneapolis: University of Minnesota Press.

CARRIER, JAMES G. (1990*a*). 'Gifts in a World of Commodities: The Ideology of the Perfect Gift in American Society', *Social Analysis*, 29: 19–37.

——— (1990*b*). 'Reconciling Commodities and Personal Relations in Industrial Society', *Theory and Society*, 19: 579–98.

——— (1992). 'Occidentalism: The World Turned Upside-Down', *American Ethnologist*, 19: 195–212.

CHEAL, DAVID J. (1986). 'The Social Dimensions of Gift Behaviour', *Journal of Social and Personal Relationships*, 3: 423–39.

——— (1987). ' "Showing Them You Love Them": Gift Giving and the Dialectic of Intimacy', *Sociological Review*, 35: 150–69.

——— (1988). *The Gift Economy*. London: Routledge.

CLARK, CHRISTOPHER (1979). 'Household Economy, Market Exchange and the Rise of Capitalism in the Connecticut Valley', *Journal of Social History*, 13: 169–90.

CSIKSZENTMIHALYI, MIHALY, and ROCHBERG-HALTON, EUGENE (1981). *The Meaning of Things: Domestic Symbols and the Self*. New York: Cambridge University Press.

DAVIS, DOROTHY (1966). *A History of Shopping*. London: Routledge & Kegan Paul.

DAVIS, J. (1972). 'Gifts and the UK Economy', *Man*, 7/3: 408–29.

DICKENS, CHARLES (1918). *A Christmas Carol*. Philadelphia: Henry Altemus Company.

EMERSON, RALPH WALDO (1983). 'Gifts', in Joseph Slater, Alfred R. Ferguson, and Jean Fergusonn Carr (eds. and compilers), *The Collected Works of Ralph Waldo Emerson*, vol. iii: *Essays: Second Series*. Cambridge, Mass.: Belknap Press: 93–6 (1st pub. 1844).

FIRTH, RAYMOND (1956) (ed.). *Two Studies of Kinship in London*. London: Athlone Press.

GARNER, THESIA I., and WAGNER, JANET (1988). *Gift-Giving Behavior: An Economic Perspective*. Working Paper 180, Bureau of Labor Statistics. Washington, DC: US Department of Labor.

GOLBY, JOHN M., and PURDUE, A. WILLIAM (1986). *The Making of the Modern Christmas*. Athens, Ga.: University of Georgia Press.

GREGORY, C. A. (1980). 'Gifts to Men and Gifts to God: Gift Exchange and Capital Accumulation in Contemporary Papua', *Man*, 15: 626–52.

—— (1982). *Gifts and Commodities*. London: Academic Press.

HEELER, ROGER, FRANCIS, JUNE, OKECHUKU, CHIKE, and REID, STANLEY (1979). 'Gift versus Personal Use Brand Selection', in W. L. Wilkie (ed.), *Advances in Consumer Research*, vol. vi. Ann Arbor, Mich.: Association for Consumer Research: 325–8.

HERVEY, THOMAS K. (1845). *The Book of Christmas*. New York: Wiley & Putnam.

HOOD, GRAHAM (1991). *The Governor's Palace in Williamsburg: A Cultural Study*. Williamsburg, Va.: The Colonial Williamsburg Foundation.

JOLIBERT, ALAIN J. P., and FERNANDEZ-MORENO, CARLOS (1982). 'A Comparison of French and Mexican Gift Giving Practices', in Richard P. Bagozzi and Alice M. Tybout (eds.), *Advances in Consumer Research*, vol. x. Ann Arbor, Mich.: Association for Consumer Research: 191–6.

JONES, CHARLES W. (1978). *Saint Nicholas of Myra, Bari, and Manhattan*. Chicago: University of Chicago Press.

LÉVI-STRAUSS, CLAUDE (1969). *The Elementary Structures of Kinship*. Boston: Beacon Press.

MATTHEWS, GLENNA (1987). *Just a Housewife: The Rise and Fall of Domesticity in the United States 1830–1963*. New York: Oxford University Press.

MAUSS, MARCEL (1985). 'A Category of the Human Mind: The Notion of Person; the Notion of Self', in Michael Carrithers, Steven Collins, and Steven Lukes (eds.), *The Category of the Person*. Cambridge: Cambridge University Press: 1–25.

—— (1990). *The Gift: The Form and Reason for Exchange in Archaic Societies*, trans. W. D. Halls. London: Routledge.

MAYER, CAROLINE (1987). 'Retailers Worry as Holiday Shopping Begins', *Washington Post* (27 Nov.): C1, C3.

MILLER, DANIEL (1987). *Material Culture and Mass Consumption*. Oxford: Basil Blackwell.

—— (1988). 'Appropriating the State on the Council Estate', *Man*, 23: 353–72.

PARRY, JONATHAN (1986). 'The Gift, the Indian Gift and the "Indian Gift"', *Man*, 21: 453–73.

RASPBERRY, WILLIAM (1988). 'Christmas Run Amok: Our Gift-Giving Has Gotten Out of Hand', *Washington Post* (4 Jan.): A13.

RICHARDS, KATHERINE LAMBERT (1971). *How Christmas Came to the Sunday Schools*. Ann Arbor, Mich.: Gryphon (1st edn. 1934).

RYANS, ADRIAN (1977). 'Consumer Gift Buying Behavior: An Exploratory Analysis', in Barnett A. Greenberg and Danny N. Bellenger (eds.), *Contemporary Marketing Thought 1977: Educators' Proceedings*. Chicago: American Marketing Association: 99–104.

SCHNEIDER, DAVID (1980). *American Kinship: A Cultural Account.* 2nd edn. Chicago: University of Chicago Press.

SICKEL, H. S. J. (1940). *Thanksgiving: Its Source, Philosophy and History.* Philadelphia: International Printing Company.

STREITFELD, DAVID (1987). 'Tip o' the Season', *Washington Post* (11 Dec.): C5.

# 4

# Materialism and the Making of the Modern American Christmas

*Russell W. Belk*

The fact that Christmas is at once the greatest religious holy day and the greatest commercial holiday in the Christian world constitutes what Pimlott (1962) calls the paradox of Christmas. The tension produced by this paradox surfaces each Christmas season when the consumer materialism seemingly stimulated by the holiday challenges the non-materialistic values enshrined by Christian theology. At least four of the seven deadly sins against which Christianity once railed are now seen by some to be venerated in Christmas celebrations: avarice, gluttony, lust, and envy (Louden 1985). The conflict is by no means uniquely American, Christian, or confined to the Christmas season, but America has contributed the uniquely American Santa Claus and has become an arbiter of Christmas celebrations around the world, primarily because of its past import of European emigrant traditions and its present export of popular culture.

Materialism is construed here as the belief that having possessions is the most important source of satisfaction in life (Belk 1985). This chapter examines the history of the American Christmas in an effort to understand better the relationship between Christmas and materialism. I also examine two major alternatives to the religious meta-narrative for Christmas: the Santa Claus myth and the story of Ebenezer Scrooge. These alternatives to the Christian metanarrative are then related to the historical development of American Christmas shopping and materialism.

## ROM and Coke

Controversy over a museum exhibit entitled 'The Real Thing at the ROM' provides a recent illustration of the conflict created by the apparent intrusion of material interests into the ostensibly Christian holy day of Christmas. The exhibit which ran during November and December 1991 at the Royal Ontario Museum in Toronto featured twenty-six oil paintings of Santa Claus by Haddon Sundblom. Sundblom was commissioned by Coca Cola during the 1930s to 1950s to create these paintings for its advertising at Christmas time. Most of the images show a sentimental depiction of Santa enjoying a bottle of Coke. The Coca Cola corporation lent the paintings to the ROM, provided promotional funding, and offered discount coupons for the show with purchases of Coca Cola products. The outrage of critics towards this exhibit was perhaps best captured by Jill Savitt of the Washington, DC Center for the Study of Commercialism: 'It is sad that an august institution like the Royal Ontario Museum would put its imprimatur on junk food . . . This further links the birth of Christ with Santa Claus, with consumption . . .' (Godfrey 1991). Coca Cola justified the show by suggesting that these Santa images transcend the soft drink and concern the creation of a modern legend. And the exhibit curator reportedly defended the exhibit by citing its ability to show 'the power of mass media to shape culture and traditions' (ibid.).

Sundblom's paintings, made accessible through Coca Cola advertising, have indeed helped shape Americans' visual images of Santa Claus and have also helped reinforce the connection of Santa to contemporary Christmas celebrations (Louis and Yazijian 1980; Munsey 1972; Waters 1978). But these latest uses of Santa Claus in secular Christmas festivities are only a small part of the development of a holiday that began its evolution before the birth of Christ. In order to understand the ascendance of materialism in the modern American Christmas, it is first useful to examine briefly the history of American celebrations of the Christmas holiday.

## Christmas Comes to America

In 1647 the British Parliament abolished religious festival celebrations, including Christmas, and the ban persisted for the duration of the Puritan Oliver Cromwell's reign (Coleman 1957; see also Miller's 'A Theory of Christmas' in this volume). The early Puritan emigrants to America also condemned Christmas celebrations as 'a wanton Bacchanalian feast' (Barnett 1954). Massachusetts Bay Colony passed an ordinance in 1659 that treated Christmas as any other working day and demanded a fine from anyone caught feasting, refusing to work, or engaging in other forms of celebration.

As more liberal Protestants began to emigrate to America from Great Britain, the Netherlands, and Germany, they brought Christmas traditions with them (Golby and Purdue 1986; Shoemaker 1959; Snyder 1985). By 1836, the earliest of the American states and territories began to recognize Christmas as a legal holiday and by 1890 it had become a national holiday.

Even so, religious opposition to excesses in the secular celebration of Christmas has continued to emerge periodically in twentieth-century America (Barnett 1946, 1954; Hirschman and LaBarbera 1989). It was not until the mid to late nineteenth century that Christmas became a sanctioned lesson topic in church Sunday schools (Coleman 1957; Richards 1934). The ambivalent religious support for and opposition to the American Christmas attests to the polyvocal nature of what in the past 100 years has become both the biggest religious and the biggest commercial celebration in America.

## The Evolution of Santa Claus

Because the Santa Claus myth is so integral to contemporary Christmas celebrations, it is a good starting-point for examining the beliefs and values encoded in these enactments. As Malinowski (1948) suggested, myths are mirrors for culture and reflect its social practices, changing when these practices change. That modern myths are partly shaped and changed by commercial and media institutions makes them no less revealing of modern culture. The most direct ancestor of the modern American Santa Claus is, ironically, the Christian Saint Nicholas. Saint Nicholas, who is also the patron saint of sailors and pawnbrokers, was the fourth-century Bishop of Myra (in what is now Turkey), and is reputed to have performed miracles (including raising the dead) as well as lesser charities such as tossing bags of gold through the windows of poor girls to serve as their dowries (de Groot 1965; McGinty 1979; Shlien 1959).

But Saint Nicholas is only one of the European ancestors of the modern American Santa Claus; others include the British Father Christmas, the French Père Noël, the Dutch Sinterklaas, the Danish Jules-Missen, and the Romanian Moş Craicun. To varying degrees such figures all retain vestiges of religious associations such as a Bishop's robe, hat, and mitre. Many of the European Christmas figures also are portrayed riding a horse and served by an often sinister assistant. Because Martin Luther objected to the practice of gifts being given to children in the name of Saint Nicholas, he introduced Christkindlein—a messenger of Christ—as the gift-bringer. Christkindlein, through mispronunciation, came to be known as Kris Kringle, who became another variant brought to the United States by protestant immigrants from northern Europe (Coleman 1957).

Although these European Christmas figures have influenced the American Santa Claus, there is considerable agreement that the American Santa is more than an amalgam of these characters and is instead uniquely American (Belk 1987; Carver 1982; Golby and Purdue 1986; de Groot 1965; Hagstrom 1966; Jones 1978; Opie and Opie 1959; Oswalt 1970; Wolf 1964). Belk (1987) characterizes five major differences:

1. Santa Claus lacks the religious associations of such gift-bearing figures as Santa Lucia, Saint Nicholas, Christkindlein, and the Three Kings.

2. Santa Claus lacks the riotous rebelliousness of figures such as Saturn and Knecht Ruprecht.

3. Santa Claus lacks the punitive nature of Sinterklaas (with his companion Zwarte Piet), Knecht Ruprecht, Hans Trapp, Pelze-Nichol, and Saint Nicholas.

4. Despite his mythical nature, with his North Pole home and with his many appearances on streetcorners, in stores and shopping malls, and in homes, Santa Claus is a more tangible character than his predecessors and counterparts.

5. Santa Claus is a bringer of numerous and substantial gifts, not merely the fruit, nuts, and simple homemade toys of the traditional European figures. (Belk 1987: 87)

Evidence of these differences is found in Caplow's study of Muncie, Indiana, Christmas celebrations by more than 350 families (Caplow 1982, 1984; Caplow *et al.* 1982; Caplow and Williamson 1980). That study found, for instance, that costly gifts 'from Santa' were never withheld or lessened because of children's bad behaviour, that parents often used costumes to play Santa, and that Santa was clearly believed to have a home, family, and friends. If certain of these characteristics now appear in European Christmas celebrations as well, it seems likely that they have been adopted from the American Santa Claus. Support for this claim is found in the European adoption of the American visual image and American media portrayals of Santa Claus (Buday 1954; Carver 1982), as discussed below. Although many contemporary Christmas customs originated in Europe (see Miller, 'A Theory of Christmas', this volume), the increasingly global contemporary Santa Claus appears to have been largely created in America.

The contemporary visual appearance of Santa Claus was shaped primarily by Clement Moore's 1822 poem, 'A Visit From St. Nicholas' (often known by its opening line ' 'Twas the Night Before Christmas') and by Thomas Nast's drawings of Santa Claus which appeared in *Harper's Weekly* between 1863 and 1886. Sundblom's portraits for Coca Cola advertising beginning in 1931 were refinements on these themes. Moore's poem introduced Santa's reindeer-drawn sleigh (possibly drawing from an unsigned lithograph of the previous year—McGinty 1979), disposed of the idea of assistants, and suggested that Santa was jolly and fat. Gone are any hints of religious ancestry or mentions of the nativity. However, the poem still portrays Santa as a small elfin character. Nast's pen and ink drawings showed Santa Claus as a somewhat larger (if obese) Caucasian sporting a white beard and a fur-trimmed outfit with boots and a large belt. He carries numerous toys in his bag and has a ruddy laughing countenance (see Figure 4.1). Sundblom's colour paintings sixty years later retained these conventions, made Santa larger still, made clear that Santa dressed in red and white, and removed Santa's pipe (replacing it with a bottle of Coca Cola).

The evolution of the Santa Claus myth has also been influenced by popular American literature, film, and broadcast media. Shlien (1959) first recognized that in many of these media treatments Santa is given a coherent life story that helps to fulfil many of the criteria suggested by Ragland (1937) for a folk hero:

1. A distinguished or divine origin
2. Mysterious portents at birth
3. Perils menacing his infancy
4. Initiation or revelation
5. A quest
6. A magical contest
7. A trial or persecution
8. A last scene
9. A violent or mysterious death
10. A resurrection or ascension.

Frank Baum, who also wrote the magical tales *The Wizard of Oz* and *The Art of Decorating Dry Goods Windows* (Culver 1988), wrote a series of stories that provide a biography for Santa fulfilling many of these criteria (Baum 1986). The song 'Rudolf the Red-Nosed Reindeer' anthropomorphized Santa's reindeer as aids on Santa's quest and resulted in a number of seasonal American comic books embellishing these mythical themes (Belk 1989). The films *Miracle on 34th Street*

Fig. 4.1. 'Merry Old Santa Claus', Thomas Nast, *Harper's Weekly*, 1 January 1881

(1947), *Here Comes Santa Claus* (1984), *One Magic Christmas* (1985), and *Santa Claus, the Movie* (1985) also help to flesh out the myth of Santa Claus. The plot of the last film is indicative of such heroic myth-building. The story begins in the Middle Ages, when the wood-cutter Claus and his wife Anya are taking the wooden toys he has made to his nephews for Christmas. Their reindeer-drawn sleigh is stopped by a snowstorm and Claus and his wife fall asleep as the snow drifts over them. They 'awaken' at the North Pole where they are attended by elf-like Vendequm who explain that they are both now immortal and that Claus (henceforth to be known as Santa Claus) is to fulfil the prophecy of 'the ancient one' by delivering toys to all the children of the Earth. Because the childless Claus loves children, he pursues this mission with vigour until one overly eager Vendequm, named Patch, disgraces Santa by producing shoddy toys on a production line that he convinced Santa to substitute for handcrafted production. In hopes of redeeming himself, Patch goes to Earth (which, incidentally, situates the North Pole in heaven) and agrees to help a ruthlessly greedy toy manufacturer by using magical stardust. They make a magical sucker which briefly allows children to fly, and Patch (using his high-tech 'Patchmobile') distributes it to delighted children at Christmas. The toymaker seizes the opportunity for huge profits by planning a 'Christmas II' on 25 March and sets Patch to work making magical (but unknowingly dangerous) candy canes that the toymaker plans to sell for very high prices.

Through the toymaker's young ward and the orphan boy she has befriended, Santa becomes aware of the danger and takes his sleigh and reindeer to Earth. There he thwarts the plot to distribute the dangerous candy canes. As a result, Santa regains the love of the world's children, Patch returns to the North Pole, and Santa and Anya adopt the two orphans. In such stories we see a more complete version of the myth of Santa Claus, even if they are created by popular media rather than folk stories. We also see antipathy toward mass produced toys from factories and a removal of any association of Santa's gifts with market-place transactions—a theme that will be considered further. As such stories refine the American Santa Claus myth, Santa continues his apotheosis.

The American Santa Claus has a distinctive appearance and dress, is married, lives at the North Pole, delivers gifts in a sleigh drawn by flying reindeer, and answers the wishes of children around the world. Adoption of this Santa scenario, along with other parts of the American Christmas celebration pastiche (e.g. Christmas trees, decorations, stockings, feasts) emerged as a mark of acculturation for nineteenth- and twentieth-century European immigrants. Not only was this true among Christian immigrants to the USA (Sereno 1951; Shoemaker 1959), but among Jewish (Goldin 1950; Heinze 1990; Matz 1961; Stark 1983; Witt 1939) and Hindu immigrants (Mehta and Belk 1991) as well. But more recently, the unique American Santa Claus has begun a reverse migration back to Europe and other parts of the world (Barnett 1954; Belk 1987). Thanks in part to American exports of music, films, television, tourists, and advertising, and in part due to the ability of the American Santa Claus to represent modernity and Western values, even Japan has now begun at least to superficially adopt Santa in some department stores during the Christmas and New Year's season (Moeran and Skov, this volume; Plath 1963; Stenzel 1975; Wanks 1984; Yates 1985). This diaspora of the American Santa Claus is not unlike the diaspora of Coca-Cola as an emblem of American modernity. But while his unique features have differentiated the American Santa Claus from the more religious Saint Nicholas, the development of the Santa myth has made him increasingly Christ-like. In many ways Santa has now become not only a hero, but a god.

Both Hagstrom's (1966) sociological parody and Shlien's (1959) semiotic analysis contend that Santa Claus is a sacred figure for a secular world. Several more specific parallels between the stories of Santa and Christ extend these arguments (Belk 1987):

1. *Miracles.* Santa has flying reindeer, a bottomless bag of toys, and visits all homes with children in a single night.

2. *Gifts.* Just as Christ brought gifts of love and salvation to Earth and then ascended to heaven, Santa brings gifts of toys and treats to homes and then ascends up the chimney from whence he entered.

3. *Prayer.* Children's letters to Santa can be seen as prayers offering a sacrifice of good behaviour and seeking material blessings. In fact, some of these letters are addressed to 'heaven' (Snyder 1985) and children are not infrequently observed praying to Santa (Bock 1972; Sweitzer 1986; Waits 1978).

4. *Omniscience.* Santa knows if children have been bad or good, holds them accountable for their actions, and blesses them accordingly. He is immortal, is normally unseen, and is capable of forgiveness.

5. *Other Parallels.* In addition to these similarities, Santa's elves act as apostles, his reindeer may be seen as manger animals, children's mantelpiece gifts of cookies and milk represent additional offerings to Santa, Christmas carols about Santa can be seen as secular hymns, belief in Santa constitutes faith, and Santa lives in a heavenly place of whiteness and purity.

Striking as these similarities are, there are also important differences that are equally critical to understanding the Santa myth (Belk 1987):

1. *Physical Image.* Santa is old and plump while Christ is young and thin.
2. *Clothing.* Santa is dressed in rich reds and furs; Christ is dressed in humble white robes.
3. *Demeanour.* Santa is jolly; Christ is serious.
4. *Type of Gifts.* Santa's gifts are toys and luxuries while Christ's gifts are health and necessities. Christ often condemned the material focus that belief in Santa Claus' gifts seems to promote.

These similarities and differences between Santa Claus and Christ suggest that Santa is a secular version of Christ, with one key difference. While Christ reigns in the realm of the spirit, Santa's realm is that of material abundance. Despite attempts to suggest other roles for Santa Claus (e.g. Jekels 1936; Meerloo 1960; Proctor 1967; Sterba 1944), including a role as a symbol of *anti*-materialism (Oswalt 1970) and an attempt to reconcile Santa Claus and Christianity through one story of Santa praying at the manger (Bakewell 1984), the evidence seems strongest that Santa is first and foremost a symbol of material abundance and hedonistic pleasure. Thomas Nast drew Santa with an appearance that is reminiscent of his drawings of the corrupt and corpulent plutocrat William 'Boss' Tweed and is strikingly similar to his depiction of a drunken Bacchus (Figure 4.2). Nast said that he was inspired by the furs of the Astors in drawing Santa's now popular fur-trimmed outfit. The good things Santa brings are never everyday necessities, but exciting toys and games. Santa's bag of toys is a cornucopia and the Christmas stockings he fills are smaller cornucopias. The office parties, family feasts, and candies of Christmas similarly celebrate abundance and encourage gluttony and self-indulgence.

The jolly demeanour and fat belly of Santa Claus are in keeping with his role as a symbol of hedonistic indulgence—not only of material desires, but for some adults perhaps indulgence in pleasures of the flesh as well. Such sexual indulgence is detected in Santa by Hall's (1984) analysis of Christmas issues of *Playboy* and *Penthouse* magazines. In these issues, which outsell all other months' issues, Santa is portrayed as a lecherous old man who fits well with these magazines' general enthusiasm for sexual and material pleasures.

In addition to promoting Coca Cola, Santa has also been routinely used in promoting indulgence in various brands of alcohol and cigarettes in American advertising (Coleman 1957). Finally, the success of the emphasis on material indulgences in the Santa Claus myth is

KING DEATH'S DISTRIBUTION OF PRIZES.
BACCHUS TAKES THE FIRST PREMIUM.

Fig. 4.2. 'King Death's Distribution of Prizes: Bacchus Takes the First Premium', Thomas Nast

supported by the highly materialistic requests in children's letters to Santa Claus in comparison to their wishes in other contexts (Bradbard 1985; Caron and Ward 1975; Downs 1983; Richardson and Simpson 1982). We encourage children to make lavish material requests of Santa and suggest that if they do as we parents and society desires, these wishes will be granted. For children the vision offered through Santa Claus is that of a magical economy without scarcity or need of paying for the luxurious indulgences they are encouraged to believe in and wish for (McGreevy 1990). All of these differences support the view that Santa Claus is to American material faith what Jesus Christ is to Christian spiritual faith. But Santa Claus is only part of the secular mythology offering a materialistic alternative to the religious Christmas mythology. The other major part of the secular mythology came from England in Dickens's *A Christmas Carol*.

## *A Christmas Carol*

Christmas celebrations were dying out in Europe and America before Charles Dickens's 1843 publication of *A Christmas Carol*. Although Barnett (1954) may exaggerate in claiming that Dickens single-handedly revived Christmas through this and subsequent Christmas stories, other than the Santa Claus myth, *A Christmas Carol* is clearly the most prominent and most often repeated secular Christmas tale on both continents (Bolton 1987; Davis 1990; Viola 1986). More than 357 scripts have been written for performing this story, which has achieved its greatest popularity during the second half of the twentieth century (Bolton 1987). While eight stage productions of the story opened in the two months following its publication and it was nearly universally known in England and America (Ley 1906; Hewet 1976), many Victorians regarded the story as being too 'sacred' for the stage (Bolton 1987). A sacred Christmas text it remains, although in a strictly non-religious sense involving myth, ritual, hierophany (showing itself to be supernatural), communitas (provoking a transcending cama-raderie), and mystery (Belk *et al.* 1989).

The story of Dickens's *A Christmas Carol* dramatizes the opposing Christmas ethos of Ebenezer Scrooge and the Bob Cratchit family. Scrooge's transformation makes him more like the Cratchits and thereby more attuned to the 'true spirit' of Christmas. This transformation or conversion experience involves five major dimensions of change (Belk 1989):

1. Status differentials
   a. From Privilege Accorded Age to Privilege Accorded Youth
   b. From Privilege by Virtue of Wealth to Privilege by Virtue of Poverty
2. Emotions
   a. From Lack of Emotion to Joy and Sorrow
   b. From Concentration on the Pragmatic Present to Concentration on a Nostalgic Past and a Hopeful Future
3. Work, home, and family
   a. From Individual-orientation to Family-orientation
   b. From Factory-focus to Home-focus
   c. From Work emphasis to Leisure emphasis
4. Money, self, and others
   a. From Miserliness to Generosity
   b. From Selfishness to Brotherhood
   c. From Love of Money to Love of People
   d. From Avarice to Altruism
5. Money and spending
   a. From Saving to Spending
   b. From Austerity to Lavishness
   c. From Utilitarianism to Hedonism

Unlike the Santa Claus myth, the message of *A Christmas Carol* seems to run counter to everyday American values and experience in most of these five themes.

The first of these transformation themes is an old one that is evident in medieval and even pre-Christian holidays as rites of reversal in which master and servant, the fool and the scholar, and the high and the low change places in carnival inversion (Babcock 1978; Bakhtin 1968; Miller, 'A Theory of Christmas', this volume). Early in *A Christmas Carol*, Scrooge suggests that the poor and orphans should be housed in gaols. But following his transformation on Christmas Day, Scrooge tips the poor newsboy, gaily gives away money, and brings lavish gifts to the poor Cratchits. More generally, for at least this one day or season, the powerful attend the powerless, as adults give gifts to children and the rich offer charity to the poor. In the long run, however, these may be inversions that serve to ease tensions between the strong and the weak and thereby reinforce the status quo (Gluckman 1959, 1963). Barnett (1954) suggests that the growing popularity of *A Christmas Carol* in America is due in no small part to its ability to lessen tensions felt between rich and poor. In this respect it is much like Christianity and may perform similar tension-diffusing functions without an explicitly religious motif (Belk 1983).

The second transformation of Scrooge is from passionless pragmatism to poignant emotions, complete with laughter and tears. Victorian sentimentalism is evident throughout the tale, but it is focused most heavily on crippled Tiny Tim Cratchit. Parallels to the biblical story of Lazarus have been suggested by Walder (1981). Scrooge is moved by nostalgia for the past when he is made to remember his childhood and lost love and is filled with remorse when he is shown a future that includes his own unattended grave and the grave of a youthful Tim. But hope blossoms when Scrooge awakes on Christmas morning to find that he has a chance for a different future. As with the general Victorian retreat into the home as an escape from the dehumanizing effects of the industrial revolution, Scrooge's retreat is into the past and future. More broadly still, Christmas is a nostalgic holiday that brings families together for meals, gifts, and selective photographs which will subsequently call forth memories of 'happy times'. Christmas cards commonly show nostalgic scenes of hearth, home, and nature in a pre-industrial age (Buday 1954; Coleman 1957; Hill 1969; Holder and Harding 1981; Johnson 1971). And children are urged to dream and to list the gifts that they imagine will bring them the greatest delight. In light of the tale's idyllic emphasis on awakening positive emotions, it is ironic that for many participants, Christmas seems instead to provoke drudgery, depression, and unhappiness (Eisenbud 1951; Fischer and Arnold 1990; MacLean 1899; Otnes *et al.* 1992; Rubin and Rubin 1988; Sherry *et al.* 1992; Yao 1981).

The third of the transformations in *A Christmas Carol*, involving a change of focus from the individual at work to the family at home, can also be seen to accord with the cult of domesticity that arose in Europe and America during the period of Dickens's writings (Clark 1988; Mathews 1987). The tale suggests that there is more to life than work and that the family is a haven in a heartless world. This theme also accords well with Carrier's reading (this volume) of the familial rituals of Christmas. Scrooge's initial disregard for orphans is especially vile, because orphans are deprived of the bosom of home and family and do not benefit from Christmas largesse of parents. As van de Wettering (1984) and Barton (1989) note, such Victorian emphasis on the home also involved an emphasis on abundance, wholesomeness, success, and plenty. The burden for nurturing this home and family, including preparing the Christmas feast and bearing much of the responsibility for successful gift-giving, falls primarily on women who participate disproportionately in the moral economy of gift-giving (Cheal 1988; Fischer and Arnold 1990; Sherry and McGrath 1989; Wallendorf and Arnould 1991). For if giving and nurturing family are 'women's work', a man is not held too accountable in society for his failure in these roles.

In the transformations of Scrooge from avarice and miserliness to altruism and generosity there is a turning from thoughts of self to thoughts of others. In *A Christmas Carol*, the ideal proposed is very like the Christian ideal of emphasis on charity and community overcoming antisocial emphasis on the self. This is one of the chief functions of gift-giving in small-scale communities and groups (e.g. Cheal 1986; Hyde 1983; Mauss 1925; Stack 1974). But there is some evidence that in modern or post-modern society this ideal of selfless Christmas giving is seldom met. Mick and DeMoss (1990) found that one apparent effect of the commercial displays of Christmas gifts is a substantial number of 'gifts' to the self at this time of year. Advice columnist Judith Martin ('Miss Manners') summarized the letters she receives for Christmas gift advice in the following way:

Presents are never given because they are felt to be obligatory, but because people enjoy expressing their affection and appreciation in tangible form. You choose a present when something catches your eye and suggests itself as a source of delight for a particular person. When you receive a present, your pleasure in it and in the feeling it symbolizes obliterates any awareness of its material worth. Do you believe this? Miss Manners is trying to. People keep interrupting her by asking if they have to give something to this person or that, how little they can get away with spending, how they can get others to give them something they really want rather than something of that person's choosing, and what do they do about people who give cheap presents or none at all. What a nasty, troublesome business it all seems to have become. Miss Manners is beginning to think that nobody deserves to get anything until we all manage to get greed under control. (Martin 1982: 521)

Once again, the ethos of many Christmas gift-givers seems to be more like that of the unrepentant Scrooge than of the Cratchits.

The final theme of Scrooge's transformation is from being a frugal utilitarian to being a free-spending hedonist. This is the one theme that seems most in keeping with everyday values in America. Poor though they are, the Cratchits exhibit this spirit in splurging on a Christmas goose and a plum pudding they can ill afford. On Christmas morning the transformed Scrooge too begins to spend extravagantly and joyously. Such is the hedonism of modern consumer culture (Campbell 1987). It is this spirit of spending with little thought for tomorrow that prompted Boorstin (1973) to call Christmas 'the National Festival of Consumption' and Lévi-Strauss (1963; this volume) to call it 'a giant potlatch'—an interpretation echoed by Moschetti (1979). As in the romantic model of love (Belk and Coon 1991), to be overly careful in spending at Christmas threatens to profane the ideal. The more accepted tendency toward free spending, as well as the tensions detected between the other themes of *A Christmas Carol* and the practice of everyday American life, suggest a more careful consideration of commercial influences on Christmas practices in America.

## The Development of American Christmas Shopping

With the secularization of society we have relegated the sacred to the material world. In so doing, the control of transcendence has shifted from the central authority of the church to the diffuse authority of the media and the merchant (Belk *et al.* 1989; Belk forthcoming). It is not surprising that material values have come to be emphasized over (but sometimes under the banner of) spiritual values in Christmas celebrations given these circumstances. As Miller ('A Theory of Christmas', this volume) and Kryth (1954) stress, spending money (on others) at Christmas is not a new phenomenon. But Pimlott (1978) notes that most of the Christmas expenditures until the nineteenth century were for food and drink for feasting and toasting others.in the family or community. This pattern changed shortly after mid-century in America, just as the post-bellum rise of American industry was beginning to pump excess goods into the market.

Along with the acceptance of Santa Claus came the shift of giving presents at Christmas rather than at New Year. Moreover, gifts no longer expressed a legal relationship but instead became an intimate exchange with friends and relatives. At the beginning of the nineteenth century, the chief household expense at Christmas was for food and drink, but with the increased popularity of giving gifts, they emerged as the costliest part of the festival. The commercial importance of Christmas was becoming enormous. (McGreevy 1990: 36)

Besides prior Puritan restraints on personal gift-giving or other celebrations of Christmas in early America, English immigrants were inhibited by the traditional pattern of giving Christmas gifts only to servants and the poor (Snyder 1985). Just as Christmas itself was not officially recognized and sanctioned in the United States until the mid to late nineteenth century, Christmas gift-giving did not become common until the same period. Between 1820 and 1870 advertising in Philadelphia and New York newspapers for Christmas gifts was uncommon, with New Year's gifts or 'holiday gifts' being more commonly mentioned (Snyder 1985). But by about 1870 Christmas gifts started to be promoted more heavily. In Victorian America, charitable bazaar 'fancy fairs' promoted home-made gifts created by women at Christmas time (Gordon 1986; O'Neil 1981). As with the emphasis in Santa Claus tales on handcrafted gifts, factory-made Christmas gifts were not yet acceptable.

Starting with an 1874 Macy's Department Store display of $10,000 worth of imported dolls, Christmas window displays of manufactured goods became a part of the promotion of Christmas buying and gift-giving (Snyder 1985). Numerous other department stores also began to promote Christmas gifts heavily at about this time (Schmidt 1991). Between 1880 and 1920, Waits (1978) found that popular American magazine advertising in November and December began to encourage the purchase of manufactured gifts instead of home-made gifts. Santa Claus featured prominently in these ads. The idea of giving personal (sacred) gifts that were manufactured and sold in impersonal (profane) factories and stores was still a troublesome one for Americans to accept. Waits (1978) discovered that retailers helped facilitate the shift to store-bought gifts in several ways. Department stores ordered special merchandise which was designated as 'Christmas gifts' rather than as ordinary stock. Wrapping paper was introduced in the late nineteenth century and the ritual of removing price tags and wrapping gifts to be presented in highly ritualized Christmas exchanges became a common means of 'decontaminating' and 'singularizing' (Appadurai 1986) products bought in the market-place. Caplow (1984) found that the practice of wrapping gifts is now universal and calls this unstated Christmas norm 'the wrapping rule'. Gifts of money (also profane— Belk *et al.* 1989) are generally taboo, unless given (as charity) from someone older and higher in status to someone younger and lower in status (Burgoyne and Routh 1991; Carrier, this volume; Webley *et al.* 1983; Webley and Wilson 1989). Businesses began to give Christmas bonuses during this period, so the money spent on Christmas gifts was not ordinary (profane) money, but special sacred money (Barnett 1954; Belk and Wallendorf 1990). And banks began to offer non-interest-bearing 'Christmas Club' accounts in which customers could save for Christmas gifts without the contamination of receiving profane interest on their savings (Barnett 1954). Santa Claus may be seen as performing a similar sacralizing function so that gifts to children are not seen as things that parents have purchased in the same way that they purchase ordinary goods and services. As Barton (1989) suggests, Santa also served as the god blessing Christmas materialism in early department stores:

Victorian parents taught the same habits of accumulation and display to their children, especially at Christmastime, when the 'fetishism of commodities' was most pronounced and glorified and valued things were most numerous and mysterious. The irony here is the transformation of an antimaterialist's birthday into a commercial celebration. It is difficult to imagine a more pointed and effectual socialization for consumption than Christmas, wherein concrete enjoyments are hoped for and appear out of nowhere, apparently under the benevolent sponsorship of a supernatural prosperous elder. (pp. 70–1)

It is not surprising that Santa became a fixture in department stores, which slowly realized that exploiting the growing Christmas emphasis on children was good business. If Santa is the god of materialism, what better place to enthrone him than in the department store which did so much to foster consumer culture (Bowlby 1985; Hutter 1987; Lewis 1983). As Schmidt (1991) observes, 'If after the Civil War the early department stores emerged as the new cathedrals of the culture of consumption . . . the holidays came to be its ultimate incarnation' (p. 889). More recently, the shopping mall has eclipsed the department store as the current cathedral of consumption in which supplicant and fearful children bring their wishes to Santa at Christmas (Kowinski 1985; Zepp 1986). Like special Christmas gift merchandise, wrapping rituals, exchange rituals, and Christmas clubs, the presence of Santa Claus helps sacralize these retail sites and facilitate the Cratchit-like spirit of spending with little concern for cost. While the secular god, Santa, was normally employed in department stores, Schmidt (1991) notes that store displays sometimes directly incorporated religious symbols to sacralize their wares. In 1898 the Philadelphia Wanamaker department store used a nearly life-size model of a church (complete with a performing choir and organ) above the silk department (Leach 1989). Although large city stores led the way in commercializing Christmas, rural emporia were not far behind (Schlereth 1989).

If there is lingering opposition to the prominence of selling and

Santa Claus in the Christian holiday of Christmas, it is deftly dealt with in the perennially popular Christmas film *Miracle on 34th Street* (1947). The film begins with the event that, until recent efforts to start the season earlier, marked the beginning of the American Christmas high shopping season: the Macy's (department store) Thanksgiving Day Parade on the third Thursday in November. The man hired to play Santa Claus in the parade shows up drunk, so he is replaced by a man named Kris Kringle who thinks he is Santa Claus. Kris is asked to stay on through the holiday season to play the Santa in Macy's main store on 34th Street in New York, and there he meets the store's pragmatic publicity woman, the divorced Doris, and her young daughter Susan. Although Susan initially doubts the existence of Santa Claus, Kris together with Doris's quixotic boyfriend, Fred, reawaken her faith in such magic. Kris initially angers Macy's management by referring customers to arch-rival Gimbels for items they cannot find at Macy's. But when the store begins to benefit from the goodwill this inspires, Macy's management decides to capitalize on it by portraying Macy's as 'the store with a heart', even though profit is their sole motivation for doing so (Luke 1989–90).

The crisis in the film comes when Kris must undergo a sanity hearing after he irks the store's hard-headed personnel director by insisting that he is Santa Claus. When the US post office delivers him letters addressed to Santa Claus (because Susan's letter to Santa was sent in care of the court), he is declared sane to the delight of Susan, Fred, and Doris. Kris disappears on Christmas Eve and the next morning the local zoo reports that its reindeer which disappeared the previous evening are back and look well lathered. Doris marries Fred, Susan now has a complete family, and the film ends with the good feelings that Susan and Fred's faith in Santa is justified, that Santa has shown the department store a more caring way to conduct its business, and that Christmas is a time when cold reason must be cast aside and disbelief suspended for the course of this magical season. The implicit message is that despite the apparent incompatibility between the values of Santa Claus and the values of the department store, there is really no conflict; Santa's compassionate caring and Macy's profit-motivated business practices can flourish together after all.

That Americans should acquire their Christmas gifts in department stores was no longer an issue by the time of *Miracle on 34th Street*. Post-war prosperity at the time of the film made such shopping seem an entitlement. Still, the shopping depicted was for gifts to friends and family. None of Mick and DeMoss's (1990) self-gifts were in evidence. But by the time of the shopping mall Christmas portrayed in the film *Scenes from a Mall* (1991), self-gifts had become the entire focus of the shopping experience depicted (Belk and Bryce forthcoming). Although this extreme of Christmas self-indulgence is still not typical in America, it is perhaps not far removed from the spirit of self-interest cultivated in children through a focus on Santa as a bringer of all good things. When the Martin advertising agency was asked recently to be one of seven firms preparing advertisements *for* one of the deadly sins of medieval Christianity, they drew greed. Their ad in *Harper's* magazine showed a photo of a Santa Claus in a business suit with the headline, 'The World's Foremost Authority Speaks Out on the Subject of Greed'. The ad's copy read:

Do you remember all of the things you told me you wanted as a child? Well, your list may have changed, but I'll bet it hasn't gotten any shorter. Perhaps you shouldn't be worried about that. Greed has always motivated men and women. It has motivated inventors to make better mousetraps, artists to create greater art and scientists to find cures for diseases and pathways to the moon. Just be sure to use your greed to good ends. Be greedy for knowledge. Be greedy for the kind of success that helps you, your family and your friends. Be greedy for love. Remember, I'll always be the first one to know if you've been bad or good. So be good for goodness sake.

Advertising often attempts to assuage feelings of guilt about self-indulgent purchasing, but if such attempts to change avarice from a vice to a virtue have been successful, then the materialist message of the modern American Christmas has fully succeeded.

## Conclusion and Criticisms of Christmas Materialism

The movement toward a more materialistic and self-indulgent Christmas has not gone unopposed in America. American newspaper comics at Christmas have often concentrated on ridiculing the materialism that seems so evident during this season. In the words of one such comic strip, Christmas gifts help us to 'fulfil each other's greeds' (Belk 1989). While most prior treatments of gift-giving emphasize the social cohesion and feelings of community support that gift exchange engenders (e.g. Belk 1979; Carrier, this volume; Cheal 1987; Mauss 1925), another function of routinized gift-giving among adults is to acquire luxuries (as gifts) without suffering the concomitant guilt of self-indulgence that might accrue from buying these same things for ourselves, at least without resorting to the rubric of giving well-deserved 'gifts to ourselves' by, in effect, taking over from our parents to become our own Santas. It is the occasional transparency of this mutual cleansing of objects acquired to fulfil our material desires that is often ridiculed in the newspaper cartoons and critiques such as that of 'Miss Manners' presented earlier.

Such transparency occurs under several conditions. When we hint or ask for specific gifts we risk destroying the pretence of viewing gift exchange as an act of altruism and social affirmation. Similarly, when we give money (or gift certificates), make too much of an issue of monetary gift exchange equivalence, or demand to know what someone really wants for Christmas, we threaten to make the materialistic aspects of Christmas gift-giving overly obvious. But if we can instead explain our giving as due to a love of others or as a replica of Christ's love for humanity, then rather than suffer guilt from participating in an exercise in greed, our Christmas gift exchange is ennobled and elevated as selfless, Christian, and praiseworthy. Going to church at Christmas time and donating money and other gifts to the poor, even if such behaviours only occur at this time of year, may have a similar effect in making us feel altruistic enough to justify the egoistic rewards of receiving extravagant gifts that we lust after and covet. The shallowness of such seasonal 'caring' has led to a number of religious attacks on materialism that are also most commonly offered during the Christmas season (e.g. Barnett 1954; Blenkinsopp 1971; Montgomery 1968). These criticisms may be framed as attacks on the secularization and commercialization of Christmas, but the deeper concern seems to be with egoistic motivations disguised too thinly with a veneer of seeming altruism.

Paradoxically, at the time of year when charitable contributions peak, commercial appeals to buy also peak, resulting in the parading of a bewildering array of consumer luxuries before the eyes of the American masses who watch television, listen to the radio, see outdoor advertising, view merchants' window displays, and read popular magazines. The poor who can least afford such luxuries become acutely aware of the desirability of consumer goods at this time of year. It is perhaps among the poor and the lonely that the spiritual message of the religious Christmas and the Dickensian emphasis on the simple pleasures of home and family offer the greatest solace. Thus, as Thompson (1988) observes, home and family are the predominant emphases in American television Christmas fare. Yearly television Christmas specials draw large audiences and offer a quasi-family to viewers who feel reunited with familiar, if digitized, faces (Benney *et al.* 1959; Caughey 1984).

Clearly, as Carrier (this volume) argues, the contemporary Christmas is a family celebration involving products that have been appropriated from their commercial contexts and singularized as gifts. This in no way obviates criticisms of the holiday's celebration of materialism, made manifest, for instance, in the consumer credit difficulties caused by Christmas expenditures (Faber and O'Guinn 1988). The family is also implicated in these criticisms, as McGreevy (1990: 40) observes: 'Christmas celebrates the division of society into small private bands and thereby serves the economic system it seems to oppose by encouraging the growth of independent functional consumption units with ever-expanding desires.' That many of the excesses in Christmas shopping are carried out under the veneer of love (just as with overwhelming parental expenditures on their children's college educations and weddings, and on their parents' nursing homes and funerals may be), does not mean that such materialism is benign (Schudson 1986). Isaacs (1935) found that we learn from childhood to interpret the withholding of a gift from us as a withholding of love. Later we conflate our own giving of material gifts with the giving of love. With emotional symbolism so salient in gift-giving it is perhaps too easy to succumb to the material messages of Christmas encouraging us to spend and buy.

Because it is advertisers who promote the cornucopia of consumer goods, it is facile to blame these advertisers for the 'commercialization of Christmas', and to ignore the deeper issues of consumer materialism that this paper has argued Christmas brings to the fore. Nor are merchants wholly to blame for seducing us to spend freely at Christmas time. If department store and shopping mall Christmas displays continue to be extravagant celebrations of abundance and invitations to celebrate Christmas with financial abandon, they are often matched by the lavish home Christmas decorations of American consumers (Cohen 1988; Kirshenblatt-Gimblatt 1983; Oxley *et al.* 1986; Pollay 1987). This is not to deny the role of advertising and commercialism in stimulating materialism, but consumers are not passive or unwitting pawns in this yearly frenzy of material desire. We instead submit to it willingly and knowingly. Such is the increasingly powerful spirit of the romantic secular Christmas.

The romantic secular Christmas is opposed by a number of people and organizations in the United States, including SCROOGE—the

Society to Curtail Ridiculous, Outrageous, and Ostentatious Gift Exchanges—founded in 1979. In their annual newsletter, this group encourages 'sensible spending' at Christmas and gives suggestions such as buying gift certificates for self-improvement classes, smoke alarms, and first aid kits. Similarly, some family counsellors (see Rubin and Rubin 1988) recommend spending less time with family (because too much togetherness is bound to prompt conflict), focusing less on Christmases past (which will only lead to morose nostalgia), and stripping gift-giving of its emotional significance (which wrongly equates gifts with love and nurture). There is, however, a danger in such a rational approach to Christmas gift-giving that is as sinister as the most excessive materialism. The danger is that by rationalizing and deromanticizing Christmas we remove the myth and mystery needed for sustaining a key contemporary ritual in the home. Just as rationalizing love or religion precludes the chance for ecstatic experience and bonding (Ennis 1967; Lüschen *et al.* 1972), so does rationalizing Christmas celebrations. It is not surprising that in a consumer culture consumption has become the vehicle (not only in gifts, but in decoration and feasting) for celebrating family, friends, and community at Christmas. But when consumption becomes the end rather than the means of celebrating Christmas, then it precipitates a destructive materialism which Csikszentmihalyi and Rochberg-Halton (1981) appropriately labelled as terminal materialism. And both the terminal materialism epitomized by self-gifting and the desacralizing rationalization of Christmas urged by critics and counsellors threaten to deprive us of the greatest chance for contact with the numinous in many of our lives.

## Note

This paper has benefited from a dialogue with James Carrier and comments by Daniel Miller. I am thankful to both for acting as a critical sounding board for these ideas.

## References

APPADURAI, ARJUN (1986) (ed.). *The Social Life of Things: Commodities in Cultural Perspective*. Cambridge: Cambridge University Press.

BABCOCK, BARBARA A. (1978). *The Reversible World: Symbolic Inversion in Art and Society*. Ithaca, NY: Cornell University Press.

BAKEWELL, NICHOLAS (1984). *Santa and the Christ Child: A Christmas Legend.* Los Angeles: Kneeling Santa.

BAKHTIN, MIKHAIL (1968). *Rabelais and his World,* trans. Helen Iwolsky. Cambridge, Mass.: MIT Press (1st edn. 1965).

BARNETT, JAMES (1946). 'Christmas in American Culture', *Psychiatry,* 9: 51–65.

—— (1954). *The American Christmas: A Study of National Culture,* New York: Macmillan.

BARTON, MICHAEL (1989). 'The Victorian Jeremiad: Critics of Accumulation and Display', in Simon J. Bronner (ed.), *Consuming Visions: Accumulation and Display of Goods in America, 1880–1920.* New York: Norton: 55–71.

BAUM, FRANK L. (1986). *The Life and Adventures of Santa Claus.* New York: Signet Classic (1st edn. 1902).

BELK, RUSSELL W. (1979). 'Gift-Giving Behavior', in Jagdish Sheth (ed.), *Research in Marketing,* vol. ii. Greenwich, Conn.: JAI Press: 95–126.

—— (1983). 'Worldly Possessions: Issues and Criticisms', in Richard P. Bagozzi and Alice M. Tybout (eds.), *Advances in Consumer Research,* vol. x. Ann Arbor, Mich.: Association for Consumer Research: 514–19.

—— (1985). 'Materialism: Trait Aspects of Living in the Material World', *Journal of Consumer Research,* 12 (Dec.): 265–79.

—— (1987). 'A Child's Christmas in America: Santa Claus as Deity, Consumption as Religion', *Journal of American Culture,* 10/1: 87–100.

—— (1989). 'Materialism and the Modern U.S. Christmas', in Elizabeth Hirschman (ed.), *Interpretive Consumer Research.* Provo, Ut.: Association for Consumer Research: 115–35.

—— (forthcoming). 'Carnival, Control and Corporate Culture in Contemporary Halloween Celebrations', in Jack Santino (ed.), *Halloween.* Knoxville, Tenn.: University of Tennessee Press.

—— and BRYCE, WENDY J. (forthcoming). 'Christmas Shopping Scenes: From Modern Miracle to Postmodern Mall', *International Journal of Research in Marketing.*

—— and COON, GREGORY S. (1991). 'Can't Buy Me Love: Dating, Money, and Gifts', in Rebecca H. Holman and Michael R. Solomon (eds.), *Advances in Consumer Research,* vol. xviii. Provo, Ut.: Association for Consumer Research: 521–7.

—— and WALLENDORF, MELANIE (1990). 'The Sacred Meanings of Money', *Journal of Economic Psychology,* 11 (Mar.): 35–67.

—— —— and SHERRY, JOHN F., Jr. (1989). 'The Sacred and the Profane in Consumer Behavior: Theodicy on the Odyssey', *Journal of Consumer Research,* 16 (June): 1–38.

BENNEY, MARK, WEISS, ROBERT, MEYERSOHN, ROLF, and RIESMAN, DAVID (1959). 'Christmas in an Apartment Hotel', *American Journal of Sociology,* 65/3: 233–40.

BLENKINSOPP, JOSEPH (1971). 'Why Keep on Celebrating Christmas?', *Commonweal* (Dec.): 302–3.

BOCK, E. WILBUR (1972). 'The Transformation of Religious Symbols: A Case Study of St. Nicholas', *Social Compass*, 19: 537–48.

BOLTON, H. PHILIP (1987). *Dickens Dramatized*. Boston: G. K. Hall.

BOORSTIN, DANIEL (1973). *The Americans: The Democratic Experience*. New York: Random House.

BOWLBY, RACHEL (1985). *Just Looking: Consumer Culture in Dreiser, Gissing and Zola*. New York: Methuen.

BRADBARD, MARILYN R. (1985). 'Sex Differences in Adults' Gifts and Children's Toy Requests at Christmas', *Psychological Reports*, 56: 959–70.

BUDAY, GEORGE (1954). *The History of the Christmas Card*. London: Rockliff.

BURGOYNE, C., and ROUTH, D. A. (1991). 'Constraints on the Use of Money as a Gift at Christmas: The Role of Status and Intimacy', *Journal of Economic Psychology*, 12: 47–69.

CAMPBELL, COLIN (1987). *The Romantic Ethic and the Spirit of Modern Consumerism*. Oxford: Basil Blackwell.

CAPLOW, THEODORE (1982). 'Christmas Gifts and Kin Networks', *American Sociological Review*, 47 (June): 383–92.

—— (1984). 'Rule Enforcement without Visible Means: Christmas Gift Giving in Middletown', *American Journal of Sociology*, 89/6: 1306–23.

—— BAHR, HOWARD M., CHADWICK, BRUCE A., HILL, REUBEN, and WILLIAMSON, MARGARET H. (1982). *Middletown Families: Fifty Years of Change and Continuity*. Minneapolis: University of Minnesota Press.

—— and WILLIAMSON, MARGARET H. (1980). 'Decoding Middletown's Easter Bunny: A Study in American Iconography', *Semiotica*, 32/3–4: 221–32.

CARON, ANDRE, and WARD, SCOTT (1975). 'Gift Decisions by Kids and Parents', *Journal of Advertising Research*, 15: 15–20.

CARVER, SALLY S. (1982). 'Santa Claus: A Man for All Seasons', *Hobbies*, 95 (Dec.): 104–10.

CAUGHEY, JOHN H. (1984). *Imaginary Social Worlds*. Lincoln, Nebr.: University of Nebraska Press.

CHEAL, DAVID J. (1986). 'The Social Dimensions of Gift Behaviour', *Journal of Social and Personal Relationships*, 3: 423–39.

—— (1987). ' "Showing Them You Love Them": Gift Giving and the Dialectic of Intimacy', *Sociological Review*, 35 (Feb.): 151–69.

—— (1988). *The Gift Economy*. London: Routledge.

CLARK, CLIFFORD E., Jr. (1988). 'Domestic Architecture as an Index to Social History: The Romantic Revival and the Cult of Domesticity in America, 1840–1870', in Robert Blair St George (ed.), *Material Life in America, 1600–1860*. Boston: Northeastern University Press: 535–49.

COHEN, JOHN (1988). *Christmas in America*. San Francisco: Collins.

COLEMAN, ARTHUR B. (1957). *Keeping Christmas Christian*. New York: Greenwich Book Publishers.

CSIKSZENTMIHALYI, MIHALY, and ROCHBERG-HALTON, EUGENE (1981). *The Meaning of Things*. Chicago: University of Chicago Press.

CULVER, STUART (1988). 'What Manikens Want: The Wonderful World of Oz and the Art of Decorating Dry Goods Windows', *Representations*, 21 (winter): 97–116.

DAVIS, PAUL (1990). *The Life and Times of Ebenezer Scrooge*. New Haven, Conn.: Yale University Press.

DOWNS, A. C. (1983). 'Children's Letters to Santa Claus: Elementary School-Age Children's Sex-Typed Toy Preferences in a Natural Setting', *Sex Roles*, 9: 159–63.

EISENBUD, JULE (1951). 'Negative Reactions to Christmas', *Psychoanalytic Quarterly*, 10: 639–45.

ENNIS, PHILIP E. (1967). 'Ecstasy in Everyday Life', *Journal for the Scientific Study of Religion*, 6 (spring): 40–8.

FABER, RONALD, and O'GUINN, THOMAS (1988). 'Consumer Credit Abuse', *Journal of Consumer Policy*, 11/1.

FISCHER, EILEEN, and ARNOLD, STEPHEN (1990). 'More Than a Labor of Love: Gender Roles and Christmas Gift Shopping', *Journal of Consumer Research*, 17 (Dec.): 333–45.

GLUCKMAN, MAX (1959). *Custom and Conflict in Africa*. Glencoe, Ill.: Free Press.

—— (1963). *Order and Rebellion in Tribal Africa*. London: Cohen & West.

GODFREY, STEPHEN (1991). 'Sponsorships Essential, ROM Says', *Globe and Mail* (9 Nov.): C1, C4.

GOLBY, J. M., and PURDUE, A. W. (1986), *The Making of the Modern Christmas*. Athens, Ga.: University of Georgia Press.

GOLDIN, GRACE (1950). 'Christmas-Chanukah: December is the Cruelest Month', *Commentary*, 10: 416–25.

GORDON, BEVERLY (1986). 'Playing at Being Powerless: New England Ladies Fairs, 1830–1930', *Massachusetts Review*, 27 (spring): 144–60.

GROOT, ADRIAN D. DE (1965). *Saint Nicholas: A Psychoanalytic Study of his History and Myth*. New York: Basic Books.

HAGSTROM, WARREN O. (1966). 'What is the Meaning of Santa Claus?', *American Sociologist*, 1 (Nov.): 248–52.

HALL, DENNIS (1984). 'The Venereal Confronts the Venerable: "Playboy" on Christmas', *Journal of American Culture*, 7/4: 63–8.

HEINZE, ANDREW R. (1990). *Adapting to Abundance: Jewish Immigrants, Mass Consumption, and the Search for American Identity*. New York: Columbia University Press.

HEWET, EDWARD W. (1976). 'Christmas Spirits in Dickens', *Dickens Studies Newsletter*, 7 (Dec.): 99–106.

HILL, C. R. (1969). 'Christmas Card Selections as Unobtrusive Measures', *Journalism Quarterly*, 46: 511–14.

HIRSCHMAN, ELIZABETH C., and LABARBERA, PRICILLA (1989). 'The Meaning of Christmas', in Elizabeth C. Hirschman (ed.), *Interpretive Consumer Research*. Provo, Ut.: Association for Consumer Research: 136–47.

HOLDER, JUDITH, and HARDING, ALISON (1981). *Christmas Fare*. Secacus, NJ: Chartwell Books.

HUTTER, MARK (1987). 'The Downtown Department Store as a Social Force', *Social Science Journal*, 24/3: 239–46.

HYDE, LEWIS (1983). *The Gift: Imagination and the Erotic Life of Property*. New York: Random House.

ISAACS, SUSAN (1935). 'Property and Possessiveness', *British Journal of Medical Psychology*, 15: 69–78.

JEKELS, LUDWIG (1936). 'The Psychology of the Festival of Christmas', *International Journal of Psychoanalysis*, 17/3: 57–72.

JOHNSON, SHEILA K. (1971). 'Sociology of Christmas Cards', *Trans-Action*, 8/3: 27–9.

JONES, CHARLES W. (1978). *Saint Nicholas of Myra, Bari, and Manhattan: Biography of a Legend*. Chicago: University of Chicago Press.

KIRSHENBLATT-GIMBLATT, B. (1983). 'The Future of Folklore Studies in America: The Urban Frontier', *Folklore Forum*, 16/2: 175–234.

KOWINSKI, WILLIAM S. (1985). *The Malling of America*. New York: Athenium.

KRYTH, MAYMIE R. (1954). *All about Christmas*. New York: Harper & Brothers.

LEACH, WILLIAM (1989). 'Strategies of Display and Production of Desire', in Simon J. Bronner (ed.), *Consuming Visions: Accumulation and Display of Goods in America, 1880–1920*. New York: Norton: 99–102.

LÉVI-STRAUSS, CLAUDE (1963). 'Where Does Father Christmas Come From?', *New Society*, 63 (19 Dec.): 6–8.

LEWIS, RUSSELL (1983). 'Everything under One Roof: World's Fairs and Department Stores in Paris and Chicago', *Chicago History*, 12 (autumn): 28–47.

LEY, J. W. T. (1906). 'The Apostle of Christmas', *Dickensian*, 2 (Dec.): 324–6.

LOUDEN, JOHN (1985). 'Experiments in Truth', *Parabola*, 10 (winter): 19–23.

LOUIS, J. C., and YAZIJIAN, HARVEY Z. (1980). *The Cola Wars*. New York: Everest House.

LUKE, TIM (1989–90). 'Xmas Ideology: Unwrapping the New Deal and the Cold War under the Christmas Tree', *Telos*, 82 (winter): 157–73.

LÜSCHEN, GÜNTHER, STAIKOF, ZAHARJ, HEISKANEN, VERONICA

STOLET, and WARD, CONNOR (1972). 'Family, Ritual and Seculariz-ation: A Cross-National Study Conducted in Bulgaria, Finland, Germany and Ireland', *Social Compass*, 19/4: 519–36.

MCGINTY, BRIAN (1979). 'Santa Claus', *Early American Life*, 10/6: 50–3 ff.

MCGREEVY, PATRICK (1990). 'Place in the American Christmas', *Geographical Review*, 30 (Jan.): 32–42.

MACLEAN, ANNIE M. (1899). 'Two Weeks in Department Stores', *American Journal of Sociology*, 4/6: 721–41.

MALINOWSKI, BRONISLAW (1948). 'Myth in Primitive Psychology', in *Magic, Science, and Religion and Other Essays*. Garden City, NY: Doubleday: 91–148.

MARTIN, JUDITH (1982). *Miss Manner's Guide to Excruciatingly Correct Behavior*. New York: Athenium.

MATHEWS, G. (1987). *Just a Housewife: The Rise and Fall of Domesticity in America*. New York: Oxford University Press.

MATZ, MILTON (1961). 'The Meaning of the Christmas Tree to the American Jew', *Jewish Journal of Sociology*, 3/1: 129–37.

MAUSS, MARCEL (1925). *The Gift: Forms and Functions of Exchange in Archaic Societies*. London: Cohen & West.

MEERLOO, JOOST A. (1960). 'Santa Claus and the Psychology of Giving', *American Practitioner and Digest of Treatment* (Dec.): 50–3.

MEHTA, RAJ, and BELK, RUSSELL W. (1991). 'Artifacts, Identity, and Transition: Favorite Possessions of Indians and Indian Immigrants to the United States', *Journal of Consumer Research*, 17 (Mar.): 398–411.

MICK, DAVID, and DEMOSS, MICHELLE (1990). 'Self-Gifts: Phenomenological Insights from Four Contexts', *Journal of Consumer Research*, 17 (Dec.): 322–32.

MONTGOMERY, JOHN W. (1968). 'Remythologizing Christmas', *Christianity Today* (20 Dec.): 251–4.

MOSCHETTI, GREGORY J. (1979). 'The Christmas Potlatch: A Refinement of a Sociological Interpretation of Gift Exchange', *Sociological Focus*, 12 (Jan.): 1–7.

MUNSEY, CECIL (1972). *The Illustrated Guide to the Collectibles of Coca-Cola*. New York: Hawthorn Books.

O'NEIL, SUNNY (1981). *The Gift of Christmas Past: A Return to Victorian Traditions*. Nashville: American Association for State and Local History.

OPIE, IONA, and OPIE, PETER (1959). *The Lore and Language of School Children*. Oxford: Clarendon Press.

OSWALT, WENDELL H. (1970). 'A Particular Pattern: Santa Claus', in *Understanding our Culture: An Anthropological View*. New York: Holt, Rinehart, & Winston: 6–11.

OTNES, CELE, KIM, YOUNG CHAN, and LOWREY, TINA M. (1992).

'Ho, Ho, Woe: Christmas Shopping for "Difficult" People', in John F. Sherry, Jr., and Brian Sternthal (eds.), *Advances in Consumer Research*, vol. xix. Provo, Ut.: Association for Consumer Research: 482–7.

OXLEY, DIANA, HAGGARD, LOIS M., WERNER, CAROL M., and ALTMAN, IRWIN (1986). 'Transactional Qualities of Neighborhood Social Networks: A Case Study of Christmas Street', *Environment and Behavior*, 18: 640–77.

PIMLOTT, J. A. R. (1962). '. . . But Once a Year', *New Society*, 12 (19 Dec.): 9–12.

—— (1978). *The Englishman's Christmas: A Social History*. Hassocks: Harvester Press.

PLATH, DAVID W. (1963). 'The Japanese Popular Christmas: Coping with Modernity', *Journal of American Folklore*, 76/302: 309–17.

POLLAY, RICHARD W. (1987). 'It's the Thought that Counts: A Case Study in Xmas Excess', in Melanie Wallendorf and Paul Anderson (eds.), *Advances in Consumer Research*, vol. xiv. Provo, Ut.: Association for Consumer Research: 140–3.

PROCTOR, JANE T. (1967). 'Children's Reactions to Christmas', *Oklahoma State Medical Association Journal*, 60: 653–9.

RAGLAND, FITZ ROY (1937). *The Hero: A Study in Tradition, Myth, and Dress*. New York: Oxford University Press.

RICHARDS, KATHERINE L. (1934). *How Christmas Came to the Sunday-Schools: The Observance of Christmas in the Protestant Church Schools of the United States: An Historical Study*. New York: Dodd, Mead & Company.

RICHARDSON, JOHN G., and SIMPSON, CARL H. (1982). 'Children, Gender, and Social Structure: An Analysis of the Contents of Letters to Santa Claus', *Child Development*, 53: 423–36.

RUBIN, CAROL, and RUBIN, JEFF (1988). ' 'Tis the Season to Be Fighting', *Psychology Today*, 22 (Dec.): 36–9.

SCHLERETH, THOMAS J. (1989). 'Country Stores, County Fairs, and Mail-Order Catalogues: Consumption in Rural America', in Simon J. Bronner (ed.), *Consuming Visions: Accumulation and Display of Goods in America, 1880–1920*. New York: Norton: 339–75.

SCHMIDT, LEIGH E. (1991). 'The Commercialization of the Calendar: American Holidays and the Culture of Consumption, 1870–1930', *Journal of American History*, 78 (Dec.): 887–916.

SCHUDSON, MICHAEL (1986). 'The Giving of Gifts', *Psychology Today*, 20 (Dec.): 26–9.

SERENO, RENZO (1951). 'Some Observations on the Santa Claus Custom', *Psychiatry*, 14: 387–98.

SHERRY, JOHN F., Jr., and McGRATH, MARY ANN (1989). 'Unpacking the Holiday Presence: A Comparative Ethnography of Two Gift Stores', in Elizabeth C. Hirschman (ed.), *Interpretive Consumer Research*. Provo, Ut.: Association for Consumer Research: 148–67.

——— and LEVY, SIDNEY J. (1992). 'The Disposition of the Gift and Many Unhappy Returns', *Journal of Retailing*, 68 (spring): 40–65.

SHLIEN, JOHN (1959). 'Santa Claus: The Myth in America', *ETC: A Review of General Semantics*, 16/4: 27–32.

SHOEMAKER, A. L. (1959). *Christmas in Pennsylvania: A Folk-Cultural Study*. Kutztown, Pa.: Pennsylvania Folklore Society.

SNYDER, PHILLIP (1985). *December 25th: The Joys of Christmas Past*. New York: Dodd, Mead & Company.

STACK, CAROL B. (1974). *All Our Kin: Strategies for Survival in a Black Community*. New York: Harper & Row.

STARK, ELIZABETH (1983). 'Yes, There is a Jewish Santa', *Psychology Today*, 17/3: 24.

STENZEL, JIM (1975). 'Western Christmas—in a Japanese Sense', *Christian Century*, 92: 1183–5.

STERBA, RICHARD (1944). 'On Christmas', *Psychoanalytic Quarterly*, 13: 79–83.

SWEITZER, CATHY (1986). 'The Man in the Red Flannel Suit', *Parents Magazine*, 61 (Dec.): 123–8.

THOMPSON, ROBERT J. (1988). 'Christmas on Television: Consecrating Consumer Culture', paper presented at Popular Culture Association Annual Conference, New Orleans, Mar.

VIOLA, TOM (1986). 'Dickens' Well-Seasoned Story', *Guthrie Theater Program and Magazine* (Dec.): 47–50.

WAITS, WILLIAM B., Jr. (1978). 'The Many-Faced Custom: Christmas Gift-Giving in America, 1900–1940', unpublished doctoral dissertation, New Brunswick, NJ: Rutgers University, Department of History.

WALDER, DENNIS (1981). *Dickens and Religion*. London: Allen & Unwin.

WALLENDORF, MELANIE, and ARNOULD, ERIC (1991). ' "We Gather Together": Consumption Rituals of Thanksgiving Day', *Journal of Consumer Research*, 18 (June): 13–31.

WANKS, DAVID (1984). 'In Japan Gift-Giving is Often Just Another Business Deal', *Christian Science Monitor* (28 Dec.): 24.

WATERS, PAT (1978). *Coca-Cola: An Illustrated History*. Garden City, NY: Doubleday.

WEBLEY, PETER S., LEA, STEPHEN E. G., and PORTALSKA, R. (1983). 'The Unacceptability of Money as a Gift', *Journal of Economic Psychology*, 3: 223–38.

——— and WILSON, R. (1989). 'Social Relationships and the Unacceptability of Money as a Gift', *Journal of Social Psychology*, 129: 85–91.

WETTERING, MAXINE VAN DE (1984). 'The Popular Concept of "Home" in Nineteenth-Century America', *Journal of American Studies*, 18/1: 5–28.

WITT, LOUISE (1939). 'The Jew Celebrates Christmas', *Christian Century*, 56: 1497–9.

## 104      *Russell Belk*

WOLF, ERIC R. (1964). 'Santa Claus: Notes on a Collective Representation', in Robert A. Manners (ed.), *Process and Pattern in Culture: Essays in Honor of Julian H. Steward*. Chicago: Aldine: 147–55.

YAO, MARGARET (1981). 'Gift-Giving Spirit Haunts Some People Who Can't Afford It', *Wall Street Journal* (24 Dec.): 1 ff.

YATES, RONALD (1985). 'Japanese Merrily Leave the Christ Out of "Kurisumasu"', *Chicago Tribune* (22 Dec.): 1, 16.

ZEPP, IRA G., Jr. (1986). *The New Religious Image of Urban America: The Shopping Mall as Ceremonial Center*. Westminster, Md.: Christian Classics.

# 5

# Cinderella Christmas: Kitsch, Consumerism, and Youth in Japan

*Brian Moeran and Lise Skov*

## Sounds and Images

In Japan, as elsewhere, Christmas comes with a cacophonous vengeance. Throughout December 'Jingle Bells' rings out subdued but clear in hotel lobbies, airport lounges, neighbourhood shopping streets, supermarkets, banks, coffee shops, 24-hour convenience stores—in fact anywhere people go during the last heady weeks of December as they prepare to say farewell to one year and to greet another. Planted firmly in the middle of the year-end *oseibo* gift giving 'season' and just before the few days' respite from work that the Japanese traditionally enjoy over the first days of the New Year, Christmas has its own special place now in the cycle of seasonal events that constitutes Japan's domestic consumer economy.

So, while Japanese pop groups sing *'Merī Kurisumasu'* to one and all, store announcements inform us that Christmas (to give the word its English spelling)[1] is near and that 'Santa Claus is very busy so get your orders in early'. This busyness is partly to do with the way in which Santa finds himself suddenly obliged to decorate streets, shops, and advertisements all over the country. But this physical splitting of his personality is taken further when it comes to naming the red-suited gift-bearer. As 'Saint Nicholas'—the way in which he is toasted in a French Restaurant in Harajuku—he is still recognizable;[2] as 'Uncle Chimney' in a Ginza department store, he is somewhat less so. A few years ago, he was even found in a nativity scene in another Ginza department store, where he was acting as stand-in model for the new-born Christ.[3] Such transformations of Santa's persona continue apace. This year he takes to the streets as Colonel Sanders outside Kentucky Fried Chicken stores, and even appears disguised as a woman shop assistant in a local bakery.

Christmas, of course, means gifts—of snowman pyjamas, Yves Saint Laurent's heart-shaped compacts, chunky hand-knit sweaters, bottles of *rosé* champagne, strawberry topped cakes, and 'friendly pants' (*nakayoshi pants*). It is the time to buy toy purring cats, singing birds, and 'flower rock' swaying plastic flowers for your friends. But Christmas is also more than just gifts. In Japan, it is an expensive dinner for two on a yacht that cruises around Tokyo Bay, a night out at a luxury hotel lining the Yokohama waterfront, a skiing holiday on candlelit slopes in the Japan Alps. It is also a young lady in blue satin dress who sits down at a grand piano on the third floor of Mitsukoshi Department Store and from time to time trills out a somewhat classical version of numerous well-known carols. It is the music playing in neighbouring Takashimaya's sales pitch for an 'oseibo symphony', in a bank advertisement's 'Bonus carol echoes',[4] and in the ubiquitous phrase 'silent night' (*seiya*) found in both English and Japanese in advertising of all shapes and sizes.

As this hodge-podge of activities suggests, 'silent night' is a far cry from the kind of 'family Christmas' with which the tune is associated in the West. Also referred to by the English word 'eve', silent night conjures up a wide enough range of associations to make the proverbial rabbits on the moon prick up their ears in astonishment. It is true that one English company maintains the family image of Christmas with 'Mother's reminiscences and Wedgwood—Everyone comes back here on Christmas Eve',[5] but for the most part Christmas Eve in advertising takes on different connotations. 'Classic chocolate for silent night' reads the caption to a visual of candles, holly, two cups of coffee, a silver jug and sugar pot, and porcelain statue of Mozart.[6] Two glasses of champagne, red berries on a wreath, and an open box of chocolates (with half a dozen more on a china plate) are all encapsulated by 'Silent night's sweet message for him' (Figure 5.1).[7] '"I love you" comes back to life on December 24th' promises a close-up black and white photograph of a boy and girl kissing passionately, with their names—Garray and Vivian—handwritten inside a pink heart across their bodies.[8] 'A night to wear kisses . . .' claim another couple locked in their 'private session' embrace (Figure 5.2).[9] 'The satisfaction of (Christmas) Eve', smiles a blonde girl who sits demurely on a red suitcase beside three bottles of champagne and some empty wine glasses, with a large axe slung over one shoulder.[10] 'Dreams dance in the forest of the silent night' features Santa Claus astride a reindeer, a wolf standing on its hind legs chewing at a decorated fir tree, and a girl who has tumbled over to the ground, upsetting a basket of fruit and stars.[11]

FIG. 5.1. *Silent night's sweet message for him.* Courtesy of Mary's Chocolate Company and Ken Huang (a.k.a. K. Ko).

FIG. 5.2. *A night to wear kisses.* Courtesy of Melrose.

あの人へ、聖夜のスイート・メッセージ。

This strange mixture of fairy-tale elements is echoed in 'Become beautiful, Cinderella Christmas' (Figure 5.3), in which a Japanese girl in gold lamé strapless swimsuit with a coronet on her head, and holding a large gold starred wand, stands at the bottom of a spiralling red carpeted staircase leading into illuminated spires and castle-like buildings.[12] Is this the 'Urban ecstasy' referred to by a fashion house, or merely an echo of Tokyo Disneyland's 'Christmas fantasy'?[13] A child angel standing on a red rose answers: ' "Oh! My God" God Save the Christmas' (Figure 5.4).[14]

## Christmas Kitsch

How are we to make sense of these myriad sounds and images that incessantly invade our senses from all sides? Christmas in Japan seems to be made up of a vast unstructured accumulation of Western styles and Western commodities put together in a way that bears hardly any resemblance to Christmas in Europe or America. How are we to understand this Japanese reworking of a 'Western' Christmas?

Our hypothesis is that Christmas in Japan is a phenomenon of consumerism, and that when we walk around department stores, leaf through magazines, and look at advertisements, we are in fact inhabiting consumerism's semantic core. The extremely varied nature of consumerism, however, together with the plethora of meanings that it generates, makes it difficult for us to put forward an extended, rational argument in the usual academic manner. Instead, we will attempt to write in such a way that our style is itself a reflection of the phenomena under discussion.

The fascinating image of the *bricoleur*, who uses what is at hand to create new things out of rubbish, has frequently pervaded post-1960s analyses of popular culture. These tend to re-evaluate the idea of cultural forms as expressions of a dominant ideology and to talk instead in terms of the active participation of individuals.[15] Such dichotomizing can be simplistic. It is true that we all rummage around display shelves, picking up things here and there, looking at the prices before putting them back on the shelves (or even into our shopping baskets). We do this, not so much because we are 'subversive consumers' who are fighting the system, but because department stores are constructed exactly for this kind of behaviour. It is only at the abstract or metaphorical level that Japanese Christmas can be called *bricolage*. Empirically we are dealing not with old rubbish, but with phenomena that are

FIG. 5.4. *'Oh! My God' God Save the Christmas*. Shop In. Courtesy of Aramonoya Ltd.

FIG. 5.3. *Become beautiful, Cinderella Christmas*. Courtesy of Takano Yuri Beauty Clinic.

clean, well ordered, and brand new. Thus, when we gaze at the jewellery display cases or teddy bear shelves in Tokyo department stores, when we listen to Christmas carols in the city's covered shopping streets, or read about Christmas in Japanese magazines, the academic image of the *bricoleur* contains and, in a paradoxical way, is confronted with its own discreetly hidden contempt for the modern consumer. Consumerism is based upon a desire to discard the old and acquire the new, and this the concept of *bricolage* does its best to deny.

There is, of course, a 'dominant ideology' at work here (although not, perhaps, as 'dominant' as some critics might suggest), but there is also 'active participation' on the part of individual consumers, who indulge in a kind of trial and error approach to creating their own 'life-styles' by means of juxtaposing commodities that have come into their possession. The concept which best captures this ambivalence in the context of Japanese Christmas is *kitsch*, which we see as signifying industrially produced aesthetic objects that have a certain hold over the emotions, together with a whiff of tradition. On occasion, kitsch has been analysed in relation to art,[16] but here we would rather draw attention to the way in which emotional value can be added to things, and to the way in which aesthetic styles and objects are generated in contemporary society. Our point is not that feelings, or thoughts and sensual impressions mediated through things, are unreal or fictitious (in the sense of 'false'). On the contrary, we can take the resistance argument one step further by saying that commodities have already been 'subverted' before they reach the consumer, and that they can thus only be adapted in a process of 'subversive consumption'. Kitsch thus transcends the opposition between structure and agency which is at play in the debate over 'dominant ideology' and 'resistance'.

Let us illustrate our use of the concept of kitsch by examining the Christmas edition of the Japanese magazine *éf* (whose front cover describes itself in English as 'Fantastic monthly for young women').[17] This edition devotes most of its printed pages to an extended feature about 'The Proper Way to Spend Holy Night', starting out with 'Authentic Christmas in Austria' where, apparently, it is possible for the reader's heart to be 'washed' and so be purified for the emotional sincerity of the occasion. Amply illustrated with colour photographs, the text first tells us the story about how the hymn 'Silent Night' was composed in the small town of Oberndorf, near Salzburg. Then it describes how the town is decorated, before explaining how children enjoy Christmas in Austria. Finally, a box in the text informs one and all that 'Christmas in Austria' is the theme of a photographic exhibition mounted at Seibu Department Store in downtown Tokyo, and we begin to understand that this section about 'Authentic Christmas' is little more than an advertorial for Seibu.

Later on, the same report in *ef* uses a photograph of two long-haired blonde girls to tell us more about 'Tender Holy Night in Austria'. We learn how to have a quiet but happy Christmas at home, in the way that Austrians do, starting from Advent, which comes four weeks before Christmas itself. We are told where we can buy German imitation Christmas trees (for ¥16,000), candles, wreaths, angels, santas, and other decorations. Then we are told how children in Austria write, not to Santa Claus, but to 'Christkind' in the hope that they will receive what they want when they go into the room where the Christmas tree has been lit after dinner on Christmas Eve. This text is accompanied by photographs of gifts (alarm clock, glasses, pen, teddy bear, music box, leather purses, and so on—all of them purportedly from Austria), which have captions giving prices and retail outlet—Seibu Department Store once more. Finally, there are three or four more pages of photographs of goods that can be bought for Christmas—Austrian wine, Austrian cakes, and clothes—together with information about special 'ski and Mozart' tours to Austria. In the way in which it is depicted in magazine reportage, photographic exhibition, and department store, Austria is treated as kitsch whose imagery is imbued with the hallowed ring of tradition.

The question of whether there is such a thing as 'authenticity' has been examined, and frequently dismissed, in other contexts.[18] Nevertheless, the idea of authenticity, of an 'authentic Austrian Christmas', can and still does circulate—in Austria itself as well as in countries like Japan. This idea is easy enough to put down, of course, since no Japanese could ever celebrate Christmas according to 'Austrian custom'. However, the challenge here is for us to understand the authenticity of 'Austrian Christmas' as a *style*. It is not quite true to say that the actual place of Austria does not matter at all, since it is exactly because Austria is a real place with its own history and geography that the style of 'authentic Christmas' can point beyond the imagery to a social reality behind it. This reality may itself very well be a fiction (as every anthropologist worth her salt will sagely admit), but regardless of whether the people of Oberndorf really do decorate their town in the manner illustrated, and regardless of whether Austrian children really do write to Christkind or not, it is this model of reference to reality that succeeds in adding emotional sincerity to the product. Thus Austria, as country and image, comes to be arrayed on shelves of Christmas sections in Japanese department stores as a sample of *Eurokitsch*.

A reworking of Christmas elements also takes place with Christmas trees, which are found all over the city—outside a Revival Church in Nogata, between platforms at Kinshichō station, at the entrance to department stores—and which are all gaudily bedecked with gold and silver tinsel 'fairy hair', coloured glass balls, large gold bells, and even the occasional red rosette. To the eye accustomed to European Kitschmas, it would seem as if there are no aesthetic rules at work in this kind of decoration and that everything has been crammed in any old how, with as many ornaments attached to tree trunk and branches as possible. The overall stylistic effect thus comes to seem like one of total disorder. And yet this is in fact exactly the way in which Japanese bedeck riverside trees during their Tanabata festival in midsummer. The point here is that the decoration of Christmas trees reflects the way in which various styles are first detached from their geographical, seasonal, and cultural ties, before being reassembled according to different aesthetic criteria. As part of the same stylistic currency, 'Austrian' and 'Japanese' can be added to each other, precisely because they are subordinate to and consumed according to taste.

Exactly the same process takes place in the presentation of food. In 'Christmas Party on a plate', the *ef* feature goes on to give a selection of dishes that can be prepared for Holy Night dinner. The first of these consists of a 'delica[tessen] tree', made by sticking pieces of broccoli, asparagus, fried chicken, and croissants to a vertical *daikon* white radish (!); a second of Italian-style macaroni with tomato sauce, fried egg-plant, steak cooked in lemon and butter, chicken, potato, or seafood salad with mozzarella or parmesan cheese, and dried stick bread; and a third—also with cooking instructions where necessary—of 'a stylish Indian plate, with an ecological touch', consisting of 'Indian roast chicken', small stuffed pumpkins, and mushroom, tomato, and bean salad. If this is not to our taste, *ef* encourages us to bring in friends and prepare all kinds of *hors d'œuvres* to go with drinks—for example, a 'gorgeous' French loaf sandwich, filled with Brie cheese, caviare, and lemon, to go with the champagne; or platefuls of miniature pizzas to accompany our margaritas; or Mediterranean 'fritters' (cuttlefish, green peppers, zucchini) with which to wash down the sherry. Then, to take Holy Night quietly on, there are 'Christmas sweets' which should be served on 'slightly artistic' plates. The feeling of 'merry Christmas' will be fully savoured because these are 'romantic sweets' whose sweetness adds to the sweetness in our hearts. *ef* thus invites its readers to create their Christmas dinner from a selection of foods consisting of a dish which in itself looks like a Christmas tree, even though it is almost certainly not part of any Christmas 'tradition' anywhere in the world, as well as of Italian, eco-Indian, or French cuisine. The dinner is to be rounded off by romantic sweets, and everything celebrated within the mood paradigm of authentic Austria.

Let us make one thing clear here. By using the term 'kitsch' to describe this plethora of stylistic elements, we do not subscribe to the purist idea that macaroni is for Italians, that Christmas trees are not for eating, that sherry should be drunk while making polite conversation at cocktail parties, or that the blurring of advertising and information only deceives those who peruse it. Rather, we wish to draw attention to the surplus availability of styles—styles that can only be adopted as consumer choices. This is not to say that there is a lack of feeling and sincerity in Japanese Christmas. All its different styles and images are imbued with emotional qualities and meanings (we eat Mozart balls so that the sweetness of the chocolate can melt into our feelings), and it is precisely this which makes it kitsch.[19]

## A Cinema-like Drama

A cinema-like drama is about to begin. Concealing the nervousness of both hero and heroine, the curtain of Holy Night goes up. A twinge of excitement. Rather romantic. Tokyo Dressy Night—a style that beautifully reflects the finale of 1991. The heart made to throb with the pleasure of dressing up to express one's self. Two hearts—one of enjoyment, the other of playfulness —filled to the brim. Time for a twinkling party when the hour hand is forgotten. The actors are gathered on stage. Merry Christmas!

Thus runs the opening paragraph of a Tokyo department store's Christmas catalogue, entitled *Twinkle Heart Christmas* and carrying as its visual the made-up face of a blue-eyed, red-lipped Western model with a large starfish affixed to the lobe of one ear (for sale on the department store's ground floor Accessories Department for ¥38,000). It is time for us to close in on the actors who participate in Christmas Eve's theatre of consumption. We have already seen that Christmas imagery centres on youth, couples, and exclusivity. Throughout the 1980s young couples have tended to celebrate Holy

Night by having dinner alone together at an expensive European restaurant and by making an exchange of expensive gifts, before spending the night together in a hotel. This is 'a night of dreams, the dreams of a night'[20] for which—according to the rules of Western gallantry —the man pays.

There are, of course, variations on this Christmas pattern. We find a number of them in the young women's magazine *Peach* (playfully subtitled *Miss Asobision*[21]) which introduces its twenty-five-page Christmas special by a flow chart game in order to help the magazine's young women readers decide the best course for their Christmas Eve experience.[22] Situations range from the likes of 'You often go out for a drive when dating at weekends and holidays' to 'Your boyfriend is normally a pretty manly type, but once you are alone together he demands a lot of attention (*amaembō*)', by way of 'When he gives you a present, he chooses a teddy bear rather than flowers'. By answering either affirmatively or negatively to each situation, readers are able to proceed through a series of boxes until they arrive at one of nine suggested venues for their Christmas Eve date. These include a Yokohama seaside hotel (where prices go up in the days—or nights— around Christmas), Tokyo Disneyland (which has put on a special 'Christmas Fantasy'), the capital's newly developing seafront of Harumi, travelling abroad, the entertainment area of Shibuya, and a 'home party'.

Let us pause here for a moment, poised between boxes that take us from one theoretical comment to the next. The idea of 'being together' constitutes the social kernel of a Japanese Christmas, but unlike the West where 'being together' means being with one's family, in Japan Christmas has become a major celebration of romantic love. Three points follow from this, concerning dating, youth, and women.

In the first place, romantic love is articulated in Japan when people come together in what is known as a 'date', where both the word itself and its enactment are very definitely Western. It has been argued that both romantic love and consumerism are closely connected to the romantic versions of Christianity prevailing in Europe at the beginning of the nineteenth century. This complex of elements is linked by the experience of being overwhelmed by our feelings.[23] It is perhaps not surprising that the Western phenomenon of Christmas in Japan should be taken up by young people who as a social group are generally the most sensitive to trends and influences from abroad.[24] Romantic love makes us step out of our serious working lives for a moment. We thus yield to a form of individualism that leads us to believe that the 'truest' part of an individual is his or her feelings which can only be expressed in this intimate relation.

For young Japanese the date has become *the* form of romantic love today. As with any social interaction with a high degree of formalization, style and manner tend to take precedence over function and substance. A young man, for example, might start his Christmas preparations in midsummer by booking a hotel room for Christmas Eve, even though he does not have a girl-friend at the time. The idea or the feeling of being 'in love' thus takes on a significance of its own, detached from the loved one. This gives rise to the *staging* of love and to the preshaped, well-known roles that actors play when expressing their deepest emotions. Although it might be argued that we already know this emotional repertoire (which can be seen as comprising a whole dictionary of gallant clichés) the performance that ensues does not necessarily lack in sincerity. This touch of kitsch is a feature that romantic love shares with consumerism. Everything has been seen, said, and heard before, so that it is as easy to put down the experience when we observe it from a detached distance, as it is impossible to avoid getting entangled in the sticky clichés of kitsch when we try to express our feelings.

Secondly, as part of Japan's youth culture, Christmas shares many features with youth cultures elsewhere[25]—including a rejection of adult values (which in Japan have been sustained by neo-Confucianist elements including a strong 'work' ethic) in favour of what has been called 'hedonist consumption'.[26] Such consumption of romantic love (however structured that consumption might be) has helped upset the hitherto prevailing generational hierarchy in Japan, since Christmas is an event that takes place *outside* the family, in the city. Hence we find the media devoting attention to discussions of whether a young girl should or should not accept an invitation from her boy-friend to spend Christmas night together. In December 1991, a poll revealed that of the 100 mothers who were asked whether it would be all right for their daughters to stay out all night, 98 said categorically 'no', while the two who did not object were talking in general terms and not about their own daughters! The daughters, however, were of a different opinion—and this was taken to illustrate just how great the 'generation gap' in Japan is becoming these days. According to the poll, 68 of 100 girls were prepared to accept the invitation if the man were 'Mr Right'. We can thus see that when a young woman considers what to do with her boy-friend, she does not listen to the concerned voice of her mother, but to a voice coming from deep within herself, asking whether her feelings really are sincere.

This kind of youth culture has been labelled 'hedonist' because this form of consumption does not involve purchasing commodities for others in the way that it does for—say—a housewife shopping on behalf of her husband and children. Instead, 'hedonist consumption' is focused on the body and the self, on emotions and romantic love. At the same time, the idea of 'hedonism' has a pleasure-seeking, un-structured connotation which counters the structured form of the date and young women's introspective attitudes towards their own emo-tional sincerity. For this reason, we prefer to use the term *consumerism* —in the sense of a distilled form of consumption in which the act of consumption itself becomes an experience.

The third point concerns the ambivalent connection between women and consumerism. For a start, the main group of consumers in Japan consists of young women from their mid to late teens through their twenties. The language of advertising is very obviously that of and for young women, while visual images accompanying Christmas circulate almost entirely around the female body. Young women con-sumers are invited to be mistresses of their own physical appearance. 'You can definitely become beautiful by Christmas', claims one 'esthé salon',[27] while another assures us that 'If your body changes, your heart changes too'.[28] We find, then, a multifaceted play, in which women consumers, their images, and the commodities they consume are all transformed in the flexible mould of consumerism.

It is also consumerism which plays tricks with our already subverted friend, Santa Claus. The bearded old man suddenly appears as a dark-haired, brown-eyed, smooth-cheeked Japanese girl—on the cover of a magazine (Figure 5.5), in a bank branch window, on stage in a department store.[29] In a Japan Railways ad informing the com-muters of the introduction of automatic wicket gates at three of Tokyo's commuter stations 'round about the time jingle bells are ring-ing' the young woman Santa reveals her feminine nature by pulling her beard and moustache half off.[30]

Such transformations of young women can have an almost magical effect. For example, the beauty salon whose headline is 'Cinderella Christmas' suggests that a young woman can be transformed into the heroine of a fairy-tale, worthy of the love of some handsome prince in his castle. The Cinderella dream (which reappears in an advertise-

Fɪɢ. 5.5. *McSister*. Front Cover, January 1992. Courtesy of Fujin Gaho-sha.

ment for pink champagne[31]) is that of a sudden transformation which leaves behind the everyday humdrum world for a single night. 'Always at my side, proud prince', reads a brochure which then answers on the young man's behalf: 'Longing to see your face—just a little luxurious'.[32] This fairy-tale quality of Christmas is reinforced by the frequent images of stars falling from the heavens—whether in department store brochures, jewellery advertisements, or a poster for a French restaurant. Whether it really is possible for those concerned to be transported 'to a wonderland, to dreams'[33] is irrelevant. This is the way in which Christmas is acted out and celebrated.

## *Make me into Eve*

We have been moving through a series of wrapped boxes in the Christmas flow chart, examining more closely those who appear in the scene of Japanese Christmas and the roles that they act out in the play of consumerism. Faced with a confusing hodge-podge of images, we discarded other box options to enter into 'kitsch', where we applauded the idea that emotional value can be added to things. We then found ourselves witnessing some peculiarities surrounding the concept of 'dating'. Having accepted that the date is the contemporary form of romantic love in Japan, we found ourselves firmly placed in 'youth culture', and giving a sidelong glance at the appearance on stage of an old friend, 'generation gap'. From our box, we followed the arrow that led to 'consumerism'—consumption itself transformed into an experience—only to find ourselves circling through an intricate maze of ribbon-like paths and carefully wrapped boxes which stage continual transformations of young women consumers and their images under the deft directorship of consumerism itself. Stalled and in danger of retracing our steps right back to the start, to find that kitsch is but the most emotional form of all these elements of consumerism, we must somehow move on in our flow chart to other, more magical, transformations of feelings and time, of things and people, as they occur on Christmas Eve.

One highlight of Christmas Eve in Japan is the exchange of gifts. In recent years, Tiffany jewellery has been seen as *the* item to give as an expression of romantic emotion. Tiffany's is only found in Mitsukoshi department store (and one or two hotels), and during the weeks leading up to Christmas young people queue outside the prestigious section of Tokyo's premier department store, in order to be able to buy a diamond there. On 23 December 1991—the Emperor's birthday and a national holiday—the place was in total chaos as couples rushed in to purchase presents for each other.[34] Rather than go out independently to buy gifts for their loved ones, young people use Christmas shopping as a pretext for yet another date.

The Christmas gift market in Japan comes to approximately ¥670,000 million, and it was in the late 1980s posting a 25 per cent annual increase in turnover. Along with Tiffany jewellery, best-selling gift items advertised in magazines and department stores include expensive rings, accessories, and watches, together with limited edition perfume and cosmetic sets (put out for the most part by brand names such as Lancôme, Givenchy, and Elizabeth Arden), and to a lesser extent such items as handbags, wallets, and ties. Giving this kind of present is in itself an expression of one's sincere feelings, and when the loved one wears or uses the gift for all to see, it can merge smoothly with his or her personality. We find in these presents, then, a diffusion of feelings between person and gift which mirrors the way in which kitsch itself consists of emotional values added to things. For young Japanese the exchange of gifts is an integral part of consumerism itself. A survey of young people from middle school to university revealed that the average cost of the gifts that they intended to exchange with their Christmas dates came to between fifteen and thirty thousand yen (£62–125). Those questioned explained that it was important to give something to remind each other of their Christmas Eve together several months later, and that in this respect the expense itself was irrelevant.[35] Affection can thus generate both expense and luxury, and seems to be forever balancing on a tightrope slung between emotional expression and cool display.

Our discussion of gifts leads us to our next point concerning consumerism: Christmas *preparations*. As we have already noted, hotel rooms are booked in the hot and humid months of summer; fitness clubs and esthé salons put their ads out from the autumn; and magazines devote the issues that come out in December almost totally to features about different ways to celebrate Christmas and different kinds of presents to give. As we have also seen, advertising copy, photo reportages, and editorials all make use of a language taken from theatre and film. Headlines like 'Curtain rise on a holy day fantasia'; 'Beautiful presentation'; 'Wanting to have an incomparable eve through a highly valued dramatic presentation'[36] point convincingly to the fact that Christmas is a play that is well rehearsed.

私をイヴにしてください。

TISSÉ
*from*
SEIKO

FIG. 5.6. *Make me into Eve please.* Tissé from Seiko. Courtesy of the Seiko Corporation.

For the fairy-tale nature of Christmas Eve to materialize, preparation and timing are vital. During the starlit Holy Night, the progressive time of the clock almost magically coalesces into one emotionally significant moment, around which there is a strong sense of before and after.[37] It is a moment of social magic when, as if in accordance with some unwritten contract, thousands of young people decide to go out and spend time together. Christmas Eve itself can also at times be turned from the temporal occasion of Holy Night into the very embodiment of consumerism—a young woman. 'For all the Eves', promises one advertisement headline; 'Make me into Eve', requests another (Figure 5.6).[38]

At the same time, various seasonal commodities are made especially available over Christmas. Thus, although it is possible to buy cakes and ice-cream all year round, *Christmas* ice-cream is sold with special decorations of silver frosting, while *Christmas* cakes are topped with plastic holly and the first strawberries of the season. Not that this staging of Christmas means that it is in any way false. On the contrary, just as romantic love perfectly fits the prescribed frame of the date, so too is the ability to create a moment in which time stands still a central skill of consumerism itself.

*Charting the Flow of Events*

Just as Christmas coalesces into a single substantial moment, so does it dissolve into thin winter air. Outside one local neighbourhood store, a plastic, blow-up snowman in a green scarf, blue hat, and red gloves has acted as an advertisement for Christmas 'stockings'. Called 'Fantasy Boots', these novelty-filled stockings were being retailed in the days leading up to Christmas at ¥1,000, but as Christmas Eve drew towards a close, prices came tumbling down—first to ¥600, then ¥500 in the late afternoon, and ¥400 by early evening. Less than twenty-four hours later, Christmas was over and it was difficult to remember what could have been so special about it. The covered shopping streets had stopped piping their Christmas carols, and offered instead an equally jolly medley of 'old favourites'. All traces of the festival were being removed from the shop windows. Left-over bottles of bubbly were being stored with the rest of the wines in the liquor shops; the video rental assistants were removing miniature plastic Christmas trees from their display cases; and Colonel Sanders in front of Kentucky Fried Chicken had reverted to his former white-suited self. In the meantime, JR and Mitsubishi Bank had changed their Santa ads, while the smooth-cheeked woman Santa hanging from the photographer's store ceiling had been transformed into a kimono-clad young Japanese *ojōsan* wishing all customers a Happy New Year. At the bakery nearby, shop assistants were wiping the windows clean of frosting and reindeer. Instead, the ferns, straw, pine, bamboo, and mandarin decorations that adorn house entrances at New Year were emerging everywhere. There was only a week to go until the end of the year and a whole new commercial festival was about to begin.

This experience is typical of consumerism, and it invites us to visualize time, not as an ever-progressing hymn, but as a slowly revolving stage below which an orchestra of tuxedo-clad marketeers plays unceasingly variations on Vivaldi's *The Four Seasons*. In the world of consumerism, time is measured by the shifts between one commercial festival and the next, and is reflected in the seasonal commodities that accompany each. The eight days that take the Japanese from Christmas to the end of the old year and into the new are remarkable in that they include major celebrations of four different world religions or belief systems: Taoism, Christianity, Buddhism, and Shinto. In order to put the Eurokitsch of Christmas into perspective, therefore, we need to consider this commercial festival *vis-à-vis* other celebrations that take place during this season.

Celebration of Taoism is found in the annual year-end gift-giving season (*oseibo*), during which gifts are exchanged between neighbourhood or community households, between junior and senior colleagues at work, between companies, and between married couples and the go-betweens (*nakōdo*) who officially brought them together. Just as the midsummer gift-giving season (*ochūgen*) leads up to the return of the ancestors, *oseibo* rounds off the year by reinforcing social ties at the community level. Buddhism makes a fleeting appearance on the last night of the year (*ōmisoka*), when temple bells toll at midnight to rid the human race of its 108 afflictions. This is followed by New Year itself, a Shinto celebration both of the Japanese nation and of the family (and thus acts as a structural equivalent, perhaps, to Christmas in the West).

In many respects the way in which Christmas is celebrated in Japan acts as a negation of the Taoist and Shinto celebrations. Christmas is located in the realm of mass culture, the city, and is thus placed beyond the reach of both local community and family. Young couples escape their social obligations for a night when they go out to celebrate themselves, romance, and consumerism. At the same time as Christmas is set apart from *oseibo* and New Year at a structural level, all three of them coalesce when it comes to spending and consumption. It may even seem as if Japan's marketeers have cleverly created a Christmas niche for the social group which simultaneously consists of Japan's biggest spenders while not being kept occupied by the usual December hanky-panky. As an event that is constructed with reference to Western tradition, Christmas falls neatly into place beside other Japanese events such as (St) Valentine's Day (14 February) and White Day (14 March).[39] All are primarily characterized by exchanges of gifts between young men and women, by the prevalent feeling of romance, and by further opportunities for a special form of dating.

We have noted how time revolves around yearly events, and how seasonal celebrations become occasions for spending. Social life, consumption, and promotional marketing are interwoven in such a manner that they cannot be separated—a complex process which is itself the subject of one Christmas ad for a production company (see Figure 5.7). With visual of a snowman, a sack of balloons made up from the Union Jack and Stars and Stripes, and with two Japanese children—the boy with glasses, false nose, and yellow helmet complete with antlers; the girl in red Santa cap and boots blowing a kiss at the camera—the headline reads: 'Promotional activities so that annual events do a good

FIG. 5.7. *Social life, consumption, and promotional marketing.*
Courtesy of ASP.

job in consuming your life'.[40] This advertisement neatly encapsulates
the way in which Christmas leads into the New Year, which itself is
linked to Coming of Age Day (*seijin no hi*, 15 January), which leads
on to St Valentine's Day, which is inseparable from White Day, which
harks back to Girl's Day (3 March) and forward to Boy's Day (5 May),
which themselves are part of Mother's Day (10 May), not to mention
Father's Day (6 June) or Old People's Day (*keiro no hi*, 15 September),

and so on and so on, so that these occasions lead us round and round like the boxes in our flow chart. Consumption is indeed a whole way of life.

## Santas Do it with their Claws

The image that we have depicted here of Christmas in Japan is very much one of the 1980s and of the beginning of the 1990s. In the decade prior to that, it was also celebrated by young people, although they tended to go out in groups to discos or student parties, rather than as couples on dates together. Before that, in the 1960s, Christmas was celebrated only briefly by families with children, who marked the event by consuming special Christmas cakes or ice-creams that became a hit when they were introduced onto the Japanese market. In the 1950s, Christmas provided businessmen with a chance to give some inexpensive present of accessories to their favourite bar hostess.[41] The question that remains for us to examine now is whether young Japanese will continue to celebrate Christmas throughout the final decade of this century in the way that they did in the 1980s, or whether further changes are likely to occur.

In the weeks leading up to Christmas 1991, the media paid a lot of attention to precisely this question. 'Trend-setters', in the form of ad agency spokesmen, marketing representatives from department stores, and magazine editors, were asked to forecast the future. Their unanimous point of departure was the Japanese economy, and their equally unanimous conclusion was that the economy had reached its peak, and was on its way down. The bubble that had floated over the Tokyo stock exchange had burst and the nation was entering a new 'post-bubble era'. The international economic and political climate also looked gloomy, and in such a time, the trend-setters concluded, young people would be reluctant to go out and spend their money at expensive restaurants. Instead, it was more likely that they would prepare a nice plate of food, arrange their dinner table with candles, Christmas wreath, and other decorations, and spend Holy Night quietly reading or listening to music with friends. It was on the basis of such a line of thought (which appeared in numerous versions in Japanese newspapers and editorial commentary towards the end of December 1991) that the country's trend-setters came up with such keywords as *handmade*, *body warmth*, and *authenticity* to set this year's Christmas apart from that of former years. These keywords caught on and could be seen and heard everywhere—on television and the radio, in advertising and magazines, as well as in the financial pages of the national dailies —and they were discussed in relation to three elements in particular: hand-knit sweaters, Christmas trees, and home parties.

According to this trend-setting discourse, it was hand-knit sweaters above all else which expressed the new mood of 1991 and which proved to be popular gifts. Already back in September young women were buying knitting kits, especially for really bulky, chunky-knit sweaters. In answer to a survey, young women all stated that they did not knit to save money so much as to express their affection for their boy-friends, even though the sweaters in question cost about ¥40,000 to buy, and only about ¥15,000 to make oneself.

The second main commodity in this do-it-yourself trend was the Christmas tree. Marui department store (which welcomed us with the punning slogan *Marui Kurisumasu*) encouraged its customers to buy Christmas tree sets, whose blurb read (in English): 'Make your Christmas special by doing it the hand-made way', encouraging us to believe, perhaps, that Santas do it with their claws. Several department stores reported that, whereas the maximum height for a tree last year was 120 cm., this year even the 180 cm. tree sold well for ¥18,900.[42] Accompanying this demand for trees was one for proper Christmas tree lights (a 140-bulb set with controls cost ¥12,000 and sales more than 300 per cent up over the previous year), as well as for smaller items like wreaths, cards, and ribbons.

The third thing that was interpreted as representing the new trend was the 'home party'. As we have had occasion to note, *éf*, the 'fantastic monthly for young women', provided recipes for such a celebration and, in a feature about how to dress up for Christmas, also reminded its readers that they could spend this year's traditional festival quietly, as though it were part of a scene from a film. Half a dozen full-page colour photographs of Western girls modelling clothes in various Christmas settings were accompanied by short pieces of text telling readers how Holy Night could start with the uncorking of champagne bottles, before friends played cards through the night while listening to old records (for instance, of classical choral music). Earlier that day, suggested *éf*, people could hang up their socks under the Christmas tree to remind themselves of their childhood days.

In other words the hand-made trend marked a change in the direction of quiet Christmas nostalgia, rather than a continuation of conspicuous dating. The trend-setters, however, did not attempt to elucidate social reality as a whole, but only chose temporal elements of it, so that, in their discussions of the hand-made trend, they overemphasized new elements (according to the very nature of fashion and consumption) to the detriment of an overall continuity that was obviously also present. Nevertheless, market analysis data can be very informative, and Erica Carter has even argued that it can be the best material for the study of such phenomena as youth and consumerism, because market research follows very closely the lives of young people —in particular of women.[43] There are three points that we would make here in connection with this.

First, market analysis provides evidence to suggest that change is occurring, not just in Christmas but also in the New Year. In its quarterly report,[44] the Hakuhōdō Institute of Life and Living analysed newspaper and magazine articles, headlines, and advertisements, before suggesting that people were prepared to accept that the economic 'bubble' had burst for good and that there would be no harm in their turning back to seek out what was best in their lives. Words like 'the real thing' (*honmono*), 'tradition' (*dentō*), and 'origin' (*genten*) were seen to reflect the new values. At the same time, it was noted in discussions within the Institute that New Year celebrations in 1992 were somewhat muted in comparison with those of previous years, and that people had been in their most festive mood over Christmas. The 'Japaneseness' that had hitherto characterized the Shinto festival of the New Year was seen to be strangely lacking. Whereas in the old days, there was a sense of 'family unity' (*ikka*) when everybody bathed before the end of the old year and shared the coming in of the new year together, this had not been present in 1992. Moreover, housewives had apparently not carried out the customary 'big cleaning' (*ō sōji*) that marked the end of the old year; nor had they bothered to prepare the special foods that accompanied the New Year.[45] Finally, women went to pay their respects at shrines in ordinary clothes, rather than in kimono, and a lot of young people spent New Year's Eve on yet another all night date, although this time in groups with friends.

Precisely what this change signifies is hard to tell as yet, but it may be that the New Year is in the process of coming to be celebrated by friends, rather than by family. In which case, it is possible that Christmas (couples) and the New Year (friends) will come to form a closely linked pair of events, in the same way that St Valentine's and White Days have become inseparable in the marketeers' orchestral repertoire. At the same time, there are hints that young people continue to celebrate Christmas after marriage in the same way that they used to when they were courting—which suggests that the present distinctions between families (in which two or three generations are together), lovers (who go dating), and friends (who gather together in groups) might become blurred. These are, of course, mere hypotheses, but our aim is to show that Christmas is not a static event and that any changes that occur to it are likely to be reflected in other events and relationships that make up the cycle of consumerism.

Secondly, as we have seen, the bursting of the economic 'bubble' played a crucial part in trend-setters' arguments for the new trend. Of course, this is by no means the first time that political events and economic changes have helped shape new fashions. But the severe competition within the Japanese consumer market seems to have made the search for novelty more organized and more systematic here than anywhere else, and to some extent the close observation of this market has constructed a new kind of 'economic determinism'. In this respect, the economy no longer plays the role of society's 'base', but acts as a bank of ideas whose fluctuations are perfectly reflected in the flowing surface of consumerism's stream.

Our final point concerns the way in which market analysis operates. As we have already indicated, changes in market trends are interpreted by analysts in extremely quantitative terms—in the height of Christmas trees, for example, in the size of *kadomatsu* front-door decorations for New Year, in the diameter of seasonal cakes, or in the frequency of certain words in advertising and other media. Out of this floating system of co-ordinates trend-setters, with their special intuition for the new, proceed to select certain moments as turning-points which then indicate a 'trend'. The flow of time is thus conceptualized with the aid of a number of 'keywords'.

This process of interpretation, whereby something in a state of flux is fixed through linguistic concepts, is practised by all those who are involved in social analysis of one sort or another, and who are obliged to use concepts as tools of communication. Even though all concept making is marked by an element of imagination and construction, in market analysis, however, this element tends to dominate. The reason for this is simple. In contrast to sociology and anthropology (ideally speaking, at least), market analysis uses concepts not just as a means towards interpretation or diagnosis of elements (events, consumer groups, statistical data), but also to generate and accelerate a new trend.[46] For this purpose, it is not sufficient to explore the meanings that invest old words (as we have done with our interpretation of kitsch). Instead, market analysis resuscitates old words and imbues them with new meanings.[47]

As we know, it is impossible to find a stepping stone that places us 'outside' the social context that we are examining, because every text is read, reinterpreted, and acted upon. It is exactly this ambivalent aspect of social analysis that market analysis consciously makes use of. First, it isolates a particular aspect of the data being analysed. Then it sets it apart as a new trend, only for it to be consumed and so subsumed under current fashions. In this process market analysis perpetuates the dialectic of consumption and analysis itself. For sociologists and anthropologists, the irony here is that today the most objectifying form of analysis (represented by the endless number of tables and diagrams found in marketing data) is the one most unproblematically used to generate this genuinely cultural process in which analysis and consumption go hand in hand.

## Culture and Consumerism

We have suggested that the term 'consumerism' be used to describe the complex of consumption, romantic love, and youth in which women play an ambivalent but crucial role. By being closely connected to marketing techniques of timing, consumerism thus comes to refer to the ultimate form of consumption which pervades the whole of society, and which is to a great extent indistinguishable from culture.

In the department stores, shopping streets, and women's magazines that make up the semantic core of Japanese Christmas, we were assailed by a myriad of sounds and images which led us to adopt the concept of kitsch as our theoretical base. Kitsch signifies the process of accumulation and generation in a tightly woven network of feelings and things—a process of which it is practically impossible to make sense in such terms as 'subversion' or 'dominant ideology'. On the one hand, Christmas's emotional value is already prefabricated in a wide range of commodities, from Tiffany's jewellery to teddy bears; on the other, an emotional transformation of things only works when it is reworked by individual consumers. In this process of consumption there is no real or original meaning, and kitsch is thus an endless chain of 'subversions'. This ambivalence is not limited to commodities, but can also be found in people's relationships, such as the way in which young couples date on Christmas Eve.

The material presented in this paper consisted for the most part of young women's magazines and Christmas brochures from department stores. These we have read as 'manuals for consumerism'. In our interpretation they fill exactly that space between structure and agency that most social theory leaves empty, for the manuals show the repetitive patterns within and upon which individual agents act. As manuals the magazines and ads are at the same time testimony of certain sociological facts, as well as prescriptions which inevitably are reinterpreted and reworked by young Japanese as they celebrate—and cerebrate—Christmas together.

## Notes

1 For the sake of clarity and ease of reading, we have departed from usual practice in the romanization of Japanese and written all Western language loanwords in their original form.

2 If the toast were with wine, one could have sampled the dry delights of Chateau St Nicholas's White Christmas Cuvée, vinted by one John Wesley in the sunny state of California and sold for ¥1,500 a bottle in Tokyo liquor stores. With such ironies is the kit of kitsch assembled.

3 One unconfirmed source informed us that one of Tokyo's department stores had at its entrance a crucifixion of Father Christmas, with the words 'Happy Shopping' inscribed above the cross.

4 *Bonus carol hibiku*, Mitsubishi Ginkō.

5 *Haha no omoide-banashi to Wedgwood. Eve no yoru wa, minna koko e kaette kuru*, Wedgwood.

6 Mirabell's 'Mozart balls'.

7 *Ano hito e, seiya no sweet message*, Mary's.

8 *1991.12.24, I love you ga iki kaeru*, Platinum Love (jewellery).

9 *kiss o kiru eve, Session Private Christmas*, Melrose (fashion).

10 *Seiya (Eve) no manzoku*, Lancel Paris (bags).

11 *Seiya no mori ni yume ga odoru*, Juchheim's (cakes).

12 *Kirei ni natte, Cinderella Christmas*, Takano Yuri (Beauty Clinic).

13 Seed; Tokyo Disneyland (advertorial in *McSister*, Jan. 1992).

14 *Motto, hallelujah . . .* , Shop In (novelty chain store).

15 It might well be argued that Lévi-Strauss (1966) did not intend his metaphor of the *bricoleur* to have much significance beyond a highly abstract theoretical level, and that the romanticization of *bricolage* emerged when the concept was adopted by others to describe the realm of things (e.g. Hebdige 1979).

16 Cf. Adorno (1984: 339–40), who defines a clear distinction between real

and fictitious feelings, true art and vulgarity. 'Fickle as an imp, kitsch defies definition. The one enduring characteristic it has is that it preys on fictitious feelings, thereby neutralising real ones. It is useless to try and draw a fine line between what constitutes true aesthetic fiction (art) and what is merely sentimental rubbish (kitsch).'

17 *éf*, Dec. 1991.
18 Cf. Hobsbawm and Ranger 1983.
19 As an explanatory concept 'kitsch' can, of course, also provide a key to Western Christmas. But that is not really what we want to discuss here.
20 *Yoru no yume, yume no yoru*, fashion reportage. *Marie Claire Japon*, Jan. 1992. One should note here that January issues of most magazines are in the shops from early to mid-December.
21 A punning amalgam of the Japanese word *asobi*, 'play', and the English word 'vision'; *Peach*, Jan. 1992.
22 *'91 Christmas daisakusen, Peach*, Jan. 1992, pp. 60–1; the flow chart is an extremely common form in Japanese women's magazines, in the same way that it used to be in Western publications of this nature. These simple and instructive charts are designed to help readers take complex decisions simply by answering 'yes' or 'no' to a series of basic questions. Is it possible that they have acted as an important source of inspiration both for those interested in the currently dominant computer aesthetics, and for those employed in academia who believe in a step-by-step approach to theoretical arguments?
23 Cf. Campbell's *The Romantic Ethic and the Spirit of Modern Consumerism* (1987), the title of whose work suggests that his thesis is at the same time a critique of, and supplement to, Weber's concept of the Protestant ethic. The 'spirit of consumerism' can also be used to supplement Confucianism, the oriental cousin of puritan rationality, which has been used to explain Japan's successful modernization in both economic and political arenas (see, among others, Bellah 1957). As a philosophy which espouses work and a male-dominated hierarchy, the Confucianist argument may satisfactorily account for the productive side of Japan's burgeoning post-war economy, but it totally fails to deal with the 'spirit' which sustains that production—consumerism (see Moeran's '*Homo Harmonicus* and the Yen-joy Girls', 1989). In Japan, these two rationalities are divided not only according to gender and different spheres of life, but also according to a 'native'–foreign distinction.
24 This play between youth and foreign influence does not take place only between 'Western' and 'non-Western' cultures. American influence has also, for instance, been a major productive factor in the creation of youth cultures in post-war Britain (Chambers 1986).
25 See e.g. the work carried out by those in one way or another affiliated to the Centre for Contemporary Cultural Studies in Birmingham in the 1970s

and 1980s (Hebdige 1979; Willis 1977; McRobbie and Nava 1984; Chambers 1986).

26 This idea is found not only in youth culture studies, but also in Campbell (1987), who describes the emotional experience arising out of consumerism, novel reading, and romantic love as 'romantic hedonism'.

27 *Christmas made ni zettai kirei ni naru*, Tokyo Beauty Center ad in *Nonno*, 5 Dec. 1991. Note how this emphasis on training and disciplining the body is precisely the opposite to that of pleasure and laxity implied in *hedonist* consumption.

28 *Oriental Ésthetic Salon: Slim Beauty House*, *Vivi*, Jan. 1992.

29 *McSister*, Jan. 1992; *Bonus carol hibiku*, Mitsubishi Bank; Mitsukoshi Department Store Christmas party.

30 *Jingle bell ga nagareru koro*, JR (Japan Railways).

31 *Cinderella light*, Choya, Perilla Light.

32 Brochure for Marui Department Store.

33 *Fushigi no kuni e, yume no naka e*, Citizen.

34 *Yomiuri Shimbun*, Tokyo edition, 24 Dec. 1991.

35 *Nihon Keizai Shimbun*, 4 Oct. 1991; *Nihon Keizai Shimbun*, 14 Dec. 1991.

36 Fashion reportage and Clarins ad in *Elle Japon*, 5 Dec. 1991; *Totte oki no enshutsu de, tobikiri no ibu ni shitai*, Marui Department Store Brochure.

37 *Peach* magazine even reminds its readers to have their cameras ready to record that special moment on a night that takes place only once a year.

38 *Watashi o Eve ni shite kudasai*, Tissé from Seiko. Could it be that there were, after all, a few happy hours right after the Fall of Man (but before it had been discovered, of course) when Eve, naked, wandered around the Garden of Eden innocently checking the time on her Seiko wrist watch?

39 Valentine (St Valentine's) Day in Japan differs from the way in which it is celebrated in England or America in that only *women* give presents to men. The latter then have the opportunity to return the compliment one month later on White Day. It is said that St Valentine's Day was instituted as a gift-giving occasion by marketeers anxious to save the Japanese chocolate industry. In this they were more than successful.

40 *Nenjū gyōji wa jinsei o jōzu ni shōhi suru hansoku katsudō desu*. ASP (Ansell Sawada Production).

41 *Frau*, Nov. 1991.

42 *Nihon Keizai Shimbun*, 26 Dec. 1991; *Asahi Shimbun*, 8 Dec. 1991.

43 Carter (1984).

44 '*Bubble saru*', *Seikatsu Shikihō*, spring edn. 1992. Brian Moeran would like to thank Hidehiko Sekizawa and his colleagues at the Hakuhōdō Institute of Life and Living for their academic assistance and hospitality between January and May 1992.

45 This is also made possible by the growth of twenty-four-hour convenience

stores that are open every day of the year. In the past, all shops were
closed for at least three days over the New Year.

46 Admittedly, it is often difficult to see any difference between the academic
and market modes of analysis, since academics are themselves engaged in
a form of self-marketing in order to become a hit, or at least reflect current
trends. After all, who has not adorned herself—or himself—in 'the Austere
Beauty of Habermas slashed with a Daring Touch of Baudrillard' (Wilson
1990: 28) when that was in style? Like fashion clothing, which tends to
be outdated as soon as it has been displayed on the catwalk, ideas may
well become worn out just from being perceived.

47 This selection of key words is well suited to, and explains Japanese marketeers' apparent preference for, English words like 'hand-made' and
'adult mood' in their analyses.

## References

ADORNO, T. W. (1984). *Aesthetic Theory*, trans. C. Lenhardt. London: Routledge & Kegan Paul.

BELLAH, ROBERT (1957). *Tokugawa Religion: The Values of Pre-industrial
Japan*. Glencoe, Ill.: Free Press.

CAMPBELL, COLIN (1987). *The Romantic Ethic and the Spirit of Modern
Consumerism*. Oxford: Basil Blackwell.

CARTER, ERICA (1984). 'Alice in Consumer Wonderland', in A. McRobbie
and M. Nava (eds.), *Gender and Generation*. London: Macmillan.

CHAMBERS, IAIN (1986). *Popular Culture: The Metropolitan Experience*.
London: Routledge.

Hakuhōdō Institute of Life and Living (1992). 'Bubble saru', *Seikatsu Shikihō*,
spring edn.

HEBDIGE, DICK (1979). *Subculture: The Meaning of Style*. London: Methuen.

HOBSBAWM, E., and RANGER, T. (1983) (eds.). *The Invention of Tradition*.
Cambridge: Cambridge University Press.

LÉVI-STRAUSS, CLAUDE (1966). *The Savage Mind*. London: Weidenfeld
& Nicolson.

MCROBBIE, ANGELA, and NAVA, MICA (1984) (eds.). *Gender and Generation*. London: Macmillan.

MOERAN, BRIAN (1989). '*Homo Harmonicus* and the *Yenjoy* Girls: The Production and Consumption of Japanese Myths', *Encounter*, 72/5: 19–25.

NAKANE, CHIE (1970). *Japanese Society*. Berkeley, Calif.: University of California Press.

SKOV, LISE (1992). 'I modens kalejdoskop' ('In the Kaleidoscope of
Fashion'). Unpublished M.Phil. Thesis, Department of Cultural Sociology,
Copenhagen University.

WEBER, MAX (1930). *The Protestant Ethic and the Spirit of Capitalism.* London: Harper Collins Academic.

WILLIS, PAUL (1977). *Learning to Labour.* Aldershot: Gower.

WILSON, ELIZABETH (1988). *Hallucinations: Life in the Postmodern City.* London: Hutchinson Radius.

—— (1990). 'All the Rage', in Jane Gaines and Charlotte Herzog (eds.), *Fabrications: Costume and the Female Body.* London: Routledge.

## Empirical Data

| | |
|---|---|
| *Advertising* | Since the same advertisement is frequently placed in a number of different magazines and newspapers, we have not listed sources here. However, when we quote or refer to advertisements in the text, we have as far as possible referenced them in notes. |
| *Brochures* | For Marui, Mitsukoshi, and Takashimaya department stores. |
| *Magazines* | We have used material from features published in the following women's magazines: *éf, Elle Japon, Frau, Marie Claire Japon, McSister, Non-no, Peach,* and *Vivi.* |
| *Newspapers* | *Asahi Shimbun, Nihon Keizai Shimbun,* and *Yomiuri Shimbun.* |

# 6

# Christmas against Materialism in Trinidad

*Daniel Miller*

*The Critique of Christmas*

As noted in other chapters of this book the background to any analysis of Christmas is formed by a general, conventional, and oft repeated critique of Christmas as having become little more than an expression of crass materialism. In its colloquial version this states that Christmas was a good traditional family and religious festival which has been ruined by commercialization. There is assumed to be some larger force in capitalism or commerce which is forcing us to spend several weeks elbowing people in the ribs in crowded shopping centres and tormenting ourselves with instant regret as we decide that a particular relative will probably hate the gift we have finally purchased. Commerce is assisted by the fear that we would otherwise be seen as some latter-day Ebenezer Scrooge. So a welcome imperative to give gifts has been exploited by commerce and reified into an orgy of shopping and an excuse and cover for a combination of greed and hedonism. The whole phenomenon is supportive of the worst elements of what is colloquially covered by the term 'being materialistic'. The contribution of the academic critique to this analysis was noted in the introduction to this volume.

Turning to Trinidad we find this critique fully manifested in the local media. The newspapers of the season are full of articles which bemoan the inability of Christmas to be like the 'old days'. They look back to the days of carolling, noting that any carollers today would probably be torn apart by guard dogs. There is a general agreement amongst written accounts that Trinidadian Christmas has lost its authentic roots through commercialization. Indeed some of the media coverage of the 1988 Christmas was celebratory of the fact that recession was bringing to an end the Christmas that had developed in the boom time. The *Mirror* of 13 December begins, 'Do you remember the time when you couldn't get that Christmas feeling unless your home was well stocked with Europe's best whisky, cognac, brandy and wines, not forgetting the apples and grapes that lent some colour to the joyous occasion.' The Christmas Day supplement for the *Sunday Guardian* included an article called 'Return to the Real Old Time Christmas' contrasting the boom time when 'It was a straight case of who could outdo who . . . who could have the bigger staff party; who could buy the more expensive gifts'. This is compared to the new post-boom Christmas, which is described in a litany of house preparation activities such as 'the stripping of the entire house . . . scrubbing floors: hanging new curtains and putting on either new, washed or dyed cushion covers'.

Of course, the abundant adverts in the same papers contribute considerably to the sense of a crescendo of buying. The group who are allowed to be explicitly materialistic are the children who feature in the special 'letters to Santa' sections of the daily papers which include literally hundreds of requests mostly to the point, as in:

Dear Santa Claus,
I would like you to bring me a motorbike complete with hat and shades this Christmas. Thanking you in advance. TG Chaguanas

Though some elaboration can occur as in:

Dear Santa,
I hope you are holding up fine with your reindeer. I am ten years old, I would like a computer game called pac-man (small) and a game called Clue. Would you send a special gift to my father, grandma, grandpa and aunty? I have been very good during the year. Please Santa, I deserve those gifts. My parents are not working. Merry Christmas and have the brightest new year ever. SK

In addition to this nostalgia for a pre-materialistic Christmas there is, in Trinidad, an additional and equally powerful critique of Christmas as an unwarranted import which smothers the desire for promoting local culture and thereby a symbol of inauthenticity. This reliance on imports dominated the press in the 1990–1 season. The *Trinidad and Tobago Review* article for November 1990 (p. 23) 'Decking the Town with Bouts of Folly' pilloried children who, while sweating from the sun, peer in at snowmen and holly. It bemoaned the welcome given to the reimportation of apples and grapes banned for three years to save foreign exchange. Accusing the population of failing to make the transition to a 'culturally independent Christmas' it goes still further to argue 'The foreign exchange leakage by way of importing a snow-scape constitutes only the outward and visible expenses. The price-tag for loss of cultural independence is infinitely more expensive'. Similarly an article entitled 'Deck the Malls' (*Sunday Guardian* magazine, 16 December 1990) notes 'What a paradox! To find a bit of Yuletide festivity one must visit bastions of capitalism—the mecca of modern day shopping—the malls . . . They have now become little centres of Yuletide charm . . . what with its myriad decorations, festive piped music, weekend activities such as choral singing and parang, and of course, we still buy, buy, buy.'

They are not exaggerating. Many retailers noted that December sales for certain products such as curtains, exceed other months by up to a factor of 8 and make jokes about how they could be closed for the rest of the year with little loss of profits.

## Christmas Values

To reassess these critiques, Trinidadian Christmas may be considered in terms of what has also become a conventional analysis in Caribbean studies following Abrahams's importation of Geertz. Christmas is viewed by Abrahams as 'a stylized rendering of some of the central expressive and moral concerns of the group' (1983: 98–9). More specifically Abrahams relates Christmas values to what Wilson (1973: 215–36) termed 'respectability'. These values assert family continuity, the centrality of the home, order, and tradition. A contrast is then made with carnival, which is the time of the 'rudeness', that is of licentious and disordering activities. The implication of this analysis is that some Caribbean islands incorporate two opposed sets of normative values whose ideals are expressed with particular clarity in the form of festivals. I concur. Christmas is the objectification of an ideal state which is polarized against the values expressed by carnival, and each can be studied as the systematic inversion of the other; while Old Year's Night,[1] i.e. New Year's Eve, which is simultaneously the most important church service and the most important party of the year, becomes the precise point of inversion. This is of course only true through synchronic analysis. Historically almost everything now expressed through carnival was once the burden of Christmas, but I will not be discussing carnival here and so will move methodologically backwards in time from structuralism to a variety of functionalism which I believe is appropriate.

Although carnival has pride of place when Trinidadians are presenting themselves to the outside world, internally it is clear that

Christmas is viewed with a comparable degree of affection. Its importance is demonstrated in the sheer weight of labour that goes into it. Furthermore, while many Trinidadians talk of carnival as the time 'all a we is one', in practice many eschew it as immoral and it is often divisive. By contrast, it is Christmas that acts most clearly to unify virtually the entire gamut of this heterogeneous society, since most Hindus and Muslims celebrate Christmas with an intensity which is undifferentiated from that of Christians, though Hindus increasingly justify their participation by treating it as a continuity with the Hindu festival of Divali.

It is Divali which signals the beginning of the season of festivals in the Trinidadian calendar, while Christmas, in turn, marks the beginning of preparations for carnival, after which Lent closes off the festive season. These festivals are not merely special occasions, which intrude upon ordinary life. In Trinidad, Christmas and carnival, together with their associated preparations, dominate a period of several months, and the saving up of resources for Christmas, in particular, may begin almost as soon as the last festive season has finished. Christmas and carnival occupy a central place in the lives of many Trinidadians, such that the rest of the year could almost be viewed as the necessary rest, or breathing space, before the country gears itself up for the next festive season.

## Decorating the House

The period prior to Christmas is marked by three closely related activities: shopping, cooking, and cleaning the house. House interiors in Trinidad are almost invariably immaculate throughout the year. Despite this, in the fortnight before Christmas, when walking along the street, one invariably finds piles of furniture outside the house, for example, in the front porch, as the interior is swept, dusted, and 'cobwebbed'. Not every household repaints every year, but if the householders are intending to repaint the house at all that year, then this is the period in which they will do it. Ideally the entire inside and outside is repainted, more usually the rooms with most wear and tear such as the kitchen and porch area. Householders stand proud and conspicuous with paintbrush in hand, if visitors arrive during the period. Paint retailers note minor increases in their sales marking the festivals of Eid, Divali, and the season for new houses, but thanks to Christmas, December sales amount to two to three times those of other months.

A similar situation exists with regard to furniture. For most of the year the car upholsterers (which was incidentally the dominant industry in the town of Chaguanas where I conducted fieldwork) work only on vehicles, but in some cases they completely cease this work from the start of November in order to deal with domestic reupholstering. One upholsterer complained that households would only decide to make this expenditure at the last moment, and flood them with requests which they would insist should be completed by Christmas Eve.

Although Trinidadians are aware of the stress on gift-giving as the key form of Christmas expenditure in other countries such as the United States, both wholesalers and retailers in gift items confirmed that the giving of gifts is a small element of expenditure as compared to spending on new items for one's own home. Toys purchased for children are an exception here. For the gift shops, it is glassware, artificial flowers, and items used for furnishing and interior decoration which are the main focus of December sales. Gifts are given to children, between close relatives, and are exchanged by older school-children and close friends, but these are generally small items. Gifts are not only conceived of as objects purchased for others; but also encompass the often rather more expensive items which many people purchase for themselves. Christmas may be the occasion for finally purchasing that dress or those trainers which had been coveted for some time, and this is thought of as buying a Christmas present for oneself. It is the house, however, rather than the person which is the main recipient of Christmas shopping. The major expenditures, often planned for a considerable period, and aided by hire purchase schemes, are on items such as upholstered couch sets or dining suites. Ideally, the housewife puts money aside week after week during the rest of the year, in order to save for the special expenditures of Christmas, or alternatively uses the 'sou sou' (a rotating credit scheme) for the purpose of Christmas saving.

The preparations for Christmas become a focal point of discussion as well as activity. A typical seasonal radio phone-in consisted of the interviewer telephoning housewives to discuss with them the measures they were taking for that year's Christmas and any special tips about painting and cooking that might be passed on to the listeners. Each housewife would report upon which rooms were being repainted and which Christmas foods were being prepared for that year. In one of his numerous pieces on Christmas, dialect poet Paul Keens-Douglas (1975: 53–64), takes the perspective of an old-time domestic:

Lord Miss Julie, dis Christmas go' kill me,
Ah don't know why dem people feel
Dey must put up new curtain an' cushion cover
Every Lord living Chrismus . . .
De woman cleanin' house since November
Like she married to Fadder Chrismus.

One element in the decoration of the house interior is items, such as holly, Santa Claus, artificial Christmas trees, and paper festoons in white, scarlet, and green which belong to an international range of Christmas symbols. Christmas cards are displayed in more affluent areas. The calls in the newspapers for localization of images as in the headline 'Pawpaw, Cashew and Melon rinds for Christmas fruit cake' are entirely ignored as stupidness.

Such Christmas decorations are, however, in the main much less important (indeed in most cases tokenistic) compared to the work done on the ordinary furnishings of the house, which will not be put away after Christmas, including the replacement of worn items or unpacking of new ones. The focus is upon the presentability of all aspects of the home itself, whether towels have worn thin, the flooring is adequate, some paint has been knocked away, and so forth. The work is dominated by the female members of the household, but this is a time of year when men are also expected to take their domestic responsibilities seriously, and many men who at other times are free to escape domestic chores and slip away to drink with their friends (Andy Capp is a long-running cartoon in the Trinidadian press) are at this time of year strongly reminded of their domestic duties, particularly with regard to house painting and chair revarnishing.

For several weeks, most of the household members are feverishly engaged in experiencing the physicality of their home in a manner which changes their relationship to it, bringing back into focus the minutiae of furnishing which otherwise so readily become the taken-for-granted background to domestic life.

The climax to these domestic preparations is Christmas Eve. It is then that the presentation of the house interior becomes most clearly ritualized, in the sense of being framed off as an ordered sequence of actions. The normative ideal is that the family stay up late into the night completing their house cleaning and decoration, as well as their baking. There were many stories of Christmases where couples had stayed up the whole night, often inviting neighbours in to 'lime' with lively accompanying music. In some neighbourhoods in particular, the beating of bottles with spoons to the sound of the newly released calypsos accompanies the tidying and decorating. This is the time when any new items, such as towels or a new stereo system, should be unpacked and brought out for use. The established closing ritual to these activities is the hanging out of the curtains. Of all the elements of home decoration, it is curtains which are most closely associated with Christmas, as confirmed by retailers. The oil-boom may have transformed a tradition of changing curtains to one of buying new ones where possible; the less affluent replace them with a set from storage or at least wash and rehang them. Given the number of households who managed to be in the middle of hanging curtains as I visited their homes on Christmas Eve, the activity is clearly extended in time for as long as possible. Once the new curtains are up, this is commonly felt to be both the climax and the end of the task of preparing one's home.

### Christmas Visiting

After the house, the next element[2] is a tremendous time spent on home food and drink preparations such as puncha crem, sorrel, ginger beer, black cake, and ham,[3] and specially imported goods intimately associated with Christmas such as whisky, and apples and grapes.

Both the preparations of food or drink and the cleaning out of the house are intended to serve two demands. In the first instance they provide the setting for the meal of Christmas Day, which is increasingly viewed as an intensely private celebration for the immediate family. This meal takes the best of the prepared edibles, including often three kinds of meat and the expensive imports and utilizes the home at its most pristine. The family is the clear focal point of Christmas Day activities, as is clear also from the typical newspaper interviews with celebrities as to what they do on Christmas Day. This extended luncheon is intended as a quiet interlude between the feverish preparations and the commencement of intensive house visiting. In a country where loudspeakers in cars, houses, and shops provide a continual backdrop to daily life, Christmas morning is probably the only quiet time of the year.

Boxing Day represents the commencement of a period when people may be expected to drop in without invitation or formal arrangement. Such visiting is most intensive up to Old Year's Night, but in practice 'Christmas' visiting continues for three weeks and more. Such visiting varies from the perfunctory, by neighbours who feel they are merely following an established obligation, to the use of Christmas for family and friends to re-establish connections which had been in danger of becoming lost. In all cases the visitor is expected to partake in the special foods which have been prepared and, at the very least, have a piece of cake and an accompanying drink. The food, and more particularly the drink, which accumulates through these successive visits help contribute to a general expansive, festive, and immensely hospitable conviviality for this season. This is in contrast to the rest of the year when at least for the new residential areas house-to-house visiting by neighbours is for many households quite exceptional.

Christmas is recognized at work itself by pre-Christmas parties, which expanded greatly during the oil-boom. This probably followed global normative patterns established by multinational companies, though Christmas also vied with 'crop-over' time for traditional festivities in the local sugar plantations. Similar parties may also be held, at schools, government institutions, residential areas, and churches.

Men used to have a more formal role within Christmas as peer groups that went carousing, making music, and drinking their way from house to house on Christmas Eve, but in the new quiet, respectable Christmas this practice has declined, while women are more inclined to go visiting and not merely be hosts as in the past. Indeed this causes problems for the older male ethos as made clear in a play by Keens-Douglas (1979: 45–54) called 'Ah Pan for Christmas'. The play argues the non-viability of the alternative morality exemplified in the hard masculine steelbandsman. It begins with the lines: 'Fargo was in ah bad mood. It was Christmas Eve, an' he hated Christmas Eve. Because dat was de one time ah year he used to feel like nobody eh like he. Because Fargo didn't have no family to like he.' The play continues with a mysterious figure-cum-spirit telling Fargo to find some family where he could visit, and ends with him being welcomed into the home of a distant aunt, in what becomes a Trinidadian *Christmas Carol*. As in many other countries, the religious side of Christmas is muted, with Old Year's Night becoming a more important church service than Christmas. There is, however, a general feeling that the values which are being expressed through Christmas celebration are congenial with the teachings of the Church, and the Church is much involved in the season of preparations. There are some associated activities such as blessing the crèche or singing carols. On my surveys Hindus and Muslims may actually outspend Christians at Christmas.

Why should it be the home rather than the person which is the recipient of most of the shopping associated with Christmas? The term 'domestic' is rarely used in Trinidad, but there is considerable employment of the dichotomy between 'inside' and 'outside'. For example, an 'outside' woman is a synonym for a mistress (locally termed a deputy), as opposed to a legal or common-law wife. The focus of the 'inside' world is the home and it is a term which has much in common with the concept of domesticity in so far as it includes social and aesthetic as well as spatial considerations.

The aesthetics of the living room may provide a clue as to the values being 'enshrined'. In summary, these include an emphasis on covering over and enclosing forms, deep upholstery and pile carpets, and a cramming in of ornaments and artificial flowers, together with many religious and secular homilies asserting domestic virtues and pictures of family activities such as weddings. The Christmas emphasis on the restoration of such decorations and furnishings as well as adding to their stock, provides, by Christmas Eve, the immaculate setting for what is ideally the key annual ritual of family reaffirmation as a moral and expressive order.

In the first instance this ritual is one of consolidation, culminating in the Christmas meal, which is seen as exclusive to the family proper, who receive the gift of the perfectly tidy and clean house and the choicest foods, enclosed by the new, or newly cleaned curtains. The family strives towards a sense of quiet solidity, often falling asleep after a heavy Christmas meal. By Boxing Day (or late afternoon on Christmas Day), however, there is a marked change in orientation and it is as though the home and family, once secured, becomes the focal point of a process of progressive incorporation, through which the domestic becomes not merely an enclosed space but a kind of centripetal force striving to incorporate as much of the outside world as possible into itself.

This process is first evident in the pattern of post-Christmas visiting. Commonly the wider family visit first, followed by neighbours and friends, with groups such as work colleagues coming towards the end of the visiting season. This contrasts with the rest of the year, during which most people make great efforts to avoid too much association between the world of work and work colleagues and the 'inside' world of the home. But as we shall see, for Christmas the whole nation pays homage to the centrality of the home and family within the sense of being Trinidadian. This centripetal effect is by no means limited simply to the hospitality provided by the home. It is also extended to other aspects of identity formation including temporality and ethnicity. One of the most commonly expressed sentiments about Christmas is that ideally it should be as it has always been. Indeed Christmas becomes the focal point for a sentimental and nostalgic view of the past centred upon the celebration of Christmas itself.

In the case of carnival, although there is a standard structure, everyone is waiting to see how this year's carnival will be special, will be an event, based around the new styles, costumes, music, and so forth which surround it. For Christmas, by contrast, there is a strong sense of the normative. Ideally Christmas should be unchanging and there is disappointment when it does not live up to or conform to those expectations. These nostalgic newspaper articles already referred to form a genre. Typically a journalist from a rural or low-income background will tell how his family made out when he or she was a child, emphasizing all the work which was done by hand and the 'warm' atmosphere. For example, Angela Pidduck recalls (*Express*, 19 Dec. 1990) how 'My grandmother pulled out the old hand sewing-machine, she cut the curtains and morris chair cushion covers, we the children (boys and girls) took turns turning the handle . . . But there was warmth, sharing and love, not only amongst ourselves at 94 Picton Street, but in the neighbourhood. We shared pastelles and ponche de creme after midnight mass at home . . .'. In most such articles the family is usually represented in terms of longevity and descent, the grandparents juxtaposed with the children, a sense of continuity with tradition being handed down through the generations. This creates quite a problem for the many anthropological studies of the West Indian family which ignore a powerful descent-based component (Besson and Momsen 1987).

The concept of an unchanging Christmas is complemented by the use of key symbolic tokens, such as ham, apples, and grapes. In talking about the past, a shopkeeper's daughter claims that the traditional start of the Christmas season was marked by her father, who would boil up a ham in a pitch oil (kerosene) tin. Everybody in the area, even those on a very low income, would feel it essential to buy at least a token amount of ham, such as an ounce. The involvement of these items is taken as making for a specifically 'Trinidadian' Christmas.

*Christmas Ethnicity*

This centripetal aesthetic both draws people to the domestic and compresses historical time into the timeless. It also tackles what is generally regarded as the most divisive of all social dimensions in Trinidad, that is ethnicity. Trinidadian Christmas has an ethnicity all to itself, based upon the concept of 'Spanish'. A number of the special foods which are only made around the Christmas season, including pastelle and arepas are associated specifically with the Spanish traditions of Trinidad. As such, they are related to another key symbol of Christmas, which is the Parang music. This consists of small groups of musicians with instruments such as the cuatro and the one-stringed box bass, who together with singers perform traditional Christmas songs in Spanish. Traditionally these were men (and some women) travelling from house to house on Christmas evening, and the term Parang is said to derive from the Spanish *parranda*, a term for carousal groups (Taylor 1977). In 1988 Parang had become more closely associated with the competitive playing of more established groups, culminating in a grand competition. The singers often cannot understand the content of their songs, and Parang is not played at any other time of the year, but for this period it briefly dominates the radio, and is evocative, especially of some past period when it is assumed it was itself more common.

If one asks formally who are the Spanish in Trinidad, then there are a number of possible answers (Winer and Aguilar 1991), depending upon whether one lays stress upon the original colonists who ruled the country, prior to transference of sovereignty to the British, but who were never a significant demographic presence, or the Venezuelan élite mentioned by Braithwaite (1975: 74–5), or most importantly the migrating peons, also from Venezuela, who formed quite homogeneous villages of the kind depicted by Naipaul in *The Suffrage of Elvira* (1958). All of these definitions, however, would fail to evoke the actual meaning of the term 'Spanish' as used colloquially in contemporary Trinidad. First, the term 'Spanish' in its reference to the original colonists also incorporates the Carib and Arawak pre-colonial populations. Although when precision is required an individual, particularly from élite groups, may lay claims to a partial Amerindian ancestry, for most Trinidadians, it is the term 'Spanish' which is employed simply to signify an element of Amerindian blood as part of a generic sense of roots that go beyond slavery and indentured labour. Similarly, the term 'Spanish' has become, in rural areas, synonymous with the concept 'mixed'. Thus a person whose actual ancestry includes a mixture of East Indian, Chinese, French, and African might have been transmuted through the category 'mixed' into a sense of being 'kind of' Spanish. The importance of the term lies precisely in its vague aura of an alternative ancestry which is specifically not pure African, East Indian, or White. Within Spanish, then, a sense of being mixed is suffused with the connotation of being of the original or ancient inhabitation.

It is at Christmas time, that many Trinidadians manage to locate amongst their ancestry at least an element of Spanish. This provides them with a sense that they have a kind of natural affiliation with the associated music and food, but also has deeper consequences. To have an ethnicity that evokes a sense of Trinidad beyond the images of rupture such as slavery and indentured labour is to evoke a generic objectification of the land itself. This is also suggested by a figure in the rituals performed by Hindu Trinidadians. The propitiation of a spirit termed the Dih seems to have arisen as a link between the present occupants of a house or land and its original owner (see Klass 1961: 176–8; Vertovec 1992: 113, 215). The image of the Dih is also found especially at lower 'caste' Madrassi style temples, e.g. at Kalimai temples, though the worship has a much wider following in the home. A curious feature of Dih worship is that the figure represented appears to have Spanish looks and is seen as representing the ancestral lands of Trinidad.[4] When one worships the Dih one worships the property upon which one's house is based. The worship is of a syncretic variety involving typically ex-African aspects such as the use of rum and cigarettes. The main distinction made is whether one sacrifices a fowl to the Dih. For many Hindus who otherwise have nothing to do with animal sacrifice this is the one point at which such sacrifice is carried out. The Dih then represents the integration of Trinidadian land, as existing prior to the indentureship, within the wider Hindu cosmology, and indicates a strategy which was probably vital to the significance which property has come to have to this community. It is noteworthy that many East Indians who would refuse any suggestion of African elements in their ancestry seem quite comfortable with the idea that they are in part of Spanish descent.

Through these various associations the concept of Spanish ethnicity seems to evoke a generalized sense of the traditions of the land, and is probably the one strategy that enables Trinidadians, who are usually characterized (not least by themselves) as comparatively 'rootless', to conceive of their current practices as having a derivation from a general and ideally unchanging line of descent. It is noticeable that this evolution of 'Spanish' has received neither official sanction nor encouragement, but appears to represent the spontaneous dynamics of popular culture.

Christmas is then a centripetal process which starts from the family and reaches out to create a powerful sense of being Trinidadian, an image resonant of a consensual society and culture. The ideal may not last for long, and intra-family quarrels, fuelled by the availability of alcohol, may erupt even before Christmas lunch is finished (an event which may cause acute embarrassment), but is also I feel much less common here than in Christmas in other regions. Other counter-tendencies which would undermine the consistency of this ideal will be noted in my conclusion, but this should not detract from the clarity with which what Abrahams calls a stylized expression of a moral society is proclaimed by this festival.

Christmas in Trinidad as represented here lies uneasily against current trends in anthropological theory. Just as anthropologists are busy discovering that what had been described as bounded societies and cultures are actually creolized and pluralist, in Trinidad there is an evident example of a creolized and comparatively rootless region, with considerable evidence for everything from the international remittance-based family to evident dependency. Trinidad should therefore provide evidence to support this critique of the culture concept as an academic forgery. The problem is that anthropologists in their self-critique of previous fashions and methodologies must also allow for the possibility that a given group of people may well be engaged in the opposite endeavour especially when, as here, they have emerged from a history replete with fragmentation and denigration. The evidence suggests that for at least a chunk of the year tremendous effort is invested in creating a self-image of bounded society, nostalgic common culture, and sentimental roots, through what is probably the single most successful functionalist strategy within the Trinidadian repertoire. Indeed, as in Paul Keens-Douglas's play, it is the anti-establishment stylist, the dude whose movements and music are otherwise appropriated with favour internationally, who for this period is relegated to the role of Scrooge. We cannot, however, ignore Trinidad just at the moment when it does not provide the images which are currently 'required' by global, in this case disciplinary, imperatives.

*Christmas and Commerce*

Trinidad, like many other countries today, approaches Christmas by an extraordinarily intensive bout of shopping. In the malls and main streets of Chaguanas stalls are set up in front of shops and more stalls in front of those stalls, making the town virtually impassable to traffic, a phenomenon reflected in the December sales figures and the impact on ordinary people's annual budgets. It was noted in the introduction to this chapter that Trinidad has its own local and vocal version of a global discourse which critiques Christmas celebration as overly materialistic, and merely the vehicle for projects which stem from the imperatives of commerce or even capitalism. That a religious festival should become subsumed in a flurry of commerce seems a key symbol of this threat to traditional life.

To consider this further, several of the previous observations about the actual behaviour of Trinidadians at Christmas may be analysed. When asked during surveys of household interiors about when an item was purchased, people would note that the dining suite and electric fan were bought for this Christmas while the couch set and stereo were brought for the previous Christmas, and so it would go on until there was virtually no major item which was not bought for Christmas. This does not necessarily mean that everything was paid for at Christmas, but many people will use hire purchase and other schemes to ensure that the new dining suite, for example, actually arrives in time for Christmas. Indeed many people use sales at other times of the year, or especially exploit what has become a national institution—travelling on charter flights for intensive shopping to Caracas and Margarita in Venezuela, where prices are substantially cheaper. But they then store many of the main purchases unused in a cupboard until Christmas. The new items are then brought out to be used for the first time at Christmas Eve. This suggests that as far as possible Trinidadians desire to associate their purchasing of goods with Christmas; it seems as though if they could only shop this one time of the year for major items they would much prefer it.

In earlier periods the expenditure at Christmas was directed almost entirely to items consumed as part of the festival itself, that is eating and drinking, although special glasses, tablecloths, and other furnishings were a traditional feature. In contemporary Christmas the expenditure is directed largely to the refurbishment of the home. Some of this, it is true, is prompted by the festival itself, such as changing curtains and cushion covers that otherwise need not have been replaced, but this additional expenditure was essentially a feature of the oil-boom. What emerges from the details of actual expenditure in 1988 and 1990 is something else. The house repainting was both symbolic of Christmas and also discussed pragmatically in terms of what areas of the house required repainting that year; similarly with items such as bedsheets, towels, upholstery, and utensils—that is, they were all items that would be required at some stage in the year. To a lesser extent this point may be extended even to what might be thought of as short-term goods. The purchase of whisky was singled out by several informants as something which they hoped would represent their yearly investment in this element of their hospitality costs, though recognizing that with enough visitors it might only last the season. Most items are replaced because this is required, either through wear and tear or shifts in fashion. In other words the major effect of Christmas on expenditure directed to the house may not be an overall increase in expenditure, but more a seasonal concentration in certain forms of expenditure.

But why this desire to relate shopping to Christmas? At one time it was common for children in Trinidad to bring the new toys they had received for Christmas to the church for a special blessing. Indeed this practice sometimes extended to the purchase of cars and other items. Although such formal blessing has declined, the impulse behind it may account for the more general tendencies observable in the commercialization of Christmas. Even without church blessing it is clear the stage of purchase is then followed through by the ritual of incorporation. The religious element of Christmas Eve, culminating in Midnight Mass, has been gradually replaced by the secular ritual of bringing out the new goods and placing them in the home. The appropriate nature of this replacement is manifested by the centrality of Christian teaching to the values expressed in the home. Over more than a century a systematic network of values has emerged in which the very sense of being religious is directly associated with the purchase of a home and the sanctity of a church wedding. There is a powerful association throughout the Caribbean between simultaneously constructing one's own home, becoming legally married, and dramatically increasing one's religiosity. This is still the case for contemporary Trinidad.

The closing ritual of Christmas Eve, the hanging of the curtains or drapes which signify the boundary between the inside world of domesticity and religion as against the outside world with its implications of transience and sin, is therefore a manifestly clear construction of the home as temple to the project of lineal family identity and descent, a theme echoed in the details of interior decoration, whether marriage photos or symbols of education such as encyclopedias. All are opposed to the values of the street and principles that underlie the very different perspective on kinship and spending explored through carnival.

Through Christmas the home is literally enshrined as the site of these values, which in turn valorizes the expenditure on the home as a dutiful act in accordance with the highest moral authorities. The festival thereby transforms what would be a mundane impersonal process of shopping and installing goods, which might have had little other than utilitarian significance, into an activity that fills each purchase with a set of positive, if complex, associations constructed through the festival of Christmas itself.

The result seems to be less a celebration of materialism than a sacralization of shopping. Various journalistic comments about Decking the Malls have been noted, but the three malls in the town of Chaguanas are in many respects the 'proper' context for this construction of sociality. Whereas in Britain for example, a mall such as Brent Cross in North London is used for little more than the act of shopping itself, Trinidadians with very different traditions of public space seized upon the possibilities of the new malls with alacrity. In Chaguanas the malls are today where you have the best parties and fêtes. Virtually every major political and religious meeting, indeed virtually any major public event takes place within malls, so that the fact that this is almost the only site today for blessing the crèche and for singing Christmas carols may be quite appropriate. Commerce colludes for its own benefit, but to enhance rather than detract from the possibilities of public participation in anything from politics to partying.

But the imperative behind all this concern to incorporate shopping may well lie in concerns over materialism. Materialism here is not the problem of having goods. Trinidadians know too much about recent poverty to have many qualms about the accumulation of wealth. But many conversations do express a more general concern about the antisocial orientation of some 'people today', which concurs with that common theme in all the ancestors of the social sciences about the reification of goods or money leading to a general loss of sociality and a tendency for the qualitative and social to be replaced by the quantitative and abstract. This unease has come to the fore with the effects of the oil-boom of the late 1970s and early 1980s, when for the first time the issue of materialism became a very real one for many Trinidadians. It is no coincidence that the Christmas themes described here crystallize around this time of the oil-boom. Christmas thereby becomes an example of one of the many strategies which are found in modern consumption, through which popular practice attempts to reincorporate into the construction of social bonds activities which threaten to become antisocial (Miller 1987: 178–217). In effect Christmas becomes the first festival of anti-materialism. At this point there is an obvious affinity with Carrier's chapter on the transformation of commodities into gifts, though also to more general concerns about the appropriation of goods in capitalist societies.

This strategy is conducted first at the level of the family and finally at the level of the island itself. The journalists' critique of materialism is matched by their disparaging the reliance on imported images from tropical snowscapes to apples and grapes. Indeed as noted above the government banned the importation of apples and grapes for three years in order to save foreign exchange. But in 1990, when the ban was lifted, Trinidadians mobbed the port to welcome the first container load of apples and grapes as though it was some combination of Dunkirk and the return of foreign hostages. Everyone was fighting to buy the first trays of fruit. A recent television series on the Caribbean also used the image of a greedy seizure of apples as an image of postcolonial dependency. But as a Trinidadian anthropologist remarked to me, many of those in the fray would only a few weeks before have been eating apples with some nonchalance in Miami or New York. This did not, however, lessen the excitement with which they responded to their presence in Trinidad. Indeed so much fruit was imported in subsequent weeks as massively to oversupply the country, and for a short time Trinidad probably became the cheapest country in the world in which to buy apples. For most Trinidadians these fruits are defined anew by their context, they become essential for this process of nostalgia in which all true Trinidadian Christmases include the symbolic tokens of their past celebration, which in turn define the specificity of Trinidadian Christmas. After all, how would the British feel if they were told this year's Christmas pudding was to be without raisins in order to save on foreign exchange? Britain produces no more raisins than does Trinidad. Christmas may be a global festival today but as an immensely popular local song goes, as far as they are concerned 'Trini Christmas is the best'. Tropical snowscapes are utterly authentic, because it is the same process which transforms a history of alienation into the sense of inalienable nationalism through imagined Spanish roots which transforms alienable, here imported goods and images into the inalienable process of social construction. The global here is appropriated as the paradigmatic objectification of the local, just as Christmas itself is appropriated through the actions by which it is consumed.

Finally this relationship to commerce may be viewed in its historical context. All festivals in Trinidad turn out on historical investigation to have undergone extraordinary transformations; none of them bears much relation to what it was even a century ago. Taking the Caribbean literature more generally it is clear that virtually everything which today is associated with carnival was originally expressed through the celebration of Christmas. The title of Dirks's (1987) book on Caribbean Christmas, *The Black Saturnalia*, says it all. For a much later period there is recollection of elements of early twentieth-century Christmas in oral accounts from elderly people in the Chaguanas area today (see the introduction for an elaboration on this relationship between Christmas and carnival). Several such informants noted that at that time it was Christmas rather than carnival which was more likely to be associated with fighting and exceptional heavy drinking. Their accounts differ markedly from the stress on domestic calm which was found in the nostalgic newspaper accounts.

It seems, then, that the strong dichotomy in the relationship between these two festivals was not necessarily so marked a feature in previous times. It is relatively recently that Christmas has sloughed off many of the attributes which would have associated it with a sense of bacchanal and disorder. As noted in the introduction to this volume the Caribbean seems to have constructed a dualism out of the original unificatory Saturnalia over two centuries in parallel with the manner by which Europe accomplished the same feat, according to Lévi-Strauss amongst others, over two millennia. Even today there are constant threats of leakage between the two festivals, with carnival threatening to sink into an objectification of tradition (Stewart 1986), and Christmas being souped up with the arrival of Christmas calypso, where songs like 'I want a piece ah pork for my Christmas' threaten to bring carnival style sexuality back in. This structural relation is then by no means fixed. It takes its particular form today partly because it is used to work out strategies in relation to consumption.

It is then only recently that Christmas has come unambiguously to embody one particular consumption ideal, to increase goods and then consume them as sociality. It is very likely to be the existence and importance of carnival which celebrates those elements of the centrifugal and the style-centred life, which has allowed Christmas, by contrast, to gain its exceptionally clear 'Dickensian' character today. As a result Christmas seems to be highly successful as a strategy in relation to consumption. At one level Trinidad strikes the visitor as a highly materialistic country with considerable dependency upon imported goods. Few people seem to form their identity in close relation to their involvement through work with either the production or the distribution of goods. It is in consumption that most Trinidadians use goods to create themselves as social persons. Despite this, Trinidadians do not seem to share the strong sense of alienation and *ennui* which is associated with this degree of devotion to goods in Western Europe and the United States. Although they do indeed extensively copy and emulate ideas and practices from elsewhere, they rarely conform to the portrait of cynicism and superficiality as depicted by Naipaul in *The Mimic Men* (1967).

The development of these elaborate and complex Christmas rituals may therefore be related to the contradictions of modern materialism as they are faced by contemporary Trinidadians. It is this that accounts for the considerable amounts of energy and financial resources spent upon Christmas today. Christmas works as a kind of alchemy in reverse, in which the 'spirit' of Christmas is used to transmute the transient and anonymous qualities of money and commodities into the domestic symbols of the longevity of family descent and beyond that to a wider sense of Trinidadian specificity and continuity. As such Trinidad seems to bring into clearer focus one of the key reasons behind the growing importance of Christmas in the modern world, and its intense relationship to materialism. It is that Christmas has become in a sense the first ever festival of anti-materialism, an event which becomes deeply involved in the world of goods, but in order to combat what are widely seen as the negative consequences of that involvement.

# Notes

1 Old Year's Night is on 31 Dec., i.e. New Year's Eve.
2 The details of these aspects of Christmas are not included here for reasons of brevity, but see Miller (forthcoming).
3 Puncha crem is made with strong rum, eggs, and condensed milk. Sorrel is a drink made from the red blossoms of a member of the hibiscus flower which flowers at this time of year. Black cake is made with chopped dried fruit soaked in alcohol (rum or cherry brandy) and is the equivalent of the steamed Christmas pudding found in other countries.
4 This point and the general significance of the Dih was pointed out to me by Bill Guinea.

# References

ABRAHAMS, R. (1983). *The Man of Words in the West Indies: Performance and the Emergence of Creole Culture.* Baltimore: Johns Hopkins Press.
BESSON, J., and MOMSEN, J. (1987). 'A Paradox in Caribbean Attitudes to Land', in J. Besson and J. Momsen (eds.), *Land and Development in the Caribbean.* London: Macmillan.
BRAITHWAITE, L. (1975). *Social Stratification in Trinidad.* Mona: Institute of Social and Economic Research (1st edn. 1953).
DIRKS, R. (1987). *The Black Saturnalia: Conflict and its Ritual Expression on British West Indian Slave Plantations.* Gainsville, Fla.: University of Florida Press.
KEENS-DOUGLAS, P. (1975). *When Moon Shine.* Port of Spain: College Press.
—— (1979). *Tell Me Again.* Port of Spain: Keensdee Productions Ltd.
KLASS, M. (1961). *East Indians in Trinidad.* New York: Columbia University Press.
MILLER, D. (1987). *Material Culture and Mass Consumption.* Oxford: Basil Blackwell.
—— (forthcoming). *Modernity: An Ethnographic Approach.*
STEWART, J. (1986). 'Patronage and Control in the Trinidad Carnival', in V. Turner and E. Bruner (eds.), *The Anthropology of Experience.* Urbana, Ill.: University of Illinois Press: 289–315.
TAYLOR, S. (1977). *Parang in Trinidad.* Port of Spain: National Cultural Council.
VERTOVEC, S. (1992). *Hindu Trinidad.* London: Macmillan.
WILSON, P. (1973). *Crab Antics: The Social Anthropology of English Speaking Negro Societies of the Caribbean.* New Haven, Conn.: Yale University Press.
WINER, L., and AGUILAR, E. (1991). 'Spanish Influence in the Lexicon of Trinidadian Creole', *Nieuwe West-Indische Gids/New West Indian Guide,* 65: 153–91.

# PART III

*Christmas and the Family*

# 7

# The English Christmas and the Family: Time Out and Alternative Realities

## Adam Kuper

### I

In England, Christmas Day is normally spent at home, with the family: and it is regarded as a celebration of the family and its continuity. The evidence from sample surveys in the past two decades is consistent and unequivocal. Asked in December 1969 with whom they would spend Christmas, 86 per cent of an adult British sample responded that they would spend it with their family. Asked whether it was essentially a religious or a family occasion, 53 per cent said it was a family occasion, 9 per cent that it was religious, and 37 per cent that it was both equally.[1]

Twenty years later, the picture was very similar. In an NOP poll for *The Mail on Sunday* in 1988, 78 per cent of adults said they would spend most of Christmas Day with their immediate family (or partner), and a further 15 per cent said they would spend it with other relatives. Asked what was the most important part of Christmas Day for them, 58 per cent said being with the family, 18 per cent said watching children enjoy themselves, and only 7 per cent said that it was marking Christ's birth.[2]

Over Christmas, the whole nation is constructed as a series of identical family parties. Christmas is probably the only annual occasion when virtually everyone in England is doing the same thing at the same time. Pre-war differences have been ironed out.[3] To take one striking example, long-established class and regional variations in the celebration of a Christmas dinner have greatly diminished in the past generation. Christmas dinner was traditionally eaten by some families on Christmas Eve, by others in the late afternoon of Christmas Day, in the place of high tea. The main course could be roast beef, venison, chicken, goose, or turkey. Today practically every family sits down to a Christmas dinner in the early afternoon of Christmas Day, and (according to the 1988 National Opinion Poll for *The Mail on Sunday*) as many as 69 per cent eat turkey (cf. Pimlott 1978: 169). At 3.00 p.m. a large part of the population stops eating, or washing up, and watches the queen's Christmas message on television. The queen's Christmas broadcast itself is also a family occasion: viewed by the family, and presented in a familial idiom. There are signs to show that she is celebrating Christmas just like everyone else, with a tree and Christmas decorations, in the midst of her family. (When a documentary film of the royals at home was released in the 1960s, the high point was the family Christmas.)

In her speech, the queen usually evokes the nation as a family, or the Commonwealth as a family of nations. She preaches family virtues: mutual care, love. Shortly before her 1988 broadcast, a devastating earthquake hit Armenia. She recorded a postscript to the pre-recorded broadcast, to remind her audience of the *families* mourning in Armenia. In 1992, the carefully fostered image of the domestic life of the royal family was eroded by a series of marital mishaps, some spiced with scandal. The queen's 1992 Christmas message implicitly acknowledged these troubles but she suggested that Christmas was a time at which family values should be reaffirmed. If England is a nation of families on Christmas Day—and a nation of equal families—then the nation itself is also projected as a family, represented by the Royal Family, which is made to seem a family just like any other.

The queen also usually refers to the birth of Christ. Though Christmas Day is by and large a secular holiday, the Christian reference is crucial to at least a significant minority, and it is fostered by the churches and the BBC, particularly by way of popular carol services.

The English Protestant Churches were initially hostile to the secular celebration of Christmas, but the Church of England, followed by the other churches, made repeated attempts to recapture the public festival for religious purposes. The Nativity play was revived by the Church of England after the First World War. The crib, introduced by Catholics from Germany and USA in the mid-nineteenth century, spread to English Protestants after the Second World War (Pimlott 1978: 151–2). Such icons, together with practices like carol singing and religious broadcasts, sustain a Christian context which over a third of opinion poll respondents consider essential.[4] They all project a child-centred image of the Holy Family.

Some four million people in England attend Christmas church services, about a third up on normal Sunday attendances. Christmas Day, however, is less likely to be marked by church attendance than Christmas Eve, or midnight mass (a modern adoption of the Catholic practice by many Church of England congregations). The decline of Christmas Day services has been marked since the war, and there seems to be a common view that the clergy should be at home, celebrating with their families (ibid. 150).

The association of Christmas with the Christian celebration of Christ's birth presents a problem for non-Christians, and particularly for those reared in other faiths. Anthropologists from Brunel University, working in Southall, a predominantly Sikh and Asian area of London, have found a range of responses, including attempts by civic authorities to associate Christmas with Asian festivals, and they have noted the ways in which Asian children impose elements of Christmas celebration on their families (see Baumann 1992: 102–5; cf. Alibhai 1987).

Nevertheless, the national uniformity is striking. The celebration of Christmas as a national holiday in America is more strongly resisted by non-Christian minorities. American Jews have developed Hannukah into a parallel celebration. This resistance is perhaps one of the reasons for the renewed prominence of Thanksgiving, a national occasion which also brings families together, but which celebrates the integration of immigrants with native Americans, and employs a secular or non-denominational idiom.

Despite the exclusion experienced by many non-Christians, for most English people Christmas is a simultaneous celebration of the Holy Family, the Royal Family, and the domestic families across the nation.

## II

This construction of the English Christmas as a family festival— domestic and national, with religious overtones—is in evident tension with the decline of the family as an institution in modern England, and with the common experience of Christmas as a time of family tension. Those who stress the continuities of the modern English Christmas over the past century and a half are accordingly confronted with an apparent paradox, which requires explanation.

J. A. R. Pimlott's *The Englishman's Christmas: A Social History* (1978) has usefully traced the crystallization of the modern Christmas to the period between the 1840s and the 1870s. The emergence of the modern English Christmas has been related to processes of urbaniz-ation and industrialization in Victorian England, accompanied as these were by evangelical and middle-class concern for the religion and morals of the workers, and for the maintenance of family life. It has also been explained in terms of the adaptation of upper-class customs first by a middle class and then by a working class, increasingly affluent, with more holidays at their disposal, and with access to cheap con-sumer goods (see Pimlott 1978; Golby 1981: 15–26).

Whatever the causes, the fact is that the modern English Christmas emerged quite suddenly. Pimlott posits a sharp break with earlier Christmas practices around 1840. Perhaps his most telling evidence comes from Dickens, the great mythologist of the English Christmas. As he points out, there is a highly instructive contrast between Dickens's representation of Christmas in the *Pickwick Papers* (1837) and the *Christmas Carol* (1843).

Visiting Dingley Dell, Mr Pickwick and his friends paid more atten-tion to a wedding celebrated the day before Christmas than they did to Christmas itself. Christmas Eve was a secular celebration. The Wardle family and their guests joined the servants in the kitchen, where there was fun and games under the mistletoe. Dickens does not note the presence of children. Afterwards, 'they sat down by the huge fire of blazing logs to a substantial supper, and a mighty bowl of wassail . . .'

'This,' said Mr. Pickwick, looking round him, 'this is, indeed, comfort.'
'Our invariable custom,' replied Mr. Wardle. 'Everybody sits down with us on Christmas eve, as you see them now—servants and all; and here we wait, until the clock strikes twelve, to usher Christmas in, and beguile the time with forfeits and old stories.'

On Christmas Day the party dispersed without further celebrations.

In the *Christmas Carol*, the celebrations are on Christmas Day, the centrepiece is the modern Christmas dinner—with turkey—and the themes are family, children, and charity. The setting in the city and the suburbs of London also contrasts sharply with the old-world rural peace of Dingley Dell.

The other elements of modern Christmas were quickly added to the features which already defined the Christmases of Scrooge's rela-tives and dependants. The Christmas tree, a German import popu-larized by Prince Albert, spread rapidly in the 1840s and 1850s, though it was introduced into English churches only after the First World

War (and became a common church decoration only after the Second), and spread into public places only in the 1930s (Pimlott 1978: 97–9, 151, 159). The Christmas card was invented in 1843, its use becoming widespread after the cheap rate for cards and unsealed envelopes was introduced in 1870 (Buday 1954; cf. Pimlott 1978: 162). Carols, which had almost vanished from the English scene, were revived deliberately by evangelicals, the turning-point being the publication in 1871 of *Christmas Carols Old and New* (Pimlott 1978: 108–10, 153–4). Father Christmas, traditionally represented rather like Father Time, was recast in the mould of the American Santa Claus, and became a central figure in the English Christmas in the 1880s, together with stockings and chimneys.[5]

These elements have since remained stable. 'What is remarkable about the celebration of Christmas in the twentieth century,' Pimlott concludes (ibid. 171), 'is not the erosion of old forms but their persistence and reinforcement.' It must, however, appear paradoxical that the celebration of Christmas has continued with unabated enthusiasm through a period during which the English family has undergone prolonged and escalating change—perhaps even crisis—as measured by rates of divorce, marriage, and fertility.[6]

Pimlott—and other authors—have suggested that the changed circumstances of modern England may actually have caused the continuity of ceremonial forms. 'Christmas evokes in a modern, atomised society feelings of security based on close family ties. Though the scale, duration and economics of the celebration develop and evolve, past associations and old images remain of the essence' (ibid. 172). The argument is that Christmas celebrations in recent times express nostalgia for community and security, lost to us but genuinely expressed in the Victorian ceremonies. That there is an element of nostalgia can hardly be doubted. Christmas cards often evoke a rural, snow-bound, carriage-driven traditional Christmas, and the Christmas dinner may be celebrated in a style that evokes images of Victorian plenty and order. The greeting 'Merry Christmas', with its echoes of 'Merrie England', may itself hint at a world we have lost.

It is, however, one thing to concede that there is an element of nostalgia in the English Christmas, it is quite another to conclude that the whole ceremony is essentially an exercise in nostalgia. Stability in rituals is certainly a possible response to changes in social circumstances, but why should changes in the domestic sphere of English life have stimulated the maintenance of an essentially stable Christmas, while other great Victorian family rituals, such as funerals or Sunday church-going, have been eroded or jettisoned?

Pimlott's stress on ceremonial continuities also draws attention away from the changes that have occurred in the ceremonies themselves, though he did note significant shifts in timing and in context. He described the early start made to Christmas celebrations in post-war England, and commented that there had also been a more recent extension forward in time. 'The latter process which has occurred very rapidly in the sixties and seventies . . . is a reversal of an earlier trend which had reduced the Twelve Days of Christmas to comparative unimportance' (ibid. 166). This is just one indication that the ceremony itself may be in flux.

An American scholar, Theodore Caplow, also suggests that the celebration of the family at Christmas compensates for a sense of loss, but his argument is more complex, insisting on the significance of changes in the nature of the celebration as well as the changes in the social reference. His data are drawn from a recent restudy of Middletown, the Midwest community which has been systematically restudied by ethnographers since the pioneering work of the Lynds.

Middletown today is a family-oriented community. This fact is evident in its festival symbolism and also when today's festival activities are compared to those of 1890 or 1924. In 1890 Middletown displayed a great deal of patriotic and civic pride, while the 'family festivals' as we know them today were relatively undeveloped. In 1924 patriotism was still felt, but its public celebration was much diminished . . . The Lynds reported an increasing awareness in both men and women of the necessity for spending time with children and family, but this attachment apparently found little more symbolic expression in 1924 than it had in 1890. The Christmas season especially seems to have been more a time for attending parties and dances than for celebrating family solidarity.

Today, on the contrary, national holidays are less energetically marked in Middletown. 'Replacing city and country as a focus of festive attention in Middletown is the family. Every widely observed festival in Middletown now celebrates the family and the related ideas of home, mother and child, and feminine roles' (Caplow *et al.* 1983: 224; cf. Barnett 1954: 58–66).

To account for this shift to family-centred ceremonies, and for the present emphasis on the family in the celebration of Christmas, Caplow and his colleagues suggest that rituals may fulfil a homeostatic function, counteracting felt weaknesses in the social system.

We suggest, then, that Middletown's festival cycle celebrates family matters because the family is the institution most at risk in the community. It is the institution most dependent on emotions, rather than reason, for its continuance, and in this dependence lies its vulnerability. The ritual of the festival cycle appeals to the emotions, strengthens them by assuring Middletown residents of the rightness, and so ensures the continuity of the family. (Caplow *et al.* 1983: 243)

In a useful mid-century ethnography of the American Christmas, James A. Barnett made a similar argument. He noted that 'The folk celebration is centred in the family and largely controlled by women', who 'somehow symbolise the kinship and humanitarian values traditionally associated with Christmas.' He observed that this dominant position assigned to women belied the relative powerlessness of women in the larger society, and suggested: 'Perhaps they are permitted and encouraged to dominate our most important national festival as symbolic compensation for accepting the disadvantages of their social role' (Barnett 1954: 64–5). Similarly, the practice of charity, benevolence, and family love over the Christmas period was described by Barnett as an act of compensation for the neglect of these moral obligations during the rest of the year (ibid. 77, 139).

Yet the hypothesis that Christmas celebrations compensate for the loss of cherished values is at best a partial explanation for the lively continuance of Christmas as a national holiday. Ethnographers and informants do not confirm that people generally feel a sense of loss at Christmas time, or that they see themselves as yearning, over Christmas, for a better time that they imagine in the past. The experience of Christmas is generally supposed to be a happy one.[7] Informants agree that Christmas is under threat from commercialism, but there does not seem to be a widespread sense that Christmas is old hat, or that it refers to a vanished social order.

The analytical difficulty remains: Christmas is clearly a celebration of the family, and yet Christmas ceremonies have flourished, if anything becoming more family-focused than ever, just at a time when the family itself appears to be less central in the experience of very many people. I dispute the view that this intensification is a ritualized expression of a sense of loss. Alternative explanations are required.

### III

To move forward, it is necessary to recontextualize Christmas ceremonies, and to pay attention to the particular image of the family that
is constructed over Christmas.

As Van Gennep explained (1909), we define a ritual time-phase, or a
ritual place, by erecting boundaries between ritual time and normal life,
ritual places and secular places. Sacred places are decorated, people
dress up. Following Van Gennep, Edmund Leach argued that ceremonies '*create time*, by creating intervals in social life' (1961: 135). During the sacred period, special rules apply and specific values are
celebrated. Van Gennep suggested that secular, individual identity is
transcended, and we experience 'communitas', a sense of belonging to
a spiritual community. Leach pointed out that the rituals practised at
these times may directly affirm social values, which are celebrated with
exaggerated emphasis (as at weddings, parades, examinations, etc.);
alternatively, normal values and forms of behaviour may be flouted and
reversed, as at masquerades or carnivals. He drew attention in particular
to the way in which symbolic inversions may demarcate a sacred time
and place, and I shall suggest that this helps us to understand the construction of the Christmas period. But the argument can be taken
further. A ritual may set up its own definition of 'normal' values, which
it will then transform. Other rituals turn other worlds upside down (and
rituals may also be read as transformations of other rituals).

Leach also pointed out that rituals create their own annual cycle.
'Notice for example how the 40 days between Carnival (Shrove Tues-
day) and Easter is balanced off by the 40 days between Easter and
Ascension, or how New Year's Eve falls precisely midway between
Christmas Eve and Twelfth Night' (1961: 135). Other social scientists
have also commented upon the place of Christmas in a ritual calendar.
Caplow *et al.*, and also Barnett, discuss the place of Christmas in the
annual cycle of American holidays, drawing particular attention to the
clutch of year-end festivals, which runs through Halloween, Thanksgiving, and Christmas to New Year's Day. Barnett noted that 'Christmas exerts influence on these celebrations and is affected by them to
some degree. Its articulation with these other occasions sustains a high
level of excitement and contributes to the social effectiveness of the
entire period' (Barnett 1954: 130–1).

Caplow *et al.* indicate some of the structural transformations which
appear within this set of festivals. Halloween inverts central features

of the values celebrated at Thanksgiving and Christmas, turning children out to seek gifts from strangers, and threatening all with the activities of witches. Thanksgiving and Christmas celebrate the family, and during the Christmas period children are at the centre of the family, receiving unsolicited gifts from close relatives or from Santa, who is in every way the opposite of a witch. Christmas itself is bracketed by office parties and by New Year's Day, adult events—not suitable for children—marked by drinking and flirtation (Caplow *et al.* 1983: 229–37; Barnett 1954: 135).

In the absence of Thanksgiving, and with Halloween still a novelty not widely disseminated, the ethnographer of England would wish to contextualize the celebration of Christmas somewhat differently in the festival cycle. Even an abbreviated and stereotyped description of the festive period may, however, bring out some of the ways in which a sacred time is being marked off and imbued with meaning (cf. Pimlott 1978: 164–6).

In England, the build-up to Christmas is slow and cumulative. The first signs are the decoration of public spaces in early November. Elaborate light displays are illuminated at dusk. As a frenzy of shopping is stimulated, shop windows are given over to cribs or to models of Father Christmas and reindeer. Charities are active. At work-places, there is an easing of routine, and decorations are introduced which make the classroom, office, or factory floor seem less a place of work, more the site of a party.

Then come the office parties, in the middle of December. Cartoonists feature secretaries perched on their bosses' knees, skirts up, glasses overflowing. In fact most office parties seem to be decorous enough, though some companies throw famously wild dinners. Robert Bocock (1974: 116) suggests that, in England, these parties only really go if manual labourers are not mixed in with management, but in the army officers and sergeants serve the men on Christmas Day. The parties tend to break down barriers of hierarchy and sexual constraint between colleagues, and are associated with tolerated drunkenness.

In mid-December also, the carol singers do the rounds of a neighbourhood, and in the week before Christmas there are low-key parties for neighbours and friends, in which children are included. Now is the time for the decoration of the home. Christmas cards are displayed. A Christmas tree is installed in the sitting room, often in a window. Towards Christmas—in some families only on Christmas Eve—the tree is dressed and its base strewn with wrapped presents.

Christmas Eve itself is a quiet time, and the traditional moment of reverence at midnight may now be marked by attendance at a midnight mass. Presents are opened by the family in the morning. Privileged visitors may drop in. In early afternoon the family sits down to the Christmas dinner, which will include turkey, mince pies, and Christmas pudding. Then after the queen's speech they play games in which everyone can participate, and perhaps go for a walk, returning for a Christmas tea.

The restriction of national life to the home is especially marked on Christmas Day itself, but in the post-war period this feature of the holiday has been prolonged over the following week. Until recently, Boxing Day (26 December) marked a partial return to secular activity. Now the Christmas paralysis persists until New Year's Day, though mitigated by visits to relatives, outings to the Pantomime, and other children's treats.

New Year's Eve is a reversal of Christmas Eve. The New Year is launched with a party that contrasts sharply with the Christmas dinner. At Christmas, the English get together in family groups and overeat. At New Year they have a party with friends, and drink too much. Christmas begins on Christmas Eve, a quiet time, and the magic moment is midnight (when even the animals kneel down to pray and many English people nowadays attend a midnight mass). Midnight on New Year's Eve is marked by shouting, hooting, whistling, adults kissing adults, and the drinking of toasts. The benevolent, fat Father Christmas, with his sackful of presents, is matched by the sinister and scrawny Father Time, with his scythe; and the Christ child is contrasted with the very human infant in nappies who represents the secular New Year.

National leaders respect this ritual hiatus. At the end of the parliamentary term, in mid-December, the politicians sign off. On Christmas Day the queen speaks to the nation about issues on which it is united. Politicians do not make Christmas statements, and unless an election is imminent, as it was at the end of 1991, they remain silent until the New Year, when they make their competitive plugs for support on issues which divide the nation. New Year resolutions, too, have to do with everyday life. People resolve to give up smoking, to lose weight, to seek promotion. With the New Year they re-enter a secular, competitive, workaday, class-ridden, sexual world; though the decorations in the home may be removed only after Epiphany, which closes the religious cycle.

IV

Viewing Christmas in its extension brings into relief its particular rhythm, and emphasizes the specific features which distinguish it. Christmas has offered time out for alternative values. These may be summed up as injunctions. One rule is that Christmas Day in England is spent with the family, and at home. A second is that nobody should work. There is virtually no public transport, and the few people who man the emergency services are treated as heroes. A third is that peace should reign. During the First World War local truces broke out spontaneously in the trenches, causing problems for the High Command. At home, quarrels should be avoided, and are more upsetting than ever when they do erupt. A fourth rule is that this is a time for generosity, particularly to children and the elderly, the lonely and disadvantaged.

Christmas should therefore be conceived not so much as a straight-forward celebration of 'the family', but rather as the creation of a sacred time that defines and reverses certain everyday rules. These rules have to do above all with work, hierarchy, sex, and more generally with the political economy of everyday life.

The run-up to Christmas transforms relationships at the work-place and marks a shift of activity from work-place to the neighbourhood, and finally to the home. The construction of the family during this ritual period is achieved by detaching it from its secular context. Work and home are separated, and a special economy operates. This sacred time ends with a bang on New Year's Eve, which marks the restart of secular life.

V

The establishment of a special Christmas economy—marked by the absence of work and the giving of presents and charitable donations —inverts the economy of everyday life.

In a monograph, *The Gift Economy*, Cheal (1988) argues that gift-giving marks off what he calls the 'moral economy', which is ruled by the principle of reciprocity, from the cash nexus of the market economy.[8] The moral economy, he suggests, is a constant presence along-side the political economy, but it is clearly most prominent at Christmas time. (His study was based in Winnipeg, where just under 50 per cent of the gifts given by his sample were made at Christmas.)

The medium of the moral economy, the gift, carries with it a wish, an intention, which derives from love and caring. (I would extend the definition of the gift in this context to include exchanges of symbolic presents and messages, in the form of Christmas cards, visits, and telephone calls.) In contrast, a payment is a return for specific services rendered, and rendered primarily in order to earn a set return.[9] Secular work is performed as an economic necessity, while in the domestic context it is regarded rather as a service performed without calculation.

In an essay on Santa Claus, Eric Wolf (1964: 150–1) identified what he termed a 'contradiction' between the gift economy and capitalism. 'Where the real economy operates on the principle "from each according to his share of wealth, to each according to his ability to pay," in Santa's economy, these rules are reversed. Each recipient receives "according to his need"; scarcity has given way to true abundance, and the capitalist realities are confronted with a Utopian dream.'

To put it slightly differently, the Christmas economy, based upon gifts, imbued with the principles of charity and service, recalls the ideal economies which are typically supposed to sustain both Christian and socialist utopias. The French sociologist Marcel Mauss projected such economies into the distant past. In traditional societies reciprocity ruled, rather than the profit motive (Mauss 1954). This is probably a fantasy, a sociological construct that illuminates capitalism by constructing its antithesis. Like the Christmas economy, such alternative worlds serve as commentaries on capitalist normality, which they invert.

In practice, the moral economy is closely associated with family and the home. Indeed, the family could be roughly defined as the circle within which the moral economy should rule, and where the political economy is regarded as an intrusion. This helps to account for the common concern with the 'commercialization' of Christmas. The pre-Christmas shopping bonanza, associated with a glut of consumer advertising, is an inescapable contradiction at the centre of the modern Christmas, the one point at which the political economy intrudes into the family celebration; and informants regularly complain that it is threatening the essential Christmas that they desire.[10]

Dickens fixed the central features of Christmas most indelibly by evoking the dreadful anti-Christmas of Scrooge. For Scrooge, Christmas was an intolerable interruption to the serious business of making money.

'A merry Christmas, uncle! God save you!' . . .

'Bah!' said Scrooge. 'Humbug!' . . .

'Don't be cross, uncle!' said the nephew.

'What else can I be,' returned the uncle, 'when I live in such a world of fools as this? Merry Christmas! Out upon merry Christmas! What's Christmas time to you but a time for paying bills without money; a time for finding yourself a year older, but not an hour richer; a time for balancing your books and having every item in 'em through a round dozen of months presented dead against you?'

His Christmas is mean, lonely, tormented, haunted by spirits which force upon him horrifying intimations of the fate of people who only live for money, like his dead partner, old Marley; but he is also offered saving glimpses of the merry Christmas at his nephew's house, and of the charity and love which animate Christmas in the poor house in Camden Town where Bob Cratchit and Tiny Tim live. In the end Scrooge is 'reclaimed by Christmas', and 'it was always said of him, that he knew how to keep Christmas well, if any man alive possessed the knowledge'.

## VI

The ritual time that constitutes the Christmas period has a special quality. It tends to freeze history, to associate this Christmas with Christmas past. The fact that Christmas time is associated with the family induces a denial of changes inherent in the domestic cycle, including, most poignantly, the changes brought by death.

Christmas is a period for remembering the dead, but including them; and ghosts walk on Christmas too. On Christmas Eve the orphan Pip visited his parents' grave, in *Great Expectations*, and met up with the convict, who demanded food, and to whom he gave Christmas fare; an act of Christmas charity which sets the plot in motion and leads eventually to the discovery of a family for him.

Lévi-Strauss identified the association with the dead as a central element of Christmas, and suggested that children are associated with the dead, as beings beyond society. (He might have included prisoners and other outcasts.) I would prefer to suggest that Christmas constitutes an imaginary, family-centred society, which ignores time and breaches secular boundaries, which centres on children and reaches out to the dead and to outcasts.

Adults also revive memories of childhood Christmases, insisting on small rituals which recall them. Each Christmas repeats the previous

one as much as possible. The same things are done in the same order.
The same people arrive at the same moment and sit in the same places
(cf. Barnett 1954: 61).

Aside from deaths, there are cyclical changes, and these may be
difficult to reconcile with the ideal stability of the family Christmas.
Children leave home, marry, have children of their own, eventually
transferring Christmas celebrations from the homes of their parents
to their own homes. This sets up an inescapable conflict. Christmas
must be spent with the family, but as the family cycle evolves the
question becomes, whose family? Where is the home base? Will the
parents of both husband and wife attend the new family's Christmas?
If there are several grown and married children, who acts as host?
(See Barnett 1954: 63; Boholm, 1983: 158.)

In the chapter 'A Christmas Dinner' in the *Sketches by Boz*, Dickens
outlined an ideal solution:

> The Christmas family-party that we mean, is not a mere assemblage of
> relations, got up at a week or two's notice, originating this year, having no
> family precedent in the last, and not likely to be repeated in the next. No. It
> is an annual gathering of all the accessible members of the family, young or
> old, rich or poor ... Formerly, it was held at grandpapa's; but grandpapa
> getting old, and grandmamma getting old too, and rather infirm, they have
> given up house-keeping, and domesticated themselves with uncle George; so
> the party always takes place at uncle George's house, but grandmamma sends
> in most of the good things, and grandpapa always *will* toddle down, all the
> way to Newgate Market, to buy the turkey.

There are also problems caused by the growing apart of siblings,
particularly as a consequence of differential social mobility; and at the
extreme, serious family quarrels.

Even in the absence of such rifts, family tensions feed upon the
contradiction between the ideal timeless repetition of Christmas and
the reality of change. One fairly common English solution is to dupli-
cate Christmas, for instance making of the day after Christmas, Boxing
Day, a shadow Christmas at which the same ceremonies, meals, and
exchanges are repeated, but with another family set—the other set of
grandparents or the other half of a family separated by divorce. This
is one function of the extension of the Christmas period forward.
Another common option is to alternate celebrations between two sites,
for example the homes of two sets of grandparents, or the family home
and the home of a grandparent.

## VII

The celebration of Christmas constructs an alternative reality: a community without strife, caring of the weak and lonely, incorporating outcasts, in which services and gifts are motivated by love, and everyone is happy. It excludes work for gain, hierarchy, and conflict. This is a world in which family values are generalized to everyone. It is also recognizably a Christian world. However, the construct is just one particular version of family and of Christian values. Its timelessness suppresses the recognition of the changes in the family cycle (celebrated at baptisms, birthdays—especially the eighteenth, fiftieth, and seventieth—weddings and anniversaries, and funerals). Its female and child-centredness[11] plays down the different roles of adults and children—and, often, of men and women—in the everyday world, and the reflection of these activities within the family.

Ironic comments are commonly made pointing out that at Christmas nobody is supposed to work, but that women work harder than ever—the irony lying in the denial that this is 'work' (since it is done for love and not for money). Writing in 1971, Shurmer commented: 'The preoccupation of women with gift-giving and hospitality ties in with their relationship to the wider economic system. In general, their importance is in a world of social, rather than business, relationships. They are associated with the subsistence sphere of the home, rather than with the cash sphere of the outside world' (Shurmer 1971: 1244). The reality may have changed in the past two decades, but the representation of women in Christmas is probably more stable.

Just as a specific model of the family is constructed at Christmas time, so is a specific image of Christian practice. The contrast between Christmas and Easter is very marked. Easter is a religious period that marks the death and resurrection of Christ, while in England Christmas is a rather secular festival of his birth and circumcision. Christmas is centred on the child, the family, and the virtues of hope and charity. Easter is about guilt, sacrifice, suffering, and absolution.

My argument, in short, is that over the Christmas period the English construct an alternative world, with a specific social structure, economy, and morality. Other alternative worlds are similarly constructed at other places, and at other times. The tribal, male world of Saturday afternoon football; the society of the pub, with its own rules of inclusion, and its custom of immediate reciprocity; the summer holiday, which hinges on an opposition between nature (valued positively) and the urban world of work and culture.

These alternative worlds reflect upon each other. Christmas, for example, is felt by many to exclude visits to the pub, and for the past thirty years it has also excluded professional football games, once an integral part of the English Christmas Day, now (perhaps because of their increased commercial identity, or their association with men, conflict, and drink) displaced to Boxing Day. They may also merge, or serve as mutual substitutes, as when people flee the English Christmas for a weekend country cottage, or a family holiday in the sun.

Each of these alternative worlds reverses crucial elements of the world they all exclude, the everyday secular world of work, but each constructs that antithesis in its own way. Christmas hinges on a linked set of oppositions between home and work, female dominance and male dominance, food and drink, gift and purchase. Only the traditional family Sunday shares a similar pattern, though perhaps decreasingly, and Mary Douglas (1975) has drawn attention to the continuities between Sunday lunch and Christmas dinner. The recent debate on the Sunday opening of shops yokes together, in a suggestive way, sabbatarian arguments and arguments about the value of segregating the domestic world from the world of commerce.

I have characterized Christmas as a time out for alternative values, which implies also a time in which the everyday is constructed in a specific, antagonistic fashion. The reality of the Christmas community (as of other alternative worlds) is sustained by elaborate tricks of boundary maintenance. There is therefore not a straightforward incongruity in the fact that the family at Christmas may bear little relationship to the secular family, any more than in the fact that the everyday economy is not characterized by gift-giving and charity, as is the Christmas economy.

Nevertheless, one can speculate about the function of this antithesis for the operation of the secular society. It was probably Dickens again who first made the plea, 'Would that Christmas lasted the whole year through (as it ought), and that the prejudices and passions which deform our better nature, were never called into action among those to whom they should ever be strangers!' The idea is that the values of charity, caring, etc. should be sustained when we are back in the world of work. Cheal has shown that the moral economy is indeed an element of social life throughout the year, and it may be that Christmas sustains and reinvigorates this parallel economy; and even that the moral economy is a necessary ingredient for the functioning of the political economy. It is also evident that the burst of present-buying at Christmas provides a great boost to commerce, and sustains important industries (see Davis 1972). (At the same time, however, it depresses output, and this is increasingly true as the Christmas break extends itself forward.)

The identification of functions is, however, notoriously uncertain, and it is famously naïve to assume that the performance of a specific 'function' could *cause* an institution as complex and enduring as the English Christmas. Structures and structural transformations can be identified with greater precision. Christmas is a structural transformation of a particular vision of everyday social life. The modern English Christmas flourishes because the opposition which it constructs with an everyday reality has meaning: a significance fed by the increasingly secular, utilitarian, Gradgrind England of everyday experience.

## Notes

This study is based largely on secondary sources, often traced through the excellent bibliography compiled by Sue Samuelson (1982). I am grateful to Dr C. D. Field of the John Rylands University Library of Manchester, who drew my attention to a series of relevant public opinion polls. Some data were, however, collected specifically for this project. For this I was dependent on assistance, for which I am very grateful. Dr Maryon McDonald helped me organize short undergraduate projects on Christmas by a class of Brunel students. My colleague, Professor Michael Wright, wrote a splendid account of his family Christmas for me. Ms Marie Gillespie arranged for her school class in Southall to write Christmas diaries for my benefit. Mass Observation gave me access to their Christmas diaries for 1942 and 1986.

I am also grateful to Gerd Baumann, for his valuable comments on an early draft of this paper, and to members of various seminars (at Brunel University, the LSE, the Oxford University Centre for the Human Sciences, and the Department of Anthropology, State University of New York at Stony Brook), who discussed drafts of the argument as it developed.

1  *NOP Bulletin*, Special Supplement 1, Christmas, Dec. 1969.
2  *The Mail on Sunday*, 18 Dec. 1988.
3  A Gallup poll illustrates this clearly (Gallup Political Index Report no. 316, Dec. 1986):

Which of these things are you doing at Christmas?

| | |
|---|---|
| Having a Christmas tree | 79% |
| Having a turkey or other poultry | 77% |
| Staying at home | 73% |
| Having a family party | 52% |
| Filling children's stockings | 38% |
| Going to a pantomime | 1% |
| Going away to the seaside/country | 8% |
| None of these | 2% |

Do you normally go to church on Christmas day or not?

Yes   27%
No    73%

4 Opinion polls suggest that nearly a third of the population associates Christmas with a Christian message or significance. For example, the 1986 Gallup Poll included a question about the significance of Christmas, to which 34% responded that it was 'a religious festival' (Gallup Political Index Report No. 316, Dec. 1986).

5 There is a relatively large literature dealing specifically with Santa Claus and Father Christmas. See Barnett (1954: 24–48); de Groot (1965); Lévi-Strauss (1952); Pimlott (1978: ch. 10); Wolf (1964).

6 On this issue see Bennett (1981: 49–73).

7 NOP asked respondents in 1975, 'Do you think you will have a happy Christmas or not?' 88% replied in the affirmative (*Political, Social and Economic Review*, 4, NOP, Nov. 1975).

8 Davis (1972) distinguished a gift economy alongside other major subsectors of the national economy.

9 See Caplow (1982); Cheal (1988: 85–6); Shurmer (1971: 1244).

10 Asked by NOP in 1969 'Is Christmas too commercialized?', 83% agreed. 90% of women gave an affirmative response (*NOP Bulletin*, Special Supplement 1, Christmas, Dec. 1969).

11 See Benney *et al.* (1959: 239–40) for some interesting observations and comments under the heading 'Christmas and sex role'.

## References

ALIBHAI, Y. (1987). 'A White Christmas', *New Society* (18 Dec.): 15–17.

BARNETT, JAMES (1954). *The American Christmas. A Study of National Culture*. New York: Macmillan.

BAUMANN, GERD (1992). 'Ritual Implicates "Others": Rereading Durkheim in a Plural Society', in Daniel de Coppiet (ed.), *Understanding Rituals*. London: Routledge.

BENNETT, TONY (1981). 'Christmas and Ideology', in *Popular Culture:*

*Themes and Issues*. Milton Keynes: Open University Press: Block 1, Units 1/2: 47–73.

BENNEY, MARK, WEISS, ROBERT, MEYERSOHN, ROLF, and RIESMAN, DAVID (1959). 'Christmas in an Apartment Hotel', *American Journal of Sociology*, 65/3: 233–40.

BOCOCK, ROBERT (1974). *Ritual in Industrial Society: A Sociological Analysis of Ritualism in Modern England*. London: Allen & Unwin.

BOHOLM, ÅSA (1983). *Swedish Kinship*. Gothenburg Studies in Social Anthropology, No. 5. Gothenburg: Acta Universitatis Gothoburgensis.

BUDAY, GEORGE (1954). *The History of the Christmas Card*. London: Rockliff.

CAPLOW, THEODORE (1982). 'Christmas Gifts and Kin Networks', *American Sociological Review*, 47: 383–92.

—— BAHR, HOWARD M., CHADWICK, BRUCE A., HILL, REUBEN, and WILLIAMSON, MARGARET HOLMES (1983). *Middletown Families: Fifty Years of Change and Continuity*. New York: Bantam Books (1st edition 1982).

CHEAL, DAVID (1988). *The Gift Economy*. London: Routledge.

DAVIS, JOHN (1972). 'Gifts and the UK Economy', *Man*, 7/3: 408–29.

DOUGLAS, MARY (1975). 'Deciphering a Meal', *Implicit Meanings*. London: Routledge & Kegan Paul.

GOLBY, JOHN (1981). 'A History of Christmas', in *Popular Culture: Themes and Issues*. Milton Keynes: Open University Press: Block 1, Units 1/2: 9–26.

GROOT, ADRIAAN D. DE (1965). *Saint Nicholas: A Psychoanalytic Study of his History and Myth*. The Hague: Mouton.

LEACH, E. R. (1961). 'Time and False Noses', *Rethinking Anthropology*. London: Athlone Press: 132–6.

LÉVI-STRAUSS, CLAUDE (1952). 'Le Père Noël supplicié', *Les Temps modernes*, 7/77: 1572–90. (Abridged English version in *New Society*, 19 (1963): 6–8.)

MAUSS, MARCEL (1954). *The Gift*. London: Routledge (1st pub. in French 1925).

PIMLOTT, J. A. R. (1978). *The Englishman's Christmas: A Social History*. Hassocks: Harvester Press.

SAMUELSON, SUE (1982). *Christmas: An Annotated Bibliography*, Garland Folklore Bibliographies 4. New York: Garland Publishing Inc.

SHURMER, PAMELA (1971). 'The Gift Game', *New Society*, 18/482: 1242–4.

VAN GENNEP, A. (1909). *Les Rites de Passage*. Paris: Nourry.

WOLF, ERIC R. (1964). 'Santa Claus: Notes on a Collective Representation', in Robert A. Manners (ed.), *Process and Pattern in Culture*. Chicago: Aldine.

# 8

# Christmas Cards and the Construction of Social Relations in Britain Today

*Mary Searle-Chatterjee*

The sending of cards was a largely nineteenth-century British contribution to Christmas though there had been occasional medieval
prototypes on the Continent. In Britain it was a development from
the earlier custom of exchanging seasonal letters, or visiting cards,
embellished with greetings or a design. It also drew on the well-
established tradition of sending elaborate Valentine cards. A few
Christmas cards appeared in the 1840s shortly after the introduction
of the penny post, but they did not become popular until the 1860s.
By the 1870s and 1880s they were beginning to challenge Valentine
cards in popularity. It has been suggested that it was only with the
development of cheap methods of colour lithography that Christmas
cards became common. The absence of this technology, however, had
not proved any handicap to the earlier flourishing business in Valentine
cards (Pimlott 1978: 102). By the 1880s, 5 million letters and cards
were being sent at Christmas. By 1938 the number had risen to
470 million and by 1977 to 1,000 million (Finnegan 1981: 23). By
1992 this had risen to 1,560 million cards. Whereas on an ordinary
day, the Royal Mail delivered 60 million items, on the peak Christmas
postal day (16 December), they delivered 119 million in 1990. This
had risen to 122 million in 1991, the highest ever. The recession had
not produced any dent in these figures. About 10 per cent of the
annual mail consists of Christmas items. In 1991 the Post Office took
on 25,000 extra staff from the beginning of December, 20,000 extra
vehicles, and rented 100 extra buildings. They also received 750,000
letters to Father Christmas (Royal Mail Information Office). The commercial value of the Christmas card trade was estimated at £250 million in 1991 (information from the marketing department, Hambledon
Studios, the largest manufacturers of cards in Europe).

In an attempt to unravel the significance of this extraordinary
phenomenon, I shall present a detailed case-study of twenty sets of

Christmas cards, their motifs, and the practices associated with their exchange. The account is based on a sample of twelve undergraduate students in Manchester in 1991. It is supplemented by reports and materials from five other local people as well as by analysis of the cards I myself have received over the last three years.[1] I then consider whether my study of card-giving can shed any light on other familiar aspects of Christmas, particularly on gift-giving. The ethnographic material presented is derived from detailed accounts given by my respondents. Since my 'sample' is so small, I can, of course, do no more than suggest interpretations as a basis for further discussion.

Some readers might wonder whether this type of 'cold' analysis of popular custom threatens to destroy or tarnish what it examines, like the heat of a lamp on a wax mould. As my students said after their project work, 'Christmas will never be the same again.' Such anxieties imply that Christmas is a single, intact whole, like an organism, one that can be damaged by handling. In fact, Christmas customs are different among groups with varying sets of values, as will be seen when I look at patterns of gift-giving. People discuss and contest the meanings of Christmas even as they participate. They make creative changes while they are engaged in discussion. 'Cold' analysis of Christmas changed the festival for me, too, but far from making it wither away, it made me approach it with renewed warmth and thought.

As is well recognized, the sending of cards has valuable practical functions in a society like Britain with high rates of geographical mobility. An increasing number of people live far from friends and relatives. The custom ensures that people retain scattered links as potential resources for the future and as links with the past. Few contacts escape the net of at least annual communication and endangered links are made fast. It is common to send cards to relatives who may not have been seen for twenty years or more. The card keeps relationships ticking over. Contacts with old schoolfriends or cousins may then be renewed after many years, in later stages of life.

The sending of cards cannot, however, be explained in purely practical terms since cards are often exchanged by neighbours, colleagues, and relatives in regular contact. The card is also a material vehicle for symbolizing, as well as securing, relationships, past and present. It can be seen as a measure of minimal 'sociality', that is to say, of communication and co-operation (Ingold 1986), whether actual or potential. The senders of cards are people from whom one might look for some friendly hospitality or support at some time. They represent the maximum range of social relations. As such, it is highly appropriate that, encompassing the living room at Christmas, are the cards, each one a symbol of a relationship in the family's larger network of social contacts. Cards sent to individual members are usually incorporated into the family display. People are proud of, or comforted by, the number of cards they receive. Relationships may be broken or created, but mainly made manifest and incarnate, in the Card. It is expected, then, that cards be reciprocated unless there is a deliberate attempt to cut a link. People in like relationships are to be treated similarly, including, often, equidistant neighbours. An example of this is a card sent 'from all at Number 9' to 'all at Number 5'.

Some participants in the festival are reluctant to use cards simply as symbolic vehicles and emphasize the practical functions of card exchange. They try to avoid sending cards to people with whom they are in regular contact. Few are able to maintain this approach consistently, though each office or work-place has its own culture in such matters. Most adopt a symbolic approach; colleagues exchange cards. The familial focus of Christmas is revealed in the fact that families and couples often send cards collectively, even to colleagues who only know one member of the family. The names of children and even babies are included.

Many people send an identical card to everyone they know. The design, then, is emblematic of the character of the sender. This custom appears to be more common among people who have very large, but less intense, networks. A recent development is a dramatic, even extreme, version of this. The cyclostyled Christmas letter/card is one where communication of family news and the major events of the previous year are presented in identical format to all recipients. A handwritten note may be added at the end to give a more personal flavour. Most people, on the other hand, appear to choose individualized cards for up to twelve close relatives and friends; they use a more standard and cheaper card for people who are less close (Hambledon Studios).

## Card Motifs

The motifs on cards are nearly always symbolic. Only a few are purely decorative, showing flowers or attractive landscapes. The choice of theme is affected by age as well as other factors. Cards showing flowers, or Victorian scenes, idealizing the past, are more commonly sent by older people; comic themes appearing to debunk the rituals of the present, more by the young.

Analysis of twenty sets of cards showed striking patterns in the selection of motifs. Two methods were used to calculate the frequency of a particular theme. In Method 1, every card on which a motif occurred was counted even if in some cases the motif was only a minor feature. In Method 2, the only cards counted were ones on which a motif was dominant. The problem with this method was that it was very often difficult to determine what was the dominant motif. Many designers obviously work with a formula whereby a specified string of motifs must be included. However, with the exception of one motif, both methods produced similar results. As would be expected, recurring themes are winter, evergreen, birds and animals, past times, biblical themes, candles, bells, and Christmas domestic scenes, including children, and often showing, through open curtains, the contrast with the bleakness of the outer world. Of these, three themes far outweigh any others, i.e. winter, evergreens, and animals along with birds. Evergreens drop in importance if they are counted by Method 2 as they are not usually a dominating design. Christmas, then, judging by cards, is a winter festival stressing the survival of life in the form of evergreens, particularly with red berries, and in the form of creatures, particularly robins with red breasts. The colours symbolic of life, red and green, are of great importance. All other themes appear in much lower frequencies. Scenes of contemporary Christmas domesticity and childhood and of 'olden times' (often in a domestic context) are the next most important categories but they are very much below those already referred to. Biblical nativity themes appear even less.

The focus on birds and animals requires further comment, this category being the largest of all. Often the animals are young and have some association with domesticity. In some cases this is a real association, as with the farm animals, sheep, cows, and horses shown in winter fields or in nativity scenes, or the representations of household pets like cats and dogs. Mice, too, have a historic, if unwelcome, association with the home. More purely culturally contrived and symbolic is the 'cuddliness' of the rabbit and bear or the domesticity of the squirrel. Animals without such an association, such as bulls or porcupines, are practically never portrayed, nor are weasels, stoats, and snakes. It is rare for large, predatory carnivores to be presented. Even cards produced by conservationist and ecological groups tend to concentrate on animals associated with snowy environments, such as penguins. They, too, are often shown as young and fluffy. Endangered whales are not portrayed for they are unapproachable and are not associated either with winter or the domestic world. The animals shown, then, are usually from temperate or arctic zones, are 'domestic', and often young.

Very often, animals are presented in a humanized style, wearing clothes and performing humanoid activities. They are shown in 'cute' form, like idealized children, clever and mischievously lovable. If the animals are not humanized, they may be presented in a humanized context. A penguin, for example, may be presented realistically but juxtaposed with a signpost pointing to the north pole creates a humanized effect. Angels and children may similarly be presented in 'cute' form. In the trade, Christmas cards are classified into six types. 'Cute' cards are one of the most popular, constituting at least 30 per cent of the total. The 'traditional' category is the most popular. The other categories are 'religious', 'juvenile', 'humorous', and 'graphic'. The liking for 'cute' cards is peculiarly British. It is difficult to sell them abroad. The USA, the largest market for cards, regards them as 'juvenile' and buys very few. They are not popular on the Continent and only slightly in demand in Australia. Only in a few countries, such as Greece and Saudi Arabia, is there, for some unknown reason, much demand for them (Hambledon Studios). Humorous cards were common in the nineteenth century (Buday 1954: 163), but 'cute' cards are a new departure. It was only in the early 1960s that one company, Valentines, began to manufacture Christmas cards with stylized animals. By the late 1960s such cards had become so popular that a company, Image Arts, was set up to specialize in the production of 'cute and cuddly cards'. This development coincided with the increasing popularity of soft toys among children, and more recently among adults, too, both male and female ('plush' items). Oddly enough, however, although such toys are very popular in the USA, as gifts for adults, 'cute' cards are not (Hambledon Studios). We may speculate as to the social and cultural conditions that have given birth to this phenomenon. South Asian observers of the British scene sometimes speak of their astonishment at the 'strange' popularity of soft toys. They often speak of this, from an Indocentric perspective, as due to 'person deprivation' and the paucity of children in the small conjugal family.

'Cuteness' in Christmas card design differs from 'cuteness' in soft toys in that the images are presented within an ironic framework which permits the viewer to be distanced and, perhaps, protected, from senti-mentality or involvement. The context is one which is intensely struc-tured and moralistic, with its focus on childhood and family ties. The 'cute' card does not go so far as to invert these values; they are softened and treated ironically. The increasing popularity of 'cute' designs on the front of cards coincides with the loss of the moral sentimental verse within. The emergence of the 'cute' genre in card design may not have any close connection, then, with the recent rise of the soft toy to new heights of popularity, for these are not treated ironically to the same degree. It should be noted, however, that a recent paper has argued that teddy bears have therapeutic value, not just as objects of affection, but also as distancing mechanisms which enable emotions to be handled indirectly (Biancardi 1992).

Detailed examination of the motifs on Christmas cards shows that not only is there a definite pattern to the selection of themes but also that this is related to the symbolism of Christmas as a whole (for a contrary view see Pimlott 1978: 105). I have not found it necessary to explain these recurring motifs in terms of survivals from the past. Symbols on cards survive because they speak to us in the present. However, it should be said that there is no evidence that biblical themes are declining. They have never been common on Christmas cards. This was true even when the bulk of the population went to church. Only in the 1980s when church attendance began to decline did anyone begin to worry about this. A study in 1946 of the cards received by an Anglican clergyman and a Roman Catholic priest showed that they too were no more likely than anyone else to receive 'religious' cards. The former received 114 cards of which only three were religious, one of these being from a German, one from a Jewish person, and one from an actress! The priest similarly received only a couple of religious cards. If anything, there has been an increase in the selection of religious themes since 1945 (Buday 1954: 190). The sending of Christmas cards is not, for most people, associated with Christianity.

The purchase of charity Christmas cards is now increasing rapidly. In 1980 they were 17% of the total: in 1991 they were 30%. However, they are more common among the 'higher' social groups. For people in such classes it is not uncommon for 70% of all cards to be of this type (Oxfam Trading Office). Such a card is simultaneously a gift to the receiver, a recognition of a specific relationship, while at the same time being a small part of a collective gift to numerous unknown others. It indicates a sense of linkage with society at large, even beyond the shores of Britain, to people who are perceived to be less fortunate, though innocent and deserving. In that sense it is an example of generalized exchange for which no return is expected. Cards in aid of conservationist or ecological groups similarly indicate not only particularistic relationships, but also a wide and general concern for living beings as a whole in their larger natural environment.

## Christmas and Religion

It has been shown that 'Christian' themes are not, and never have been, of much importance in Christmas cards. For most people the same is true of Christmas in general. Only in primary schools is the Christian nativity story greatly stressed. Visitors and settlers from ex-British colonies, where Christmas is celebrated, comment on the absence of 'religion' in the British Christmas. Communal midnight mass is not central here as it is or was in Bombay, Goa, or Trinidad. Instead, the festival is a largely private family matter.

Although Christmas is not generally a religious occasion, it involves much ritualized behaviour. It is a ritual in the sense that it consists of widely shared and predictable routines, is a time of heightened emotion, focused on culturally prescribed activities that idealize and sanctify a key social institution, the three-generational family and its social networks. There are strong pressures on people to conform. Things must be done 'properly' and be 'special'. People must be jolly, be part of the group, and engage in group rituals. They are expected to drink alcohol, a key symbol both of 'communion' and of the 'specialness' of the season. Those who refuse to 'become pissed' or to 'lark about', whether in the home, office (in pre-Christmas parties), or elsewhere, are 'spoilsports' who are refusing to recognize 'specialness' or sacredness, and refusing to participate in group communion. They are the stern protestant nonconformists of the day, the anti-ritualists whose ancestry and subcultural socialization leads them to value individualism and the self-control and discipline which symbolizes that, more than group communion.

Though Christmas may not be 'Christian', it is certainly sacred, if by that one refers to 'things set apart ... practices which unite one single moral community' (Durkheim 1964: 37). Believers and non-believers alike lament the commercialism of the Christmas season. They contrast it, at least implicitly, with the 'true' meaning of Christmas. The festival is 'sacred' in so far as it can be profaned by commerce. The summer holiday season is a time of equally extravagant and commercialized expenditure yet no one deplores this fact for nobody expects the summer holiday to be sacred.

## The Exchange of Gifts

Card-giving delineates the maximum zone of sociality, potential as well as actual. The exchange of Christmas gifts, on the other hand, marks out the circle of those who are more likely to be providing current support. It delineates a smaller, more inclusive and closer group of contacts, mainly close relatives and a few friends. Some gift-giving occurs in individualized exchanges prior to Christmas. A yet smaller and closer circle of people is involved in the actual rituals of gift exchange on Christmas Day. This is the child-centred conjugal, or single-parent, family in association with grandparents and other members of the extended family. It is the unit on whom the major activities of Christmas are focused, the shopping for gifts, the exchange of gifts, and the Christmas dinner and tea.

Since, for many, each close relationship must be embodied and made manifest in at least one gift, presents are often exchanged in the name of babies. Domestic pets, too, may receive wrapped gifts, and even proffer them. Presents express the value placed upon the relationship and their material cost should relate to the degree of closeness. In-laws should be treated as equal to kin. Step-relatives are often differentiated. The only really acceptable asymmetry, however, is from parents to offspring. This may be very great even when all concerned are adults. Parents tend to give larger gifts than they receive. Caplow, in his American study (1984), interprets this as due to their wish to build a fund of obligation as an investment for their future old age. This is in accordance with Leonard's conclusion to her study of marriage in Swansea, showing how children and young people make very little contribution to household work (1980). This sort of approach is unduly instrumentalist and contradicts the whole drift of Christmas, with its emphasis on disguising the monetary implications of gifts, seen most vividly in the way that adults encourage children to believe in Father Christmas. Students had pretended to belief long after it had faded, 'for the sake of parents'. The device of Father Christmas also functions to define childhood as a magical time set apart. It becomes problematic for people on low incomes who may find themselves obliged to demolish the illusion in order to explain why the gifts brought to their children are smaller than average. Another custom which, if widespread, would support the view that gifts are expected to express or symbolize relationships as they are perceived to be, rather than to create them with an eye on the future, is the one whereby older brothers and sisters give disproportionately to younger ones, regardless of income. In accordance with this is the fact that, in Britain, gifts from Father Christmas are not generally said to be conditional on good behaviour. They are awarded to the child as such, by virtue of his status, not by merit (contrast Belk on the USA, 1987, and Lévi-Strauss on France, in this volume).

At school, children are socialized into a conception of Christmas as a time for doing good deeds, for giving to the unfortunate, often to unknown members of society. This non-reciprocal giving symbolizes links with society as a whole in its widest extension. Teachers may expect children to visit elderly people with gifts. Even for children, Christmas is not just a festival 'for fun'. They may be idealized but they, too, are to participate in structured symbolic giving.

## *The Rituals of Giving*

Most writing on the subject implies that there is a single, culturally shared form of Christmas observance in Britain. The Open University Unit on this topic, for example, refers only to minor cultural variations in each family (Finnegan 1981: 29). However, project work with a group of undergraduates suggests at least two major cultural variations, or poles, in patterns of gift-giving on Christmas Day.

In the first pattern, which I shall call the 'deferred gratification' type, the bulk of the gifts are exchanged in a highly regulated ritual. Individuals place presents around the family tree on Christmas Eve or morning, making them 'special', almost sacralized, one might say, before they are redistributed in a ritual of family communion. Even if the actual distribution occurs in another room at the back of the house, the gifts are first placed around the tree before being carried through. Children receive their main gifts downstairs and only token presents, sweets, and fruit in their 'stockings' (actually socks) at the end of the bed. The gift-giving is expected both to express and secure relationships within the family. Gifts must be decommoditized and made 'special' by the careful use of wrapping. Commercial wrappers, brown paper, or transparent plastic bags are not approved of. Green, red, gold, and silver are the preferred colours for wrapping paper. They symbolize evergreen, red berries, light, and royal abundance. They must be opened carefully and not greedily, by adults at least, and received with surprise and joy. Gifts of money should be disguised and are not ideal, though increasingly common in a society where many are affluent and it is difficult to provide something new and appropriate without an enormous expenditure of time.

The gift is opened publicly in a room that has been transformed, been made 'special' and different, magical even, by decoration with paper chains and evergreen foliage. Around it are the cards, symbols of the wider network; at the head is the illuminated tree, symbol and focal point of the family. It is an appropriate symbol of the branching continuity of family life. The room has not usually been made anew with fresh curtains and furnishings, ready for the start of the New Year (see the contrast with Trinidad, as described by Miller, in this volume), though sales of carpets do increase at this time. It is, however, marked by the different use of the existing curtains. This is the only time of the year when front curtains remain open after dusk in order to show forth the tree and the inner warmth. Ideally, the outer world viewed through the windows has become magically transformed by snow (supernatural one might almost say), even though in reality snow does not often fall in late December.

The events of Christmas Day proceed in a highly structured fashion. Children enjoy stockings then wake parents. Everyone washes and dresses, in some families in new clothes, before going downstairs. In one subvariant said to be common in parts of South Wales, there are strict 'rules' about the order of descent with father followed by mother, followed by children in order of age. In some families, breakfast is eaten and cleared away, even washed up, before the ceremony begins, perhaps with some ritual phrase as 'has Father Christmas been yet?' Everyone sits around the room. One member of the family, often a child, is the master of ceremonies. This is a reversal of ordinary power relations in accordance with the centrality of the child in this festival. The gifts are distributed in customary order, either alternating in an egalitarian way between the members, or, in some kind of hierarchical order. For example, presents from children may be opened either first or last. In one case the reported order is always as follows: (1) presents to father from daughter; (2) presents to stepmother from 'daughter'; (3) from father and stepmother to daughter; (4) collective family gift to the dog; (5) presents from absent people; (6) presents for nonresident son who visits later in the morning. Gifts are usually opened one at a time. Each opening may be followed by a ritual kiss to the donor. At the end everyone kisses everyone else. The ritual is followed by coffee, perhaps made by the father, or in some cases followed by breakfast. Subvariants of this type may require even more deferred gratification. Gift-giving may follow a return from church, consumption of dinner, or, in one 'extreme' case, the queen's speech. Families who practise this style of gift-giving justify it on the grounds that it teaches children 'to give to others'. It is thought important that children should, from an early age, give to adults, even though their giving must inevitably be artificially contrived by adults acting on their behalf. It is thought that children cannot begin to participate in gift-giving if they believe that all gifts are from Father Christmas.

The second cultural variant, or pole, in patterns of gift-giving, which I shall call the 'child-centred' type is reported to be common among certain traditional working-class communities (see also reference to similar practices in the nineteenth century in Lancashire, in Pimlott 1978: 121). In this pattern, practically all gifts are opened individually in bed. In practice, it is mainly children who receive gifts. Instead of the sock, there is a pillow case or sack. Gifts are given mainly to those of a younger generation, rather than to spouses or siblings, though adult offspring may give to parents. The oldest generation tend to give the more expensive gifts in descending order. Within the home, any gifts for adults may be placed under the tree but will not be presented as part of a ritual. If a gift is handed to an adult this is an individualized interaction. Individuals who follow this pattern have little to say about it, since so little ritual is involved, but insist that it is general in some localities. This lack of group ritual is, on the face of it, surprising, since extended family links are often very important in such cases. Families who practise this style of gift-giving justify it as a natural consequence of the child-centred nature of Christmas. Childhood is seen as a very special and brief phase of life, to be enjoyed to the full, before the harsh realities of adult life intrude. The group rituals of the 'deferred gratification' pattern are considered to be artificial and absurd, as well as unkind to children. They reject the view that such patterns are more likely to develop generosity.

'Moral' education is occurring in both types of practice. In the 'deferred gratification' type, the child learns that there are rules of self-control and reciprocity. In the 'child-centred' type, he or she develops a propensity to give through experiencing generosity and identifying emotionally with people who give to others. It might not be far-fetched to say that in the first case, 'morality' is seen to be rooted in the development of internal controls and norms; in the second case it is envisaged as emerging particularistically from experiencing interpersonal acts of love.

. In practice, each household has its own culture of routinized procedures.

The exchange of cards and presents, as well as the actual rituals of gift-giving, delineate distinct zones in the field of social relations, progressively smaller and more intense. The patterns can be seen in the chart. They are interrelated, hence the exchanges even of the outer zones refer back by implication to the tighter sociality represented by the Christmas Day rituals themselves. They constitute a model both of, and for, social relations. Within the inner circle is the 'family', that is to say, the extended family of parents (or parent) with children, along with grandparents, sometimes with other relatives too. Christmas, then, expresses the cultural sanctity of the child-rearing family and of the enduring links between parents and their offspring through three generations. This is the institution on which society is ideally expected to be based.

In primary schools, children are socialized into a sacred story that provides a charter for adult life in such a family, focused on the birth of a baby. The story both parallels and gives divine legitimacy to the family rituals of a contemporary British Christmas. The nativity story is a folk tradition constructed on the basis of only a couple of brief sentences in two of the Christian Gospels. Gifts are presented only by 'wise men', not kings, and are mentioned only by Matthew. Shepherds merely visit the baby in a manger (a single mention only in Luke). There is no reference to animals in either of these Gospels. In Mark, usually considered the most 'reliable' Gospel, there is no nativity tale at all. In the popular story, the Holy Family is in a stable, bereft of any material possessions. Here we have the conjugal family in its culturally pure essence, stripped of all trappings, the family where the mother, husband, and child are primary. In the sacred tale the husband has a peripheral, or at least ambiguous, role in conception; so, too, in life, at Christmas, the mother is usually the one most actively involved in creating the family and bringing individuals together. She is the one, often, who buys the cards and the gifts, who wraps them and prepares the food. The symbolic centre of this sacred tale is the divine and innocent baby, the 'miracle', nucleus and *raison d'être* of the cul-

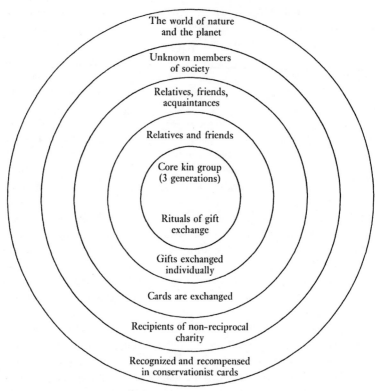

FIG. 8.1. Circles of exchange.

turally approved form of the family. Domestic animals surround the manger, completing the domesticity of the scene. In the school nativity play, extended links beyond the conjugal family are also important. Kings, and often shepherds, too, bring gifts. In the real world, extended family members bring gifts for infants, and for adults who were once infants and who may at Christmas have to struggle again with the contradictory roles of infant and adult. Conflicts arise, too, from the conjunction of the kin of one's past childhood and the 'alien' in-laws of the present. Whereas in many societies such social contradictions are given recognition in elaborated rituals, here the consensus is too fragile for this to occur. The contradictions can be resolved magically by the presence of real babies, who are greatly idealized on this occasion: 'it's all for the sake of the children', 'they make it all worthwhile', 'it's nothing without them'. When children are no longer present, the contradictions are likely to emerge more strongly and the rituals may not only be unable to reconcile them, they may become the occasion for their expression.

The parallels between life and sacred story or 'myth' are not perfect, for in many families, gifts are given not only to children but also to parents, spouses, and siblings. Egalitarian norms relating to parents and children, independent wage earning, a higher proportion of elderly people and a lower birth rate, as well as the pressure of commerce, all converge to ensure that gift-giving is not confined to such limited channels as in the sacred archetype.

It is not surprising that the gift-giving rituals of the inner circle usually involve three generations, for the links between adults and their parents provide central support mechanisms in British society. The family in this extended sense is of major importance despite, perhaps even because of, the soaring divorce rate. In any case, 'broken' marriages are hardly any more common today than they were in the early nineteenth century (Samuel and Thompson 1990). The higher life expectancy has increased the possibility of extended links with grandparents (Wall *et al.* 1983). It is the extended core kin group, based on parents with their adult children and grandchildren, rather than friends, which is the major source of help with house maintenance, financial advice, personal loans, children (Willmott 1986: 39–52; Finch 1989) and with care of the elderly (Hunt 1978; Wenger 1984). Christmas is the one occasion when the continuing significance of the larger family is actually valorized. It ritualizes and highlights major cultural ideals which, though subject to strain and challenge, still inform much of daily practice. Despite this, it is these links with the extended family that cause much of the strain of Christmas. It is one thing to provide support, but another to be closeted together indoors for several days in an intensely ritualized context, in which only communal activities are acceptable. As is the case with the Hindu system of dowry and marriage, many of those involved have deep misgivings yet feel unable to abandon the custom. Too many people would be too upset. Christmas presents an impossible ideal of perfect family unity, expressed in perfect gifts, in a mood of overflowing joy and fun. For most people this ideal cannot be achieved. For individuals living in a mobile society it is not always easy to manage the intense family collectivism expected at this time. The disjunctions referred to earlier make it inevitable that there is often conflict and disappointment (see the chapter by Löfgren in this volume). Even where stresses are minimal, Christmas is a time requiring a great deal of additional domestic labour. Usually this falls on women. Such tensions are greatly worsened by the attempts of commerce to raise the stakes of gift-giving and consumption.

For some people, the tensions are intolerable. Others do not belong to any core kin group. Hence it is that in Britain the Samaritans organization receives approximately 8,000 calls of anguish on each of the three main Christmas days, as compared with 5,000 per day at other times of the year (Samaritans Information Office).

It is clear that there are relationships between the pattern of exchange of cards and gifts. My analysis of the motifs on Christmas cards, however, at first appears to contradict the symbolism implicit in other aspects of Christmas. The dominant theme of birds and animals seems quite contrary to the rituals, with their stress on the warmth of domesticity, the centrality of childhood, and the continuity of links between the generations. In practice, there is no contradiction for cards also stress the continuity of life, but in the outer world of 'nature', beyond the walls of the domestic world. They provide a bridge between the two. Warm domestic scenes are shown to be encircled by the cold, snowy, outer world in which life still continues. Evergreen trees, red berries, bright and lively robins, and a wide range of animals, often young and in family groups, and invariably friendly, all survive and flourish. The symbolism of Christmas, then, whether in card motifs or gift exchange, is concerned with positive themes, the survival of life despite the winter and the passing of time, both within the family and society, and beyond it, in the natural world.

The exchange of cards and the giving of gifts form part of a single symbolic system. They do not provide an 'alternative' reality; they give material form to, and thus make incarnate, some of the underlying realities of social relations in Britain today.

### Note

I am grateful to my students for the work they did on this topic and for the patience with which they endured my sometimes obsessive questioning. I also benefited greatly from comments made by Danny Miller and other friends, colleagues, and relatives. The continuing encouragement of Ursula Sharma is particularly appreciated.

## References

ALLAN, G. A. (1979). *A Sociology of Friendship and Kinship*. London: George Allen and Unwin.

BARNETT, J. A. (1954). *The American Christmas: A Study of National Culture*. New York: Macmillan.

BELK, R. W. (1987). 'A Child's Christmas in America: Santa Claus as Deity, Consumption as Religion', *Journal of American Culture*, 10/1: 87–100.

—— (1989). 'Materialism and the Modern U.S. Christmas', in Elizabeth Hirschman (ed.), *Interpretive Consumer Research*. Provo, Ut.: Association for Consumer Research: 115–33.

BIANCARDI, J. (1992). 'Teddy Bear Therapy', paper presented at the 'Person-centred approach' fifth Forum, Newcastle.

BUDAY, G. (1954). *The History of the Christmas Card*. London: Rockliff.

CAPLOW, T. (1982). 'Christmas Gifts and Kin Networks', *American Sociological Review*, 47: 383–92.

—— (1984). 'Rule Enforcement without Visible Means', *American Journal of Sociology*, 89/6: 1306–23.

DURKHEIM, E. (1915). *The Elementary Forms of the Religious Life*. London: Allen and Unwin.

FINCH, J. (1989). *Family Obligations and Social Change*. Cambridge: Polity.

FINNEGAN, R. (1981). 'Celebrating Christmas', *Popular Culture: Themes and Issues*. Milton Keynes: Open University Press: Block 1, Units 1/2: 29–44.

HUNT, A. (1978). *The Elderly at Home: A Survey Carried out on Behalf of the Department of Health and Social Security*. London.

INGOLD, T. (1986). *Evolution and Social Life*. Cambridge: Cambridge University Press.

LEONARD, D. (1980). *Sex and Generation: A Study of Courtship and Weddings*. London: Tavistock.

Office of Population Censuses and Surveys (1980). *General Household Survey*. London. 198.

PIMLOTT, J. A. R. (1978). *The Englishman's Christmas: A Social History*. Hassocks: Harvester Press.

SAMUEL, R., and THOMPSON, P. (1990). *The Myths We Live by*. London: Routledge.

SAMUELSON, SUE (1982). *Christmas: An Annotated Bibliography*. New York: Garland Publishing Inc.

SANSOM, W. (1968). *Christmas*. London: Weidenfeld & Nicolson.

WALL, R., ROBIN, J., and LASLETT, P. (1983) (eds.). *Family Forms in Historic Europe*. Cambridge: Cambridge University Press.

WENGER, G. C. (1984). *The Supportive Network: Coping with Old Age*. London: George Allen and Unwin.

WILLMOTT, PETER (1986). *Social Networks, Informal Care and Public Policy*. London: Policy Studies Institute.

WILLMOTT, PETER (1987). *Friendship Networks and Social Support.* London: Policy Studies Institute.

WILLMOTT, PHYLLISS (1983). *Families at the Centre.* London: Bedford Square Press.

# 9

# Christmas Present: Christmas Public

*Barbara Bodenhorn*

In many ways, Barrow, Alaska, one of seven Iñupiaq (Eskimo) villages perched on the shores of the Arctic Ocean, could be the setting of virtually any high northern community in Siberia, North America, Greenland, or Scandinavia.[1] In late December, a translucent robin's eggshell blue outlines the horizon for a few short hours in the middle of the day. Daylight never really develops, but rarely is it truly and deeply dark. Covered by the polar ice cap, the Arctic Ocean stretches silently northward, catching and refracting any light that reaches it—whether moon or flickering aurora borealis. The surrounding tundra, swept bare in places by fierce and frequent winds, nevertheless gleams palely in the pre-dawn gloom. Dry snow crunches under foot; breath—transformed instantly into ice fog—hangs in the air for seconds, marking the path of passers-by. The sun will not be seen for another month, but the village itself is awash with Christmas lights. Children ride the bus as it shuttles its way across town (occasionally with parents in tow) simply to watch the show.

Christmas in other equally light-filled but non-Arctic locations (from village New England, rural southern Germany to metropolitan New York, Zurich, and Paris) seems to fall, in my experience, into two distinct although overlapping patterns. As several chapters in this volume observe, Christmas is often focused inward: a time for 'family' in the home. Christmas Eve 1991 in Bebenhausen, Germany, was a spectacular night—full moon, glistening, snow-covered fields—without spectators. A mid-evening walk resulted in not a single encounter. Houses were ablaze with light, but no one was about. Christmas Day in any year will be equally eerie in Central London. Christmas television programming has been advertised for weeks; videos are rented; food has been bought, prepared, and stored for easy access. Restaurants, 'wishing you and yours a Happy Christmas', have closed their doors. At the other extreme, outward-looking Christmas as well as New Year's Eve is a great excuse 'to party', to 'get legless', a chance for friends to celebrate with abandon. Even these are private events, however, held as they usually are in someone's home. As Miller suggests in the introduction to this volume, the emphasis may shift, but frequently encompasses the 'twin peak' aspects of Christmas and carnival, of 'proper' and 'improper' behaviour—the simultaneous embodiment and inversion, for instance, of 'family values'.

In Barrow, as in the other villages of the North Slope, the focus of Christmas is outward. Unlike the examples mentioned above, it is public in the sense that the celebrations take place not only with friends and relatives, but occur entirely outside individual households. For eight days, social activities are located first in the churches and subsequently in the community centre where people feast, sing, dance, and play games with barely a moment taken out to sleep.

This chapter considers Christmas in Barrow, with a nod to Leach, as both performance and performative: a ritual event that both says and does things in a way that leaves room within shared meaning for individual symbolic elaboration. I shall argue that Christmas does indeed 'act out' moral categories important to the participants. By virtue of a number of paradoxes identified below, however, it is clearly not enough simply to say that this process reflects core social values at a time of year when the world itself seems to be in a limbo of arctic darkness. Nor does it seem useful to think of the period as a ritual of reversal, playing out social values through their inversion. For a community that is predominantly and devoutly Christian, 'religion' seems to have been relegated to a minor role in the overall proceedings. In a region where inhabitants consistently identify 'sharing' as one of the most pleasurable aspects of village life, the exchange of presents is equally low key. For a people who are virtually unanimous in their emphasis on the importance of 'relatives' in their daily lives, events seem to de-emphasize 'family' at the expense of larger and more general categories. It is 'about' community—defined by participation in a multitude of activities—and it is the expression of lived Iñupiaq identity, one that focuses on the 'otherworldly' social relations between animals and humans as well as those between humans and a Christian God. Thus the reinvented tradition of Iñupiaq Christmas both takes from and expresses itself against the Christian ideology of the surrounding society. The Christ child safe in the bosom of the nuclear Nativity is present, but does not form the core metaphor around which the event is lived.

The chapter is based on Christmases experienced in Barrow between 1980 and 1986; thus, while a number of themes bear the weight of both 'tradition' and 'history', the processes under consideration are contemporary ones.[2]

## The Context

Utqiaġvik, or Barrow, has been a permanent Iñupiaq settlement for nearly two thousand years. The northernmost community on the North American continent and the largest in the region, the village today has a fluctuating population ranging from two and a half to three thousand people depending on the time of year. Iñupiat have maintained the generalized rules of access to food resources characteristic of so many hunting and gathering societies. Individual autonomy was and is protected by the openness of knowledge, by one's freedom of movement, by the right to earn 'shares' of meat with one's skill or one's contribution to the means of production. However, the hunt of *agviq* (bowhead whale), central to Iñupiaq subsistence for the last millennium, has long served as a focus for an uncharacteristically complex social organization. Headed by *umialik*—husband and wife co-captains— whaling crews involve relatively large numbers of people in enduring, interdependent relations that extend beyond both household and kinship. At the same time, for the last several centuries at the very least, highly elaborated rules of redistribution have, in combination with trading, allowed for the accumulation of durable wealth. Today Iñupiaq households continue to depend on regular supplies of hunted meat but equally must have access to regular supplies of cash—to pay for fuel, water, electricity, snow-machines and high-powered rifles, cable television, microwave ovens, computers, and home video recorders. Iñupiat define themselves as hunters; the events which mark the annual calendar correspond as much to the celebration of whaling as they do to the demands of the school year.

### The coming of the missionaries

Euroamerican contact began with the arrival of Russian explorers in the mid-nineteenth century. They were driven back without being able to land on shore, but were followed closely by British vessels searching for the Franklin expedition, which anchored off Point Barrow between 1852 and 1854. The ship employed Iñupiaq men to hunt for them, Iñupiaq women to sew much-needed winter clothing, and crew members visited the town with increasing frequency as time wore on. Multinational commercial whaling ships made their first appearance in 1864 and had become a permanent presence by the mid-1880s. By 1898, Presbyterian missionaries were an equally permanent fixture in the area.[3]

These last encountered conditions that encompassed several factors which not only had bearing on the conversion process, but also on the way Christmas is celebrated today. These included a form of social organization which brought people together in intensive communal activities during the darkest period of the winter and a shamanic tradition which emphasized public performance. The overriding idiom of social relations was, and continues to be, that of kinship. Having *iḷa*, or relatives, was extremely important; processes that allowed people to generate relatives—through adoption, namesake practices, marriage, and the like—as well as unmake them (simply by not acknowledging a kinship link) lent the system the flexibility for which the Inuit have long been noted. Thus, while 'relatives' were crucial, 'family' (for which there is no direct Iñupiaq translation) was not a bounded category.

In *Seasonal Variations of the Eskimo*, Mauss (1979) posited a dual social morphology for the Inuit: nuclear families scattered across the tundra during the summer, engaged in profane activities, whilst multiple extended families created 'community' by means of intensive ritual activity throughout the long winter months. Although Mauss missed both the sacred and the social character of summertime endeavours, much of his model holds true. Summer remains the time for family units to 'get out of town'. People go 'camping'—hunting, fishing, berry-picking—on an individual basis, or in small groups.[4] From the beginning of the fall whaling season until the final whaling celebration in mid-June, however, Barrow is the site of numerous community-focused events. Some of these, such as Thanksgiving and Christmas, have incorporated important elements of the surrounding Euroamerican culture; others, such as *Nalukataq*, the June festival mentioned above, and *Kivgiaq* (Messenger Feast), are talked about as customary Iñupiaq practice.[5] In short, from the earliest moment of missionary presence, midwinter was and has remained a period of communal celebration.

At the turn of the twentieth century, Iñupiaq religious practice followed an animist, shamanic tradition similar to many hunting and gathering societies. All adults possessed ritual knowledge; in an animated world, men and women needed to know how to operate without giving offence to the *iñua* (souls) surrounding them. Most important was the proper treatment of the souls of the animals on whom daily survival depended. *Angatkut* (shamans) were the specialists who performed individualized services of diagnosing illness, predicting and controlling the weather and the like—for a fee. In addition, however, their presence was institutionalized in the form of public performances in the *qargich*, or community houses. By day *qargich* were work-places, primarily for men but occasionally for women as well. In the evening they were transformed into community centres. Men and women would gather to sing, dance, watch shamanic displays of magical power, and tell stories. It was here that many of the rituals marking the whaling cycle would be conducted. Here too the Messenger Feasts took place, where trading partners from different villages maintained elaborate exchange relations.

*The conversion process*

Iñupiaq social organization in the eighteenth and nineteenth centuries was by any measure complex; the development of power relations, however, was minimized in a number of ways. By keeping the leadership roles of *angatkuq* and *umialik* apart, productive and ritual authority were seldom merged. Individual freedom of movement ensured that any abuse of leadership roles could easily be countered by the dissolution of followership. Thus possession of authority seldom led to the exercise of individual power.

Shifts in these relations played at least a partial role in the story of conversion to Christianity on the North Slope. For a decade, missionaries had little 'success'. During that time, however, the initial positive experience of Iñupiat with the new Euroamerican presence deteriorated.[6] The 'usual' imported diseases (measles, flu, and so on) began to exact a heavy toll; marine and land resources simultaneously entered a period of decline, generating famine conditions in many places.[7] Barrow and Point Hope, which had become magnet communities by virtue of the permanent presence of commercial whalers who were willing to pay for the skills of local whalers, now became the only sources of regular supplies. Falling prices for 'whale bone' (baleen) drove most Euroamerican whalers away, leaving local *umialit* to take over the business. Thus, by the end of the first decade of the twentieth century, both *angatqut* and *umialit* held positions which, by virtue of people's decreased mobility, gradually assumed a far greater potential for power than they had done previously. At one point, a shaman/whaling captain (unheard of until this time) essentially terrorized Point

Hope until he was finally executed. In this context of a seemingly uncontrollable environment, shamans in particular were perceived to be abusing their powers. Christian missionaries were thought to have the stronger taboos and as a consequence their messages suddenly became more attractive.[8] Conversion was rapid, apparently genuine and virtually total.

Naturally one of the first goals of the missionaries themselves was the suppression of all things shamanic. This included group singing and dancing (which in fact were meant to communicate with the animals) as well as individual shamanic practices and performances. The *qargich*, as the sites of most of these activities, were disbanded. Many of these activities have been allowed back into community life gradually, acknowledged for their entertainment value but denied their original ritual efficacy. Dancing reappeared in the 1930s. The Games in their present form were introduced by Mothers' Clubs in the 1940s and 1950s.[9] Today, although the majority of the community remains Christian, the Presbyterian monopoly has long since disappeared, supplemented primarily by Assembly of God, but including Catholic and Bahai denominations as well. In addition, a number of people have rejected any kind of church affiliation on the grounds that the original missionaries committed 'cultural genocide'. 'Being Christian' is one of the categories by which contemporary political maps are drawn.

During the latter half of this century, the character of Iñupiaq/ Euroamerican contact has changed drastically once again. Oil was discovered in the region in 1968 which, in combination with the Cold War, meant that the land itself as opposed to renewable (and removable) resources became the focus of local/national relations. Iñupiat have maintained significant control over wealth generated by the petroleum industry—mostly in the form of property taxes which do not fluctuate with the price of oil. At least in part because of this, however, Barrow has become a multicultural village, heavily involved in the world economy. Once again it is a magnet community, this time attracting Texas oil-workers, teachers from Minnesota, and accountants from the Philippines as well as Iñupiat from elsewhere in the region. Iñupiat remain the dominant population throughout the North Slope, but by the late 1980s, their majority had sunk to approximately 60 per cent in Barrow.

## Christmas Week

Currently Christmas in Barrow starts with a church pageant on Christmas Eve. There is one church service on Christmas morning, another in the afternoon which incorporates the 'Christmas Feast', and an 'Eskimo Dance' in the community hall in the evening. Rather than spend a quiet Boxing Day at home, people move to the local high school gymnasium on the 26th to begin a week of 'Christmas Games'. These break at 9.00 p.m. on New Year's Eve for a three-hour church service, and then resume for a twenty-four-hour final marathon. At the close of New Year's Day, another Eskimo Dance concludes the celebration. We will look at the components of this period individually.

### The pageant

In contrast to many European countries, Christmas Eve in Barrow is neither family-oriented, nor the high point of the season. Rather than staying at home to erect the tree, exchange gifts, or have a special meal before going to a midnight service, people go to church to watch the children put on the pageant. It is here that the 'Christmas story' is most explicit for it follows the canonical storyline of the Nativity— sometimes, although not always, performed in Iñupiaq. This is followed by singing (hymns) and food (Europeanized fare—tea, cakes, and the like) which is provided by members of the congregation.

### The feast

Christmas morning offers a church service for those who are observant. Christmas afternoon incorporates 'the feast' into another service —this one attended by observant and non-observant alike.[10] For those who do not regularly take part in either Presbyterian or Assembly of God services, the choice of which feast to attend is often made on the basis of estimating where the most whale meat will be served. The meat has been provided by all of the whaling captains in the village. Members of whaling crews have been preparing for much of the day, making soup, cutting frozen whale meat and *maktak* (whaleskin and blubber, a preferred food), and transporting hundreds of pounds of frozen fish from ice cellars to the church. Anyone—Iñupiaq or not— who shows up will be fed, regardless of church affiliation, kinship connection, residence, or participation in subsistence activities.[11] Families begin to arrive in early afternoon; by mid-afternoon, the church is full, as are the hallways and the rooms upstairs in the adjacent building. During the feast families generally sit together. These may be nuclear or extended; there are no 'rules' as to where or with whom. People bring their own eating utensils as well as plastic bin liners in which to take their 'shares' home.[12] The Church Deacons have chosen 'servers' who work in male/female pairs. To begin they approach the front of the church, each holding a plate carrying a single kind of hunted food: fish, caribou, duck, whale, and so forth. Thanks are said, acknowledging the importance of all the varieties of food, and the dependence human beings continue to have on the animals that sustain them. The servers then pass through the crowd, carrying containers of food. First *maktak*, then whale meat, and finally frozen fish or caribou are handed out. At each family grouping, the servers ask, 'how many?', i.e. how many people eat with you? The size of the commensal unit determines the size of the share. Once all the *quaq* (frozen food) has been passed out, the servers come by again with caribou soup, oranges or stewed fruit, *ugruaqtak* ('Eskimo doughnuts', or fried bread), and tea. Throughout, 'special tidbits', portions of meat especially prized by older people, have been distributed to the 'seniors'. During this time people eat and chat to each other. Some people leave as soon as they have finished eating. Others remain behind and take part in songs and testimonials of thanksgiving. Throughout this service the language of thanks and of testimonial is Iñupiaq; the deacons— who are Iñupiat—take the major responsibility in organizing the event, both 'backstage' (choosing the servers and making sure the food is available) and 'front' (saying Grace). The (Euroamerican) minister is present, but very much off to one side.

This is at once a communal meal and a redistribution of 'shares' of meat.[13] The food itself is not distinguishable from daily fare as frequently occurs in hierarchical societies. There are no Iñupiaq equivalents to crackers, flaming plum pudding, silly hats, or *haute cuisine*. Nor is the feast marked by a superabundance of daily food as is common in less differentiated groups (cf. Goody 1982). The food is scrupulously divided according to rule; participants cannot 'go back for more' as it were. But nor should they simply come to pick up their share and go home. The point is not to eat a lot, but to eat some of everything. In other contexts it was made clear to me that animals are thought to have intent, to give themselves up to hunters through their wives who generously share the meat they have received, thus acting as 'good hosts'. Part of this meal is to show hospitality and therefore respect to all the animals upon whom human hunters depend for human sustenance. Whereas, taking again from Leach (1968), some communicative events clarify and separate roles, the overriding expression of this particular event fuses many of the boundaries that separate and define Iñupiaq existence. The setting is in the church, but unlike those who attend the morning service, the participants do not form a congregation—Christians and non-Christians attend. The whaling captains provide the meat, but, in contrast to *Nalukataq*, take no further visible part in the proceedings. The food comes from the land and the sea and has been caught in all seasons, served by men and women who have been recruited neither by virtue of marriage, kinship, nor whale crew membership.[14] People may sit with relatives, but they eat together.

## The Christmas dance

After the feast people return home for a few hours' rest. Later that evening they gather in the community centre to Eskimo Dance, or *aggi-*. The musicians form two rows. Men, who will drum and sing, sit in front; the women, who sing, sit behind them. Chairs for the elders are placed along the other walls; everyone else sits on the floor or clusters near the doorway, leaving the centre of the floor open for the dancers.

The musicians chat quietly as the people begin to file in, the men tapping softly on the wooden drum rims with long, pliable drumsticks. When the drummers decide that enough people have appeared, the evening begins. An Eskimo Dance includes three kinds of dances, performed in the same order. 'Fun dances' begin the evening. These depend on audience participation and involve dances for which the movements may be invented individually; often on the spot. 'Motion dances' follow; these tell a story and involve the exact duplication of movements created by the original inventor of the dance. These may be performed by anyone who knows them, but the 'stars' of this portion of the evening are the Barrow Dancers. This is a group that meets regularly to practice and that often performs at interregional 'Alaska Native' events such as the Alaskan Federation of Natives (AFN) Annual Conference, or the Eskimo/Indian Summer Olympics. After another period of fun dances, the evening is brought to a close by a 'welcome' or invitational dance during which virtually the entire audience joins in for the final few moments.

Each of these types of dances 'says' different things. The songs for 'fun dances' generally belong to individuals, or, by extension, to families. 'Owning' in this instance usually means having the right to dance to them in public performance, and having the right to teach them to others.[15] The drummers begin the evening by drumming and singing someone's family song. If no one gets up to dance, they sit for a bit, tapping softly on the drum rims as before. Suddenly the beat strengthens and another song is sung. Eventually someone (either man or woman, but always adult) will get up to dance and the evening gets under way in earnest. The music follows the same pattern throughout. The song is sung four times, alternating in intensity between soft and resounding; the motions of the dancers likewise alternate understatement with drama. During the first round, the person who has stood up to dance will be joined by people who feel closely connected— children, siblings, spouses, namesakes. During the second half, the group in the centre is augmented by others who wish to recognize some connection with them and join in.

Women dance with both feet firmly on the ground; when they move, it is with small shuffling steps. Their expressiveness comes through the grace and wit of upper body and hand motions, although for the most part, hands and face are angled towards the floor. Men, on the other hand, move across the floor with a strong, light-footed stamp and much of their hand and face movements are up. Confident dancers —both men and women—often 'converse' through their motions, composing jokes which delight dancers and audience alike.

Once the evening has started, a person may *kimi-*, that is, show that he or she wants to do their family dance by walking out to the middle of the room and standing in front of the drummers. Occasionally someone will cross the room to give a gift—usually a pair of gloves —to someone else, which 'forces' the recipient to join the giver in a dance. This is *maglak-* (which literally means, to welcome) and in earlier times was frequently done during *kakummisaaq*, a giveaway feast. As Uyagaluk (a Point Hope elder) remembered from his youth, this event took place in midwinter, 'when the days were just beginning to get longer and longer . . .'. After 'those-with-beards' and 'those-with-no-beards' ritually fed each other, husbands and wives would *kimi-* and 'give things away'. Recipients included namesakes, the namesakes of a deceased spouse, and the relatives of those namesakes. 'When those ones to whom gifts were given all come front to join in the dancing, they would [be so many that there would be] no more room to dance in. . . . This is the time when we really finally got some Christmas presents . . . !'[16] Today such gifts are rare, although handing someone a pair of gloves continues to be exercised as a strategy to bring a reluctant dancer out onto the floor.

This portion of the dance is definitely about the importance of having 'relatives', but it is not about 'families' as domestic groups. By watching who dances with whom, one would not learn very much about residence patterns. One would learn quite a bit about strategies for claiming relatedness (and occasionally, strategies for rejecting such claims). Because of the multiplicity of ways in which relatedness may be established, the 'right' to dance with any group is almost entirely a matter of personal choice. Some people almost never sit down from beginning to end; others venture out onto the floor on a few carefully selected occasions. The more powerful families will have many more joiners than the less powerful ones. One can easily tell which family 'has the floor', as it were, but the map that is drawn reveals more about politics than kinship.

At some point, after low-voiced consultation amongst themselves, the drummers shift to motion dances. These dances are different from the preceding ones, not only because the movements have been passed down, but because the motions as well as the song itself tell stories —about hunting, travelling, meeting new people, dealing with new situations.[17] One or two of the musicians (all members of the Barrow Dancers) who are known for their skill may come forward, signalling the shift. These dances are performances in every sense of the word. The audience pays careful attention to every movement, responding to subtle visual jokes with laughter and applause. A particularly satisfying performance is often repeated. After a while younger members of The Dancers perform the dances they have been practising for months. The movements are intricate, elaborate, choreographed. The dancers themselves wear matching 'snowshirts' (loose-fitting overblouses) and skin boots, beautifully decorated with beadwork. The Dancers are a relatively new group, founded through the Community Education Program primarily to encourage young people to learn their traditional dances. It has enjoyed significant and increasing popularity amongst adolescents and their performances are warmly appreciated by the audience.

The mood shifts again and more fun dances are introduced. This may go on as long as audience enthusiasm is high and the singers' voices hold out. At the close of the evening, the drummers signify the last, invitational, dance by holding their drums above their heads as they beat the song. The floor becomes a seething mass of movement and the evening draws to a close.

The fun dances are a statement of individuality: each dancer creates his or her own motions; they are as well a statement about social connections between individuals who see themselves as related: a person's choice of when to go out onto the floor makes in effect a public statement of connection with the other dancers. The motion dances, on the other hand, are neither individualistic nor kinship-related forms of expression. Instead they tell stories about being Iñupiaq. The final dance disregards all group distinctions and is, quite explicitly, a dance 'for everyone'; it is the 'welcome dance' which is very much to rather than about the animals and their social relations with the human world.

### The games

26 December marks the beginning of 'the games'. For a week, children compete against members of their age group during the day and adults take centre stage in the evening. The children's games are 'imported': three-legged races, wheelbarrow races, potato-sack races, and so forth. Individual children are winners; their prize is money.

Adult games are markedly different; they are traditional tests and exhibitions of strength, co-ordination, endurance, and will-power— all skills that Iñupiaq women and men need to survive in an unpredict-able arctic environment—and also skills that both Iñupiaq women and men look for in considering a potential spouse. Some games, such as the 'finger pull' pit one person against another; others, such as the high kick, allow an individual to test him or herself against others' achievements; still others require teamwork.

Although the games in their present form were introduced by Mothers' Clubs only a few decades ago and today are overseen by the Barrow City Council's Recreation Department, the presence of similar activities during this time of year goes back much further. *Kaiviuniq* was customarily an extended period of competitive games which took place between the time when women had finished their winter sewing and the time during which it was taboo to sew. This 'time-to-quit-sewing' began as the returning light allowed the hunters to start hunt-ing again (early January).[18]

Each evening is divided into two parts. For the first few hours individuals compete within their age group for individual prizes. The groups begin with the '21 to 30s' and end with the 'over 60s'. Members of this last group, who no longer have the strength to compete in the subsequent games, nevertheless are able to perform feats which few readers of this paper (regardless of their ages) would be able to achieve. Each event has a 'winner'; as with the youngsters' games, the prize is money. The remainder of the evening is spent in an ongoing competition which pits 'marrieds' against 'singles'. Men and women conduct separate competitions which occur simultaneously and in the same space. The winning side is not announced until the final night and the only 'prize' is that this side can choose the first game to begin the competition the following year.

There is a general 'menu' of games with which people are familiar;[19] the winning side for any event chooses the subsequent one. It is a strategic moment since each side clearly has people who are more skilled at certain things than others; decisions are made by joint consultation with anyone who wants to join in the discussion. The players are any members of the audience who wish to participate (and anyone present—Iñupiaq or non-Iñupiaq—is put under a certain amount of pressure to do so). Although the games themselves are separated by sex, the audience is not. People sit with friends and family, often moving about during the course of the evening to visit with others, to buy 'pop' and Eskimo doughnuts, or to step out into the arctic night for a quick cigarette. The atmosphere in the hall is easy and unhurried, a contrast to the gritted-teeth determination of the competitors in the centre of the room.

The process of choosing the first contest may take from a few minutes to half an hour or more; it is made in a series of conversations with several people who are of the 'right' marital status. An outsider walking in would find several hundred people sitting four or five deep around the room, 'nothing' apparently happening. Finally a woman (or a man) walks out and sits in the middle of the floor; her challenger, after a whispered conversation which verifies the choice of game, walks out and sits opposite her. If the game sets individual against individual (various kinds of wrestling, finger pulls, arm pulls, and the like), the winner must prevail in two out of three tries. She then remains on the floor, awaiting another challenger. This continues until no one in the audience left unbeaten is willing to take up the challenge. Games in which individuals must pit themselves against the records of others (such as the high kick) are organized slightly differently. There are no restrictions on the number of attempts any individual may make; nor is there a time limit for the duration of the particular game. The only one who decides whether or not to continue the endeavour is the individual involved. When at last no more challengers are forthcoming, the marital status of the remaining man or woman determines whether the 'singles' or the 'marrieds' are the winner of this round.

There are a number of strategic choices to be made during the course of these events: if the singles choose a game they know they can win, they will then have the advantage of choosing the next game; once a game has been chosen, it is a matter of strategy when a side's strongest member should take up the challenge. If she (or he) goes out too early, for instance, she will inevitably be tired out and beaten by a long succession of challengers; if she waits too long, team-mates may strain muscles better used for other events in which they perform more successfully. Once a challenge has been won, it behoves the other side to produce another challenger quickly, before the winner has a chance to rest. Often weaker competitors will 'sacrifice' themselves at such a moment to keep the challenge going until a stronger contestant comes forward. These decisions are made without a captain and, except for the choice of game, without strategic 'huddles'. Older people may occasionally call out to correct a hold that they see is being done incorrectly; friends (who may well be on the opposing side) may 'coach' a contestant who is trying to break a record but otherwise there is no 'direction'. No one is watching the clock or organizing activity. There are no 'referees'.[20]

The games continue every night until the early hours of the morning. People drift in and out during the course of the evening, but there is a certain amount of feeling that it is not 'right' not to come every day. Part of the challenge is to put one's tired muscles to yet another test on the last days of the week; taking a rest for a day or two in the middle of the week is seen as a mild form of cheating. On New Year's Eve the games resume at midnight in order to let those who wish to attend church. At twelve the climactic twenty-four hour stint begins, concluded the following evening with another Eskimo Dance.

The games 'do' several things. In his discussion of Apache joking, Keith Basso (1979: 37) defines 'play' as those [acts] which are modelled on acts that are "not play" but which are understood not to communicate what would be communicated by these acts if they were performed unplayfully'. Iñupiaq ideology is explicit about the importance of co-operation and hospitable sociability; successful hunting is contingent on the maintenance of warm social interaction; animals come to those who are generous, kind, and thoughtful to others; in

Patrick Attungana's (1986) words 'to those who are good hosts'.[21] At the same time, however, competition is keen. According to Raymond Neakok, Sr. (Bodenhorn 1988*b*), 'competition has always been there with us' as a way of testing individual skill. The display of physical prowess (rather than fisticuffs) has also long been one way of settling disputes.[22] Here competition is publicly sanctioned, but its potentially unacceptable aggressive content is contained. These are not 'really' competitive acts because they are games. Team membership cuts across those social groups that in daily life may find themselves in competing situations: marrieds and singles include all possible combinations of family, crew, or political faction membership. Competition is possible without the real-life consequences of same. It is further set off on either end by Eskimo Dancing.

Just as the motion dances tell stories about 'being Iñupiaq', so, in other ways, do these games communicate about desirable Iñupiaq characteristics—strength, determination, and co-ordination. For singles, in fact, it is an opportunity to show exactly how desirable they are. The games provide a 'population map' of the community: by age, sex, marital status. It is a public statement, as it were, of who is where at the moment in relation to these very large categories. They say nothing about who is related to whom, who is living with whom, or who is fighting with whom. Finally, this is an event which, like the Eskimo Dances, happens within an Iñupiaq frame of rhythm and tempo. It allows for spaces and silences, for things to happen as they unfold and for an unhurried shaping of events so often lacking in Iñupiaq/*tanik* (white) interactions.

## The New Year's Dance

The final Eskimo Dance on New Year's Night follows essentially the same pattern as that described earlier. The one major difference is the performance of *Kalukaq*—a portion of the Eagle-Wolf Dance which used to last for days—a motion dance which takes up a large part of the evening. A large rectangular wooden box is suspended from the middle of the ceiling. It is left undisturbed during the fun dances; when one of the younger Barrow Dancers begins to beat it, the drum resonates and a hush falls throughout the hall. The beat of the drum is meant to resemble the heartbeat of the Mother Eagle who has lost her son to an Iñupiaq hunter. The dancers move onto the floor in procession; they wear head-dresses representing the eagle and the other spirits who have instructed the hunter how to return the slain eagle's soul to the mother and how to conduct ceremonial feasts for the animals. The processional is followed by a series of rapid, dramatic performances by pairs of dancers. Although Oquilluk (1981) clearly sets out the legend behind and the content of the Eagle-Wolf Dance, the meaning of the dance was something people in the audience 'didn't know'. Iñupiaq elders' discussion of this same feast (North Slope Borough 1981) dealt with the trading aspect, the mock battles of individuals from different communities, and the welcome dance. All mention of spirit representations was avoided. The performance of the dance, however, is keenly anticipated. *Kalukaq* is the only motion dance to be performed. After more fun dances, the final welcome dance brings the evening and the week's festivities to a close.

## Discussion

In part, these conclusions are unabashedly functionalist. Christmas in Barrow is popular and well-attended because it makes people feel good. People *like* to gather, eat, dance, play, and be merry. '*Arigaa*,' I often heard, 'it's good to do this during the dark days!' The sociological indicators are that it really 'does' what it is 'supposed' to do. In contrast to the pattern of increased social tensions found in so many places— *Weihnachtscholer* (Christmas unhappiness) as it is called in Switzerland —Barrow residents seem to feel the opposite. The numbers of alcohol-related arrests fall; the Arctic Women in Crisis Shelter has fewer emergency visits and the Children's Receiving Home must take fewer calls in the middle of the night.

You cannot drink and play a game that demands you balance on one hand and one foot, hop up, and kick a ball of caribou skin which is dangling above your head. To compete, you must be sober. If you are noticeably intoxicated, you are escorted off the floor. The question is, what is it about this entire week of events that makes them more attractive than 'going out to party', which may be a preferred activity for many during much of the year? In part, to add psychology to functionalism, I would suggest that while Christmas in Barrow is as much about cultural 'oughts' as it is elsewhere, the pressure to live up to the 'ought' is less intensely placed on individuals. In Boston, Zurich, or London, the pressure is to 'be' a happy (nuclear) family. The responsibility for producing this phenomenon often lands on a few individuals who must purchase the presents, provide the meal, the decorations, and the 'family feeling'. Parents, children, and siblings who might otherwise not choose to spend their time together are expected to gather and enjoy themselves. Tensions often run high, simmering resentments explode, doors are slammed, and tears are shed. Real violence is not uncommon. In contrast, no one individual is responsible for producing the 'proper' Christmas spirit in Barrow. The events themselves are fluid; people may choose when, where, and how to participate (or whether to participate at all). Rather than denying the existence of aggressive feelings, they may be contained in the performance of dances and games.

I have argued elsewhere (Bodenhorn forthcoming) that community in Barrow is a process of participation. People who take part do so because they feel a part of the community; by doing so, they are perceived by others in fact to be so. Christmas provides, I think, an excellent example of this. The conflicting demands of kinship obligations are potential sources of very real tension in Barrow as well as Birmingham, but they are not brought to the fore during this very public time.

Thus far we have talked about what Christmas 'does'; it is equally important to look at what it 'says'. It is relevant here to consider the distinction between community events and events that celebrate community. Basketball games and the 4th of July are community events. They are very well attended indeed, but are marked neither by communal feasting, nor by Eskimo dancing. The importance of communal feasting cannot be emphasized enough. It first and foremost maintains the proper relations with whales—whales who 'give themselves to *all* the people' and who, by being shared by all the people, feel welcome and wish to return. Dancing is also an opportunity to welcome animals as well as humans. Both activities explicitly include social relations which extend beyond 'relatives'.

Here perhaps Lévi-Strauss's (1966: 30–3) discussion of the difference between 'games' and 'rites' is useful to think with. Games, he suggests, follow rules—structure—but the outcome is open—contingent. They have a 'disjunctive' effect by creating 'winners' and 'losers' out of initially equal players; asymmetry is thus generated out of symmetry. Ritual, on the other hand, likewise operates according to rules, but they are ones in which the outcome is fixed. Ritual begins with asymmetrical relations (between sacred and profane; living and dead); the result is to bring them into symmetry, 'for all to pass to the winning side' (ibid. 32). Game-like activities may themselves be ritual, argues Lévi-Strauss, if, as with Fox adoption 'games', the 'winning side' is predetermined, thus eliminating all contingent aspects.

The week's events in Barrow are at once similar and different to this model. The games do indeed culminate in a division of participants into winners and losers which is in no way predetermined. They are definitely contingent, not only in outcome, but in conduct. What games are chosen, who participates, when and how long they are played are as open as the final score. What is not contingent is the place of the games within the entire week's activity, for they are inevitably bounded on either side by an Eskimo Dance. The form of an Eskimo Dance likewise includes open-ended possibilities and closure; neither fun dances nor motion dances are constrained by what Bloch, or indeed Lévi-Strauss, might call the limited vocabulary of ritual practice. Both are subject to individual invention and the introduction of new elements. But they do follow each other in a certain order and the evening always finishes with the welcome dance, which blurs all divisions. And here Leach's insistence on the importance of ambiguity in symbolic action is key. God (for those who are believers), animals (likewise), and humans are indeed 'all brought onto the winning side'. The disparate gathering of people who make up the 'community' of Barrow may all take part—and do.

The singing, feasting, dancing, and playing, however, are not simply about community but are also conversations about being an Iñupiaq adult with all of the connections that generates. The connection between being Iñupiaq—a real person (*iñuk*/person + *piaq*/genuine) and eating *niqipiaq*—real, or hunted, food—is profound and is often stated as an equivalence: 'I'm Iñupiaq; I eat Iñupiaq food'. The feast is a pure statement of that connection. In that people create their own movements during fun dances, and prove themselves in individual tests of strength, this conversation concerns individual skill, prowess, and inventiveness. In that the food distribution is explicitly determined by who eats together, at least some domestic relations are highlighted.[23] In so far as people sit with relatives during each of the events and dance with relatives again during the fun dances (and they generally, but not always, do), the conversation is a public statement of who considers themselves related to whom. To the extent that people feast together by eating a portion of their domestically defined 'share', 'family' is incorporated into 'group'; during the welcome dances, 'family' dissolves entirely as a meaningful category; the welcome extends from 'everyone' to 'everyone'. As the parameters of the games are defined along the axes of age, sex, and marital status, so this conversation is as well about categories that extend beyond both individual and kin. In this, as in other Iñupiaq contexts, the categories may be clear, but the boundaries are not fixed. The conversation may well say, 'we who participate are members of the community', but only on rare occasions does that message include an implicit 'and you, outsider, should not join in'. Anyone who shows up at the church is entitled to a share; all members of the audience are recruited for the games (particularly so if a visitor is strong or adept); at the raising of the drums, everyone is urged to join in the final invitational. The events are inclusive rather than exclusive; what they are not are spectacles; it is this participatory quality that makes them truly 'conversations'— conversations about 'self', about 'us', about 'other'.

Clearly what a lot of this is 'about' is continuity with pre-Christian customary practice. Throughout the chapter I have tried to point out various ways in which the feasting, games, and dancing reflect 'old' custom incorporated into present practice. One might well feel that 'Christmas' was merely an add-on, tacked onto the beginning of already existing midwinter festivities—incorporated by them rather than incorporating them into the Christmas celebration itself. Equally clearly, however, the historical developments over this past century have had profound, not surface, effects. Conversion to Christianity was genuine at the turn of the century and continues to be of central importance to many people today. The suppression of shamanic practices may have been an attempt to rid people of 'pagan' beliefs on the part of missionaries, but Iñupiaq willingness to shed such practices may have had more to do with the politics of shamanism than anything else. With the exception of the feast (which was taken out of the *qargich* and brought into the churches), the events discussed in these pages have all been reintroduced. Although they may be saying some old things, the context is new. The context is not about oppositions— community versus family, individual versus group, or even Christian versus non-Christian—so much as it is about process.

Miller suggests in the introduction to this volume that Christmas on the North Slope resembles the festival 'which integrates sociality with cosmology'. To a significant degree this is true. But it is equally true of all the other celebratory events which use the metaphor of whale/human interdependence to talk about social relations in general —*Nalukataq* being the most important of these. Significantly, the other time of year when social stress indicators drop is during spring whaling. But this view ignores the political implications of the reinvention of *Iñupiaq* Christmas. Even though the cultural 'ought' of community solidarity is an idealization—even though politics-as-usual is intense and often splits Barrow into several bitterly opposed factions—this is also a time that is undeniably Iñupiaq. In an ironic twist, this Christmas statement of self, of identity, is most pleasurably experienced when the 'other'—teachers, hospital staff, consultants, and the like—for the most part has departed for Christmas vacation. In January people will once again show up for work at 9.00 a.m., fill out report forms in triplicate and in English, take a coffee break at 10.30 and leave at 5.00 sharp. For the moment, the series of acts involving all the senses—eating, singing, dancing, playing—which combine to *be* as well as to express Iñupiaqness may be conducted on Iñupiaq terms, in Iñupiaq rhythms, and in Iñupiaq idiom.

## Notes

1  Iñupiat are one of the circumpolar peoples historically known by Euroamericans as 'Eskimo'. The term itself means 'genuine people'. The singular, as well as the adjectival form, is Iñupiaq. In 1978, the Inuit Circumpolar Conference resolved that the most appropriate umbrella term should be Inuit, which I am happy to use. It should perhaps be noted, however, that on the North Coast of Alaska, 'inuit' simply means 'people' and that 'Eskimo' continues to be used frequently by Iñupiat when talking to themselves about themselves: the Alaska Eskimo Whaling Commission, for instance, was founded shortly after the resolution was passed. The word itself is somewhat problematic in that it does not reflect the languages of Greenlanders (Kalaalimiut), the Yup'it peoples of South-west Alaska, the Siberian Yup'it of Saint Lawrence Island, or of Siberia. That being said, 'Eskimo' is even more troublesome with its multiple 'othered' origins (Amerindian, French, English), all of which carry negative connotations.

2  What I learned on the North Slope was made possible in the first instance by my attachment to the Iñupiat Community of the Arctic Slope between 1980 and 1983 as well as by fieldwork support between 1984 and 1986 from the Alaska Humanities Forum and the North Slope Borough Commission on Iñupiaq History, Language, and Culture. For material discussed in this chapter I am particularly indebted to Ernie Frankson and the Barrow Dancers, with whom anyone from the community was allowed to practice as part of the Community Education programme and from whom I learned what it feels like to dance the motion dances. Mattie Bodfish, Edith Nashoalook, Arthur Neakok, Raymond and Marie Neakok, and Melba Collette not only taught me about the games and the dances, but made sure that I took part. In Cambridge, Gilbert Lewis and Caroline Humphrey made useful comments on a much earlier version of this paper;

Simon Coleman, James Laidlaw, and Daniel Miller have all had a direct impact on the outcome of the present version.

3 Sheldon Jackson divided up the Alaskan missionary pie, allocating different denominations to different regions in the late nineteenth century. The Presbyterians 'got' the northern coast, the Catholics received large chunks of the Athapaskan interior, while the Friends (Quakers) were assigned the North-western territory around what is today Kotzebue.

4 In this case, 'family units' might include any combination of parents and children, siblings, a marital couple, cousins, in-laws, grandparents, and so forth.

5 Unlike many examples of ceremonially elaborated exchange, Messenger Feasts were not opportunities to give ('maximize outgoings' according to Gregory 1982), but to receive. The host, on sending an invitation—by messenger, hence the name—to one or more trading partners, would include a list of 'gifts' to be brought to the feast. Trading partners were never related, virtually always lived in separate eco-zones, and therefore often requested resources not available in the host's territory. In turn, of course, the guests would become hosts, sending out wish lists of their own. The relationship was conceived of as one between equals and if balanced reciprocity could not be maintained over time, the partnership withered (Burch 1988).

6 For a variety of reasons, early Iñupiaq/European relations were definitely not one-sided. Iñupiat controlled a number of scarce resources—food, clothing, skilled labour—upon which the European travellers were dependent. As long as local food resources were sufficient to supply local needs, Iñupiat were trading staples needed by the Europeans for luxury goods. They were well aware that this put them into a potentially advantageous position (see e.g. Bockstoce 1987).

7 This was in part, but not uniquely, due to overhunting by crew-members of Euroamerican ships.

8 Stefansson (1913), Brower (n.d.), Oquilluk (1981), and a number of today's elders are in agreement on this, both in terms of abuses of power, and in the attraction of seemingly stronger taboos. 'Who ever thought of making a whole day taboo,' one man was said to exclaim in relation to Sunday practices (Stefansson 1913: 412–13).

9 Mothers' Clubs were initially started by missionaries' wives in a number of villages across the Slope. They began as an attempt to educate women about necessary practices to avoid the spread of tuberculosis, which was a serious danger to community health. Many expanded to become very active, Iñupiat-run organizations involved in any number of community-oriented activities.

10 Feasts take place in both the Presbyterian and the Assembly of God Churches. As the family for whom I was 'a kid of some sort' participated

in the Presbyterian Feast, this description is based entirely on what happens there.

11  In Iñupiaq English, 'subsistence' signifies the entire complex of activities connected with hunting and gathering. It has nothing to do with providing for one's minimum needs.

12  'Shares' may be distinguished from 'sharing' in Iñupiaq distribution practices. The former refers to a specific portion of food to which the recipient is entitled. The giver is not free to decide whether or not to give someone a share (*ningik*). With the exception of these communal feasts during which all participants have the right to a share, shares are earned through participation in the hunt in some form. Sharing is much closer to Sahlins's (1972) definition of generalized reciprocity and is not earned, but rather given. See Bodenhorn (1988*a*, 1990) for a more detailed discussion of this.

13  Whales, which may produce as much as sixty tons of edible meat, are subject to extremely elaborate rules of division and distribution. Any crew helping to bring the whale into shore, pull it up on the ice, butcher, or transport it back to the village earns a share of the meat. The captain and the harpooner of each crew respectively earn a proportionately larger share than the rest of the crew. Half of the captain's share must be distributed at communal feasts and all of the captain's share must be distributed before the crew ventures out on the ice in the next season.

14  Again this differs from *Nalukataq*, the spring whaling festival, when those who provide and serve the food are directly connected to the whale crew whose feast it is.

15  This form of ownership resembles the practice of a number of hunting societies. Fred Myers (1989) discusses how ownership claims in Arnham Land are increased by giving away ritual knowledge in connection with sacred sites. The more you give away, the more you 'hold the country'. People in Barrow and Wainwright (one of the nearest villages) were by no means unanimous in relation to how this worked for them. Some people said that songs (which are in fact the essence of the dances) were handed down to individuals of one's choice; others said, nonsense, if you see a dance you like, you can learn it, and dance it. The system is by no means as strict as it is among most of the Northwest Coast societies.

16  *Puiguitkaat*, a transcript of the 1978 Elders' Conference convened by the North Slope Borough Iñupiaq History, Language, and Culture Commission (1981: 546–53).

17  There is by no means a 'fixed universe' of motion dances. Existing dances 'should' be passed on accurately, but new ones are continually being invented. Subjects include experiences with the Armed Services and with airplanes as well as thrusting harpoons into walruses or whales.

18  See *Puiguitkaat* (North Slope Borough 1981) for more detailed descriptions of these and other midwinter events.

19 During my last Christmas Games (1985), there was literally a menu: a two-page list of names of games. As far as I know, this is only to help, not to restrict. I have certainly seen people consult about choosing a game they remember only slightly, consult further to reconstruct the rules, and then explain it to the opposing side.

20 Members of the Barrow Recreation Committee are present and do in fact record the score of each round; their only refereeing activity, however, is to escort intoxicated people off the floor.

21 Attungana, in his 1986 Address to the Alaska Eskimo Whaling Commission, was referring explicitly to what makes whales decide 'to camp'— i.e. to give themselves up to a particular crew. A whale feels its soul to be hospitably welcomed when its meat is shared 'with everyone'. The 'good hosts' responsible for this are the whaling captain and his wife.

22 See Burch and Correll (1971) for a number of case-study examples.

23 This is slightly problematic since Iñupiat who eat together may not necessarily sleep in the same house. The only 'fixed' members of a single household are a married couple.

# References

ATTUNGANA, P. (1986). 'Address to the Alaskan Eskimo Whaling Commission', trans. J. Nageak, *Uiñiq: The Open Lead*, 1/2: 16 ff.

BASSO, K. (1979). *Portraits of 'The Whiteman'*. Cambridge: Cambridge University Press.

BOCKSTOCE, J. R. (1986). *Whales, Ice and Men*. Seattle: University of Washington Press.

BODENHORN, B. (1988*a*). 'Whales, Souls, Children and Other Things that are Good to Share: Core Metaphors on the North Slope of Alaska', *Cambridge Anthropology*, 13/4: 1–18.

—— (1988*b*). 'Documenting Iñupiaq Family Relationships in Changing Times', report prepared for the North Slope Borough Iñupiaq History, Language and Culture Commission. Barrow, Alas.

—— (1990). ' "I'm not the Great Hunter, my Wife is": Iñupiat and Anthropological Models of Gender', *Études/Inuit/Studies*, 14/1–2: 55–74.

—— (forthcoming). 'Public and Private on the North Slope of Alaska', in B. Bender (ed.), *Political Landscapes*. Oxford: Berg Press.

BROWER, C. D. (n.d.). 'Diaries' from *c*.1889–1927, Fairbanks, University of Alaska Archives.

BURCH, E. S., Jr. (1988). 'Modes of Exchange in Northwest Alaska', in T. Ingold, D. Riches, and J. Woodburn (eds.), *Hunters and Gatherers*, ii: *Property, Power and Ideology*. Oxford: Berg Press: 95–109.

—— and CORRELL, T. (1971). 'Alliance and Conflict: Inter-regional

Relations', in L. Guemple (ed.), *Alliance in Eskimo Society: Proceedings of the American Ethnological Society*. Seattle: University of Washington Press.

GOODY, J. R. (1982). *Cooking, Cuisine and Class*. Cambridge: Cambridge University Press.

GREGORY, C. (1982). *Gifts and Commodities*. London: Academic Press.

LEACH, E. (1968). 'Ritual', *International Encyclopedia of the Social Sciences*, xiii. Crowell: Collier & Macmillan: 520–6.

LÉVI-STRAUSS, C. (1966). 'The Science of the Concrete', in *The Savage Mind*. London: Weidenfeld & Nicolson (1st edn. 1962).

MAUSS, M. (1979). *Seasonal Variations of the Eskimo: A Study in Social Morphology*, trans. J. J. Fox. London: Routledge & Kegan Paul (1st edn. 1904).

MYERS, F. (1989). 'Burning the Truck and Holding the Country', in E. N. Wilmsen (ed.), *We are Here: Politics of Aboriginal Land Tenure*. Berkeley, Calif.: University of California Press.

North Slope Borough (1981). *Puiguitkaat: Transcript of the 1978 Elders' Conference*, trans. Leona Okakok. Barrow, Alas.

OQUILLUK, W. A. (1981). *People of Kauwerak: Legends of the Northwest Alaskan Eskimo*. Anchorage: Alaska Pacific University Press.

SAHLINS, M. (1972). 'Towards a Sociology of Primitive Exchange', in *Stone Age Economics*. Chicago: Aldine Atherton.

STEFANSSON, V. (1913). *My Life with the Eskimo*. New York: Macmillan.

# 10

# The Great Christmas Quarrel and Other Swedish Traditions

*Orvar Löfgren*

## The Moral Economy of Christmas

'I don't think I have been genuinely happy at Christmas since I was a child. What's wrong?'

'My family doesn't seem to notice all that I do for Christmas. Why can't they be more appreciative?'

'My wife and I often fight over money at Christmas. What should we do?'

These and many other laments over the shortcomings of Christmas come from readers' queries published in the new, updated handbook *Unplug the Christmas Machine: A Complete Guide to Putting Love and Joy Back into the Season* (Robinson and Staeheli 1991).

The authors of this counselling manual provide training programmes and an abundance of practical hints for creating what they see as a more authentic, more spiritual, and simpler Christmas, from rating family fun activities to recipes for low-fat desserts. Their guide to holiday enrichment can be read as a piece of 1980s Americana, but it also echoes the kind of anger and anxiety which confronted me as I was sifting through a large body of interview material on Swedish Christmas celebrations, past and present.

At first glance these interviews seemed to deal with very concrete matters: the informants described in minute detail their childhood Christmases, whether in a farm household at the turn of the century or in a teacher's home during the turbulent 1960s, or they simply presented their recollections of last year's celebrations. The texts were packed with information—how to dress the Christmas tree, what to put on the table or into the stockings—but they also dealt with frustrations about rules and traditions being abused or ignored by others.

After a while I got the feeling that all these recollections really were about something else, something more important: dreams of family togetherness or frustrations over generation conflicts, hope for the future or longing for a nostalgic past, reflections on how life has turned out and what it could have been like.

The life histories suggested an alternative reading of Swedish Christmas celebrations, as a cultural prism which enlarges or rather concentrates conflicts, utopias, and ideals of family life, which may otherwise lie hidden or forgotten in the humdrum of everyday life. That is why even seemingly trivial details can acquire a strong symbolic or emotional power, and also why the Christmas quarrel has become a tradition in twentieth-century celebrations. Christmas brings a moral economy in which expectations and obligations, demands and wishes are confronted in ways that are difficult to reconcile, and although Christmas is a festival of fun and mirth, it is also a festival that is taken in dead earnest. It is certainly no laughing matter.

It is this perspective on the tensions in twentieth-century Swedish Christmas celebrations that I will explore here, using diverse kinds of evidence, from life histories to mass media material.[1]

Outside observers are often amazed at the ferocious energy with which Swedes celebrate this holiday, and the amount of time, money, and emotional energy invested in it. Swedish Christmas festivities tend to be both longer and more elaborate than in many other national settings. Throughout December a number of pre-Christmas rituals and festivities prepare the ground. Every Sunday a new advent candle is lit; every morning the children open a window in the advent calendar; on the 13th there are Lucia celebrations at school, at work, and at home. Pre-Christmas parties are arranged with neighbours and work-mates, and so on.

'The real Christmas' starts on Christmas Eve, which is the high point of the holiday. Christmas dinner is eaten and Santa Claus (known in Swedish as the Christmas gnome) arrives in the evening to distribute presents. From then on celebrations continue well into the New Year. Schoolchildren have a three-week holiday and most adults take two weeks off work in order to get down to some serious merry-making.

There was a time when both scholars and mass media devoted a great deal of energy to deconstructing what were then commonly believed to be truly Swedish traditions. It was revealed that the Christmas tree had been imported from Germany, the idea of stockings from England, and that most peasant traditions were really late bourgeois innovations (see Daniel Miller's introduction). This kind of policing of authenticity, however, tends to miss an important point: the ways in which all kinds of cosmopolitan elements take on a very local flavour. Swedish Christmas celebrations reflect in a condensed form some basic themes and contradictions in Swedish society; some of these may be shared on a national level, while others mirror different social settings and generations.

The Swedish Christmas is thus both a modern utopia and a battle-field. Every year the Christmas person is reborn, more sensual and perhaps even more childish, able to stoop to doing things that would be inconceivable in everyday life. People overeat and overspend. Gentlemen in pin-striped suits lovingly arrange skating gnomes on a piece of reflecting glass or decorate gingerbread houses, while their wives—stressed working housewives—stuff home-made sausages and make wreaths of cowberry sprigs. But Christmas is also the dream of the good person and the happy family: a utopia of togetherness, gener-osity, warmth, and caring.

So much has to be squeezed into the busy days before Christmas, and the important hours from Christmas Eve to Christmas Day are often subjected to such acute cultural overload that they can produce family quarrels, mothers on the verge of tears, and hyperactive children.

Rather than studying Christmas as a bundle of traditions, it can be viewed as a scene on which moral dilemmas and cultural contradictions are acted out by people with widely varying experiences and expec-tations.

## *The Cultural Organization of Anticipation*

'November is such a long month. We can't wait for its last day because that's when Daddy comes home with the advent calendar.' These are the opening lines of a classic children's book from the 1940s, *Johan's Christmas*, which lovingly depicts the elaborate Christmas preparations in a middle-class Stockholm home. This constantly reprinted story reads as a detailed manual for the creation of a proper Christmas atmosphere: all the rituals and magic details needed to increase antici-pation day by day.

Every morning a new window in the calendar is opened, and in Johan's home even that minor event is turned into a family ritual: all through December the windows are opened by the children in order of age. They thus learn to wait, not only for the next window, but also for their turn. The same ritualized expectation surrounds the advent candles. Who will get to light the first of the four candles? When will it be lit? How long will it be allowed to burn? Down in the basement, hyacinth bulbs are planted, so that one can follow how new Christmas flowers burgeon each day.

Besides these rites of inspection, there is all the work that must be done in preparation for Christmas: the ceremonial cleaning, the baking, the cooking, practising Lucia songs and Christmas carols, Christmas preparations at school, evening ruminations about what presents to wish for, what presents to buy, how to wrap them in secret, and so on.

Johan's Christmas demonstrates the techniques by which waiting is transformed into expectation. All the pent-up Christmas spirit is released in a torrent on Christmas Eve: all the secrecy, all the forbidden sampling of Christmas food, all the safely concealed sweets and presents, all the tabooed attempts to start Christmas in advance. All this is overturned, as the doors are flung wide open. The expectations and promises can now be fulfilled!

In the making of the modern Swedish Christmas, the ritual of anticipation has swollen in significance. The spread of advent candles and advent calendars in the 1930s was later accompanied by radio and then television calendars for children. At a given moment, children all over Sweden now gather in front of the television to open today's window and to be reminded not to cheat by peeking in advance behind the biggest window, the one for the 24th.

Other rites of passage include the rapid expansion since the 1920s of Lucia celebrations, which have also become an export item in more recent years. White-clad, singing Lucias, with candles in their hair and coffee-pots in their hands, march not only through schools, factories, television shows, and old people's homes, but have also appeared on the cover of *Esquire* magazine (in the shape of Kim Basinger) and in Donald Duck comic books. (Lucia has even managed to squeeze herself into a recent survey of American Country Christmas traditions; see Emmerling and Mead 1989.)

In spite of all these pre-holiday festivities, the basic structure of the Swedish Christmas calls for a magic passage rite. It is on the morning of Christmas Eve that Christmas really starts. One of the interviewees summed it up in the term 'the magic wand effect': 'We save nearly everything until the evening before, so that the house is changed on Christmas Eve, as if by magic, with red curtains, candlelight, the works.' Another woman remembers how her mother achieved the great metamorphosis every year:

The weeks before Christmas were characterized by simplicity—the closer we came to Christmas, the simpler it got. Rugs and drapes disappeared, and then the copper utensils were stored away under a sheet in the attic while they were being polished. We would spend most of the last week in the kitchen. The dining room and the living room were closed off, and we felt the cold draught from the chink of the door when Mother sneaked in there carrying big boxes.

But then came the sumptuous spectacle of Christmas Morning, when the doors were thrown wide open! We went in our night-shirts from room to room, blissfully enraptured by the magical transformations. Nothing was the same. Everything shone in the light of the candles, festive and colourful; red rugs and drapes, gleaming brass, wall-hangings, spruce and pine twigs—and the most enchanting things!

Everywhere! Gnomes and angels and straw goats and Christmas scenes with little animals and sleighs and a church and angel chimes and . . . the joy just grew and grew!

The Christmas atmosphere thus rests on a solid foundation, the careful regulation of every detail, the forbidden and the permitted, which also meant the emergence of a number of taboos about the danger of anticipating Christmas, of opening one window too many, or sneaking a taste of the Christmas food. It is easy to wax ironic over the wealth of detail which people can allow themselves when listing all the things that were absolutely prohibited before Christmas Eve, but both the attention to detail and the moral indignation reveal that behind the rules there are more basic themes of life which are enacted on the Christmas stage.

The emphasis on preparations also creates a seedbed for the Christmas quarrel: preparations become demands, the things that must absolutely be done if the true Christmas atmosphere is to descend on the house on the 24th:

Then the moment arrives when you begin to panic at the thought that you won't have time to finish everything so that it will be a proper Christmas. What would it be like without curtains, or with just half of the windows cleaned, and all the tablecloths removed and the rugs rolled up and still to be beaten? And no Christmas presents ready! I haven't finished making the doily for Mother. I feel it in my bones that she will have a fit because it's too untidy and there's no Christmas atmosphere. Mother can feel things like that so well. She will think that her whole life is ruined, and Christmas too. I know that Father will try to keep the children's spirits up as far as possible, but deep inside he's sad. It shows in his eyes, as usual. He wants to give us children that Christmas peace that everyone preaches about at Christmas matins. In his childhood home there was peace both inside the house and in the barn from that moment on the day before Christmas Eve, when his father set up the Christmas sheaf for the birds in the tree outside the kitchen window. Then everything was ready. Even the birds knew that it was Christmas.

This is how Margareta Strömstedt describes Christmas nerves in her autobiographical novel *Julstädningen och döden* (Christmas Cleaning and Death). The demands about what is sufficiently clean for Christmas may have relaxed in recent decades, but other demands and expectations have increased.

## Constructing the Perfect Christmas

During the twentieth century the role of the mass media in celebrating Christmas has to some extent nationalized or homogenized the festive season. Already in the 1920s the public radio provided music for dancing round the Christmas tree on the evening of the 24th, making thousands of Swedes feel that they were joining a national event. The radio, and later on the television, has continued to provide such media arenas for expressions of a national, mass-mediated 'we', celebrating Christmas together.

Since the 1960s *the* most popular television programme of the year is an hour of Walt Disney cartoons shown in the afternoon on Christmas Eve. Attempts to change the content or the timing of this event have always met with storms of protest. Most Swedes have structured their celebrations around this media event—to miss the Disney show and the singalong with the Swedish voice-over to Jiminy Cricket's 'When You Wish upon a Star'—is to miss a sacred (and very Swedish) Christmas tradition.

The immense media output before and during Christmas has also created new parameters of comparison. In newspaper articles, magazine specials, in advertisements, in radio and television programmes, the concept of 'The Traditional Christmas' is elaborated and reified. Through this flood of images, ideas about what constitutes a 'normal' or an 'ideal' Christmas are developed.

An analysis of media material from the 1920s to the present shows a marked continuity on some levels. Media consumers are above all told two things: Christmas was better in the old days, and it should preferably be staged in a rural setting.

Media images are recycled in many of the Christmas interviews. A city girl from Southern Sweden exclaims: 'my dream is to go sleigh-riding to matins on Christmas morning', while a lawyer remembers his childhood manor-house holidays with the help of Ingmar Bergman: 'we used to have a real *Fanny and Alexander* Christmas'.

The media picture of Christmas was quick to take on a nostalgic tone, which made modern-day Christmas into a symbol of shallow vulgarization. Even back in the 1920s people wrote of how 'sleigh bells have been replaced by the angry hoots of cars and the commercial society symbolized by the tailor's dummy dressed in exclusive lingerie'. At the start of the 1970s, a woman's magazine commented: 'Perhaps we have to keep the television on all day to avoid discovering how little we have to say to each other.' Contrasted against such pictures of degeneration there are numerous variants of the genuine Christmas, epitomized in two main scenarios, Swedish peasant Christmas and Swedish manor-house Christmas. Notions of the traditional heritage were hereby cemented, particularly through advertising, which began at an early stage to market Christmas goods against a background of rural nostalgia.

A recurrent theme in media reports on twentieth-century Christmas is the triumph of tradition over modernity. In the 1920s and 1930s people anxiously wondered whether the old-fashioned Swedish Christmas celebrations would survive the new urban life. 'It is ridiculous to try to act the country household and have a traditional Christmas in a one-room flat in Stockholm,' said a newly-wed woman to the magazine reporter in 1937. Just one year later, however, she capitulated to the Christmas traditions.

A year later another reporter goes out to ask 'truly modern young couples' about their attitudes towards traditions. One of them gives the reassuring answer: 'We wanted to get rid of Christmas but it overpowered us.' The wife of a young avant-garde architect discloses that at Christmas she has opened the doors of their modernist home to tradition: 'We celebrate a truly barbarian Christmas, compared with our everyday modern life-style.'

As Swedish life was modernized and urbanized during the 1930s and 1940s, the ideal of a peasant Christmas invaded council estates and suburban homes. Just as the old peasants had saved a sheaf of oats for the birds, Christmas sheaves were posted on every balcony, and on the 24th the shining new laboratory kitchens were turned into farm interiors with copper kettles, wooden candlesticks, rustic hangings draped on the walls.

The Christmas special issue of magazines and Sunday papers

became an important instrument for the reproduction of tradition. They created a genre with strong continuity and a vocabulary of its own: the grinning gnomes, the gleaming candles, the sparkling eyes of the children. A reporter from a daily newspaper noted in one of the interviews that she could not think of a single idea in that year's Christmas supplement which had not been used before. One of the recurrent themes is the exhortation to celebrate a simpler, less stressful Christmas—a theme which has become increasingly common since the 1950s.

The picture of the proper Christmas, a genuine festivity replete with tradition, has fluctuated over the years, but the idealization has created a yardstick by which one can measure one's own efforts, thus creating further opportunities for frustration and confrontation. Yet the mass media's standardization of the perfect Christmas easily conceals the fact that the celebration of Christmas in the twentieth century in Sweden has varied significantly.

## Christmas Generations

In the interviews about 'Christmases in my Life', this breadth of variation between different childhood milieux is seen clearly. On top of this, we have the constant adaptation of Christmas to the stages of the life cycle. Generation conflicts come out clearly in the material, as for example when the recently retired Kerstin looks back.

Kerstin's mother was the daughter of a small farmer who had been able to study to become a teacher and had married into a family of teachers. This change of class made it important for her mother to live in a way suited to her new urban surroundings and her new position in society; she had to celebrate a modern Christmas. It was as early as the 1920s that they bought that new-fangled Christmas commodity, the electric Christmas tree lights.

When Kerstin herself married, on the other hand, it was her mother-in-law's Christmas routines that dominated. 'In our home we had not cared so much about the traditions, but my mother-in-law had a set pattern which I was forced to follow.' Among other things, there were rigid rules about what food should be served on the different days of Christmas, and Kerstin remembers how her distaste for her mother-in-law's Christmas sausage grew into a symbol of resistance.

Kerstin and her husband also created their own Christmas traditions. They both loved all the preparations. Together they made straw wreaths, cut and pasted decorations, played Christmas songs all through December. But their two daughters did not share their enthusiasm for this busy tinkering. 'They thought we were a bit silly. They preferred to go to other families and share in their traditions.'

When the children moved away from home they decided to create their own traditions:

My eldest daughter was part of that wave of 1968. She rejected everything, and she and her husband didn't even come home for Christmas Eve. Christmas presents and all that sort of thing were silly. She wanted an alternative Christmas. So they fell into a pattern which they maybe would like to get out of now, but it's hard for them to go back to the old. They don't have a traditional Christmas in any sense. Cleaning and tidying, changing the bedclothes, and all that, they don't worry about that sort of thing.

Now that Kerstin is a widow, she celebrates Christmas with her other daughter:

I am almost obliged to go to my other daughter, who has three small children. They take it for granted that I'll come, otherwise it wouldn't be a proper Christmas if there was no one there as a spectator. Why, I'm even given presents. My daughter is very faithful to tradition, so Christmas presents must be bought—it's important. She hasn't got time to make any herself.

Christmas for Kerstin means many conflicts of interests. She would like to go to church on Christmas Eve, but this would clash with the Disney show on television: 'Without Donald Duck's Christmas it wouldn't be Christmas. You can't deprive them of that, but it's not enough for me. It's something American or secondary, isn't it?' It is the religious dimension that Kerstin misses in her youngest daughter's Christmas celebrations:

They have rejected that. My daughter wants to stick to the traditions. She changes the curtains, brings out candles, but she doesn't read anything to her children. Perhaps a book about Santa Claus or something like that, but nothing profound, genuinely felt, beautiful, or poetic. . . . I think it's a slightly *shallow* Christmas Eve.

Sometimes Kerstin longs for a completely different Christmas, and she toys with the idea of going away somewhere and doing something 'where Christmas didn't rule my life so much. . . . But if I was alone I would probably also get sentimental and feel sorry for myself. And what would the family say?'

When she looks back on her life and all her Christmases, her daughters stand for two different kinds of renunciation. One of them has completely rejected tradition, while the other is too bound by tradition in a way that Kerstin finds excessively mechanical and empty.

Kerstin's description has many parallels in the interviews. They show how different family traditions come together, are compared, and perhaps reconciled in a newly married couple, as well as how Christmas changes in form and meaning in different phases of life. There is an art teacher, for example, who remembers with a giggle how, as a child of 1968, she burnt Santa Claus on a bonfire on Christmas Eve, but now she goes to great pains to create a traditional Christmas atmosphere for her own children.

The interviews also tell us about the ever delicate question of where Christmas is to be celebrated and who actually belongs to the family. Swedish Christmas celebrations mean a reshuffling of the everyday social landscape. In 1988 a mass survey showed that 80 per cent of the Swedish people were at home on Christmas Eve, while 17 per cent spent the night with relatives. Yet Christmas at home was not a nuclear family occasion, since most homes (61 per cent) had six or more persons on Christmas Eve, and as many as 28 per cent celebrated Christmas in more than one place.

Behind these dry statistics there is a great deal of agony and vexed discussion. Christmas Eve has become the day when the Swedish bilateral kinship system is put to its hardest test. One of the reasons for this is not just the balancing act between the paternal and maternal side, the choice of mother or mother-in-law, but also the extra complications caused by divorce: where will the children celebrate Christmas this year?

Many families have been forced to develop highly complex visiting systems, to satisfy as far as possible not only the maternal and paternal grandparents but also their new common-law families. With whom will one spend the magic hours on Christmas Eve, and who will have to be content with a flying visit at lunch-time or a dinner on Boxing Day? Other solutions are to celebrate a double Christmas, or alternating Christmases, which is not unusual in families split by divorce.

Yet another source of conflict is the vague relation of authority between parents and children which is another central feature of today's Swedish culture. Christmas raises the burning question of how long children remain children. How long can parents expect their children to come home for Christmas Eve, and when does that delicate change of scene occur whereby parents become guests instead of hosts? Some people let their Christmas celebrations take on a form which can please their ageing parents, while elderly people sigh over having to create a Christmas which has to suit their children and perhaps primarily their grandchildren.

In all these delicate deliberations, Christmas can force people to make choices they would otherwise prefer to avoid, and which bind them to problematic relations that involve showing consideration or outright submission: 'Although we are grown up and married, we are turned into children once again when we come home to my parents.' Old loyalties and dependencies are reactivated at Christmas. A middle-aged woman remembers how, as long as her parents lived, she firmly insisted that they should have the Christmas they were used to. 'But when they died and I was able to do what I wanted, well, it turned out that I didn't want very much at all.'

## Christmas and Class

At seven o'clock on the morning of Christmas Eve, the nanny came in and lit the candles in a little Christmas tree which had been put in the children's room after they had gone to sleep the evening before. All the dolls, dressed in newly washed and ironed clothes, were lined around the tree. Now there were also miniature presents in the stockings which the children had hung up at the end of the bed the night before. At eight o'clock the family assembled for coffee in the dining room, sitting at a nicely laid table together with the specially dressed servants. Also in the dining room was the Christmas crib, with the stable, the wise men, and the animals in moss. There was also a candle lit for each child, and it was said that if you had not been good during the year, your candle would not be lit. This was a great source of worry for the children. At the table, Father then read aloud from the Christmas gospel.

This account of the start of Christmas celebrations in a proper bourgeois home around the time of the First World War reveals a pattern which is seen in many other childhood recollections from the same social milieu—and from later decades as well. Christmas was planned with great care and loving attention to detail. In a way, it was the same kind of almost excessively prepared festivity as we meet in 'Johan's Christmas'.

This classic bourgeois Christmas had a fixed, secure framework, where everyone and everything had a given place, from auntie's candlestick in the shape of a gnome to big sister's rendering of Christmas songs. The virtues that were communicated were restraint, control of one's impulses, thinking ahead, assigning priority to substantial and useful things, and maintaining a balance between the Spartan and the sumptuous—celebrating without self-indulgence. In this moral doctrine, many lessons were conveyed in tiny details: Johan, for instance, had to learn to write his own name on the Christmas presents in *small* letters.

Another central theme is about instilling good taste in the young. The children were allowed unbridled experiments with their own gaudy decorations and Christmas tree crackers in the nursery, but elsewhere there were set rules about how the house was to be decked.

If we turn to look at childhood memories from the other end of the social scale, we see a very different picture. There are recollections of how a Christmas atmosphere was created with small means, of scrubbing and sweeping, of the ceremonious march of the family into the parlour which was otherwise mostly cold and empty, unused despite the cramped conditions in which they lived. Yet many of the self-evident ingredients of today's Christmas were absent. There was not always a Christmas tree, or, as one working-class man born in 1915 puts it, 'Where could we have put it? In the larder?' A crofter's son born in 1893 recalls how as a boy he stole a tree from the estate land and procured a few gingerbread men and pigs to decorate it. 'That was all the Christmas I had. It was only when I came into what you might call civilized company that I learned what Christmas meant.'

Christmas presents were still unusual in many working-class homes in the interwar years. They could make a virtue of necessity, as in the family where the children each received a pair of galoshes as their only present every Christmas. Some people remember the fantastic Christmas Eve when they actually did receive a present, but they did not need to have great expectations. 'We didn't know of any other way to celebrate Christmas,' as several of them put it.

Unlike the bourgeois Christmas, where the children were the focus of the celebrations from an early stage, many working-class informants remember their childhood Christmases as strict and boring occasions. The grown-ups stayed in the parlour while the children had to sit in the kitchen waiting for their turn.

The memory of Christmas varies with the social perspective from which it is seen. In bourgeois settings there was great joy in their attempts to recreate the feeling of the 'proper Christmases' they had celebrated as children, often with very deliberate attempts to get the children to continue the tradition. What stands out sharply in their shimmering memories is the cosy and predictable. At the same time, they feel they are at a hopeless disadvantage: how can they possibly recreate the same elaborate Christmas machinery without the domestic help that was so self-evident for Johan's mother?

By contrast, those who remember Christmas in poverty can find it important to ensure that their own children have a different kind of Christmas from what they once had to be content with. The children must have a chance to escape the tyranny of the grown-ups and enjoy a Christmas 'where they want for nothing'. Yet even the new-found material abundance can be problematic. An electrician remembers the disappointment from all the Christmases when he got no presents, and he feels a stab of pain when he sees his grandchildren in a sea of presents: 'I would have been happy if I had been given a twentieth of all that!'

The picture of their own threadbare Christmases is a composite one. Bitterness can be mingled with pride: 'We had it tough, but we had to learn to get by—unlike today's spoiled generation.' A message like this can be crystallized in a moral detail in the reminiscences: how Daddy made a church out of a piece of white cardboard, or how overjoyed one could be at the sight of oranges on the dinner table.

In Sweden, the discourse on class is rather muted (cf. Löfgren 1986 and 1991*b*), but in the Christmas interviews it surfaces in many indirect ways: in aside comments on the holiday traditions of others, as well as in situations of direct confrontation. Interclass marriages give rise to one such fairly common type of cultural confrontation, where different family traditions have to be negotiated. In the interviews these conflicts may materialize in seemingly trivial details, which nevertheless carry a heavy symbolic load. A recurrent topic in narratives of class mobility or class confrontation is the middle-class indignation over the rushed or casual ways in which gifts are dished out by 'the others'. Traditional middle-class virtues demand that presents should be distributed in an orderly manner, unwrapped and admired slowly; the gift-tags should preferably bear little home-made rhymes.

In an autobiographic novel from the 1970s, the Swedish author Ulf Lundell has given a classic picture of such a confrontation, when the nice middle-class boy spends his first Christmas in the working-class home of his girlfriend. Food and drinks are consumed not only in vast quantities but also at an exuberant speed, while the telly is on, blaring out a Brazilian carnival show.

'Is it always like this?' I whispered to Helena out of the corner of my mouth.
'What do you mean?'
'So hurried.'
'It's for the children's sake, they want their Christmas presents.'
And sure enough, there the children were every five minutes, pulling at chairs, dragging their parents' arms, and as a last resort pulling the grown-ups' clothes and feet and whining, 'Isn't he coming soon, isn't he coming soon?'

Class experiences and class values are chiefly manifested in the interviews in the great need to judge, evaluate, and reject the way other people celebrate Christmas. It can be dismissed as slovenly, meagre, tawdry, and shallow, or described as stereotyped, obsessed with tradition, or claustrophobically over-organized—all depending on one's own social vantage-point. What some people see as a deplorable lack of Christmas discipline is for other people a refreshing freedom from demands.

Another arena of confrontation has to do with the touchy subject of Christmas aesthetics. There are fine, but important, distinctions to be drawn between the festive and the vulgar, between gastronomy and gluttony, between the dressed and the overdressed Christmas tree. A recurrent theme in middle-class narratives has to do with the constant threat of the invasion of an 'Americanized' Christmas, the ultimate vulgarity with blinking red, green, and yellow lights, plastic trees, canned Santa Polyester Snow, taped muzak carols, and 'Christmas Home Memories Fragrance Spray'.

The interesting paradox here is that Christmas aesthetics and rituals in the highly secularized Sweden emphasize the sacred and the restrained: only real candles, only matching colours and natural materials; in contrast, the much more religious Americans are stereotyped as staging a far too worldly Christmas: too loud and glittery, too commercial and synthetic.

### Great Expectations

As I have shown, the laments over lost values which were found in the American manual on 'how to put love and joy back into the season' are found in both mass media and personal life histories in the Swedish interviews, but it is too easy to ironize over one's own or other people's obsession with what a real Christmas should be. Behind the seeming trivialities there is often something highly serious. In the dreams of a perfect Christmas, tiny details take on great importance. Great effort can be expended on decorating the Christmas tree according to a recipe where everything has its given place, but this makes the tree more than just a decoration: it can be read as a piece of materialized family history, where the angel inherited from Aunt Hilda and the gnome made at nursery school by the now teenage daughter have their symbolic function in the whole.

People in the interviews tend to look back at what went right or wrong. A young woman remembers how her mother forgot to come in at night with the Christmas stocking to her children in their twenties: 'Oh dear, oh dear. We were devastated. It was a huge disappointment.' Others can speak of the tremendous joy they get from seeing how little routines and traditions are passed on by the children, while others feel great regret over the loss of ostensibly insignificant things. Different stage-managing dreams are confronted: who will be allowed to direct what kind of Christmas, and who will follow or sabotage the instructions? It is sometimes a matter of a covert power struggle—who is in control of Christmas and what various (and devious) forms may the guerrilla counter-strategies of the others take, such as refusals to follow the family script, getting drunk, or retreating to the television set.

Christmas for some people is an attempt to create a monument to a lost childhood. For some it is a manifestation of their own liberation, while others try to protect the family togetherness with the aid of a fence of interwoven traditions. We can observe how the lust for ritual has become a strong urge in Swedish family life during the twentieth century: the need to produce and reproduce micro-cultures of 'our own Christmas', which in turn sets the scene for confrontations and quarrels when different family traditions have to be reconciled by new couples.

My discussion has been about Christmas celebrations as a mirror of society—the scene on which society, the family, the generations perform. Right in the middle of all the busy preparations, the gluttony, and the gift-giving, definitions of gender, class, and generation as well as fundamental moral norms can become highly visible. That is how the traditions and routines of Christmas can be concentrations and manifestations of themes and conflicts in Swedish life. It is a holiday containing many contradictions.

One of these paradoxes is that the desire for 'a Christmas with tradition' leads to the intense creation of new traditions. Preservers and builders of traditions can clash within one and the same family.

Sometimes the mother-in-law is assigned the role of policing tradition, while at other times it is the 17-year-old who doggedly insists that not a single detail in the programme may be changed.

Another paradox is the great seriousness that surrounds this relaxed and playful holiday. Christmas celebrations abound with norms and taboos. It is particularly important to achieve something authentic, genuine, proper. For some people, a home-made article takes on a special magical power at Christmas. There is profound significance about having made a Christmas present yourself, about having picked the cowberry sprigs in the forest rather than buying them at the market, or at least making the wreath yourself. You may have to buy the gingerbread dough, but you must make the house yourself. These normative and moral stances also mean that we devote great energy to our relation to other people's celebrations. The concept of genuineness is not just a matter of what is home-made and saturated with tradition, but also of what constitutes a true Christmas spirit: some experiences are rich and full, while others seem superficial or empty.

Another contradiction is concealed in the dream of community—the desire to take care of one's own folks also produces a sense of alienation. Family togetherness brings out divisions, with the ranking of siblings, branches of the family, parents, and in-laws. Being together at Christmas makes loneliness stand out more clearly. The desire for a peaceful and restful Christmas also presupposes hard work on preparations, at a time which can force women to take on a third shift in addition to their job and the normal housework. Having worked so hard, it can be difficult for them to feel the right Christmas sensation in their bodies on the morning of Christmas Eve. The dream of the perfect Christmas also includes the dream of the perfect housekeeper, wife, and mother.

Christmas is sometimes depicted as a confrontation between spiritual and material values. From this point of view, development is interpreted in terms of commercialization and degeneration, but it is not as simple as this (cf. the discussions by Belk and Miller in this volume). While Christmas has become a spending spree without which the retail trade would find it difficult to survive, this celebration has also been transformed into a time of joyful creativity. People who rarely allow themselves the time to do handwork or to play with colours, forms, and aromas give themselves a chance to tinker, to decorate, to create, with an energy which can almost make the traditional peasant seem paralysed.

Nor is it as simple as saying that the material is displacing the spiritual. The point is rather that our emotional involvement in Christmas has become greater. In this light, it is hardly surprising that Christmas does not always turn out as we expected it to, that it cannot compare with the more or less mythical past or a dreamed ideal. We can expend great energy on trying to recreate a particular Christmas atmosphere, but it is difficult to automate or reproduce a mood even if one has the same props as the last time. The spontaneity and element of surprise that once engendered the sense of happiness is not so easily repeated.

Dreaming of a perfect Christmas or mourning the loss of the real Christmas is often organized in metaphors of 'full or empty', 'profound or shallow', 'authentic or artificial'. As in the American counselling manual, the aim is to produce 'richer', 'more fulfilling', or 'truer' experiences. This utopian goal ensures that Christmas never will be good enough. As a holiday it has incorporated the main restless credo of Western modernity: things can (or must) always be improved.

The tension between fulfilled and dissatisfied expectations in Swedish Christmas celebrations involves a balancing act which is repeated year after year, despite decades of wise advice not to take Christmas so solemnly, to relax one's demands and desires. It is precisely in this contradiction that much of our Christmas energy arises: the rapid shifts between longing and dissatisfaction, between joy and tedium.

## Note

My material is taken from a considerable number of interviews and answers to questionnaires collected by students and researchers in the Folklife Archives at the University of Lund, from the 1970s onwards, as well as information from magazines and advertisements from the 1920s onwards. For a more detailed presentation of the material see Löfgren (1991*a*). Special thanks for constructive comments from Billy Ehn and Jonas Frykman and to Alan Crozier for the translation.

## References

EMMERLING, MARY, and MEAD, CHRIS (1989). *American Country Christmas*. New York: Clarkson N. Potter.

LÖFGREN, ORVAR (1986). 'Deconstructing Swedishness: Culture and Class in Modern Sweden', in Anthony Jackson (ed.), *Anthropology at Home*, ASA Monographs 25. London: Tavistock: 74–93.

LÖFGREN, ORVAR (1991a). 'Drömmen om den perfekta julen: Det stora julgrälet och andra traditioner', in Jonas Frykman and Orvar Löfgren (eds.), *Svenska vanor och ovanor*. Stockholm: Natur och Kultur: 79–100.

—— (1991b). 'Learning to Remember and Learning to Forget: Class and Memory in Modern Sweden', in Birgitte Bönisch-Bredsnich *et al.* (eds.), *Erinnern und Vergessen: Vorträge des 27. Deutschen Volkskundekongresses Göttingen 1989*, Beiträge zur Volkskunde in Niedersachsen 5. Göttingen: University of Göttingen: 145–61.

ROBINSON, JO, and STAEHELI, JEAN (Coppock) (1991). *Unplug the Christmas Machine: A Complete Guide to Putting Love and Joy Back into the Season.* Rev. edn. New York: Quill, William Morrow.

# INDEX

*A Christmas Carol* 3, 20, 66–8, 85–9, 141, 160
Abbé de Liesse 46, 47
Abbot of Youth 47
Abrahams, R. 136, 146
advent calendar 218, 219–20
advent candle 218, 220
advertising 18, 22, 75–6, 83, 90, 93, 95, 106, 108–18, 122–3
alienation 63–4
All Saints' Eve 49
alternative reality 171–2
Americanization 18, 40–1, 78, 81–2, 230
angels 50
anthropology 5, 34, 40, 128, 146
apples and grapes 135, 143, 150
appropriation 62–3, 150
Augustus 16
authenticity 111, 124–5, 135–6, 232, 233

bacchanal 29, 76, 151
Bakhtin, M. 27, 29
Barnett, J. 3, 4, 18, 19, 86–7, 163, 164
Barrow 193–212
Basso, K. 206
Baum, F. 79
begging 44
Belk, R. 18, 19, 20, 21, 22, 31, 33, 70, 71, 78
Bergman, I. 223
blessing, Christmas 148
Bodenhorn, B. 17, 24, 30, 33
bourgeois Christmas 227–8
  *see also* middle class
Boxing Day 65, 140, 142, 170, 172, 199
Boy Abbott 65
Boy Bishop 65
Bradford 57
*bricoleur* 108–9
Buddhism 122
Bussey, J. 57

cake, Christmas 67, 120, 124
calypso, Christmas 151
Campbell, C. 130, 131

candles, Christmas 42, 227
capitalism 18, 20, 31, 56, 168
Caplow, T. 57–61, 78, 162, 164, 183
cards:
  charity 181–2
  Christmas 4, 24, 30–1, 32, 40, 87, 161, 165, 176–90
  motifs 178–82
carnival 9, 27–30, 31, 86, 136, 143, 151, 152, 164
carols, Christmas 23, 110, 121, 134, 149, 158, 161, 165
Carrier, J. 18, 19, 20, 21, 22, 31, 95, 150
Carter, E. 126
Catholic Church 14, 38–9, 50–1, 158
Chaguanas 138, 147
charity 94, 163, 168, 169
Cheal, D. 57, 167, 172
child-bishops 46
child-centred 186–7
children 14, 21, 34, 39, 43–6, 48–51, 57–8, 65, 78, 85, 135, 143, 157, 169, 183–8, 221–2, 228–30
chimneys 46, 48, 161
Christ 82–3, 157, 159, 166
Christianity 10–11, 12, 22–3, 25, 32, 62, 141, 148, 171, 182, 198
Christkind 111
Christmas Club 91
Christmas Eve 92, 106, 114, 118, 120–1, 138, 139–40, 141, 148, 157, 164, 166, 167, 184, 199, 220
church service 141, 159
Cinderella Christmas 108, 116–17
class 227–30
cleaning:
  Christmas 137–40, 220, 221
  New Year 126
Coca-Cola 75–6, 82
Cohen, A. 27
Colombia 20
commodities 19, 31, 56–7, 60, 62–3, 105, 116, 128, 150
community 194
Constantine 10, 16
consumption 18, 19, 22, 89, 105–29, 150–2

contradictions, Christmas 26–8, 49, 75, 231, 233
cosmology 29–33
Cratchit, Bob 20, 67, 87–8, 91
crib 13, 158, 227
Croquemitaine 44
cross-dressing 28, 47
culture concept 146
curtains 140, 142, 148–9

dating 17, 114–15, 122
dead 21, 45, 49–51, 84, 169
decorations, Christmas 95, 139, 142, 230
deferred gratification 184–6
department stores 40, 90–3, 105, 110–13, 118, 125
Deus Sol Invictus 9, 10, 14, 24, 25, 28
devil 21
Dickens, Charles 3, 4, 19, 20, 28, 66–8, 85–8, 152, 162, 168
Dies Natalis Invicti 9
diffusion 41
Dih worship 145
Dijon 38–9, 51
dinner, Christmas 106, 114, 157, 160, 166, 170, 172
　*see also* meal, Christmas
Dirks, R. 151
Disney, Walt 222, 335
Divali 137
domestic animals 179
domesticity 12, 20, 66, 142, 148–9
dominant ideology 110, 128
*douceur* 58–9
Douglas, M. 172
drinking, Christmas 28, 141, 151, 165, 208
drummers 202–3, 207
dualism 27–8
Durkheim, É. 29

Easter 164, 171
economy:
　Christmas 168, 172
　Japanese 124, 126–7
Emerson, R. W. 56
Epiphany 10, 166
Eskimo Dance 199, 201–4, 206, 207, 210
ethnicity, Christmas 144–6
Eurokitsch 112
evangelical churches 160, 161

evergreens 179
exchange 56, 58

family 6, 11–17, 21, 29–32, 33, 63–4, 70, 88, 95, 126, 140, 157–73, 178, 183–90, 194, 203, 208–9, 224–7, 232
　divine/holy 15, 29, 158, 159, 187
　nuclear 12, 13, 15, 30, 56–7, 187
　Roman 14, 16
　royal 15, 29, 158, 159
　West Indian 143
*Fanny and Alexander* 332
Father Christmas 38–51, 67, 165, 166, 183–4, 185, 186
　*see also* Santa Claus
Father Time 166
feasting 11, 20, 21, 27, 49, 67–8, 83, 199–201
films 4, 79–80, 92–3
folklore 4, 11, 22–3, 42
food 68, 112, 141, 200
　sharing 200
Frazer, Sir James 32, 51
funerary inscriptions 14
furniture 137–9

gambling 16
games 204–7, 209, 210
Germany 193–4
ghosts 49, 50
gift-giving 6, 19, 20, 21, 48–50, 88, 93–4, 105, 119, 122, 134–5, 138, 165, 183–90, 228–9
gifts 22, 24, 31, 44, 56–64, 70, 78, 82, 105, 118–19, 138, 168
　home-made 62–4, 125, 228–9
global festival 4–5, 22–6, 31, 150
Golby, J. 3
Goody, J. 13
Gospels 11–12, 23, 187, 227
grandparents 170
*Great Expectations* 169
greed 75, 81, 86, 93, 134
Greenland 43

Hallowe'en 21, 49
Halsberghe, G. 9, 10
ham 143
Hannukah 159
hedonism 82–5, 116, 134
Hinduism 24, 137, 145
historians 5, 35

holiday 68, 76, 158, 163, 171, 174
holly 42, 44, 135
Holy Innocents Day 46
Holy Night 110, 113, 120, 124
    *see also* Christmas Eve
home 20, 21, 29, 56, 142, 147–9, 174,
    185, 221, 226
Horace 46
hospitality 20
hunting 195–6

inalienable objects 56
inheritance 14, 34
initiation rites 44–5
Iñupiat 5, 17, 24, 30, 33
inversion 15, 16, 17, 27, 28, 65, 86, 164
Islam 24, 137
ivy 4, 42, 44

Japan 5, 17, 22, 24, 26, 29, 31, 82,
    105–32
Jews 159
*Johan's Christmas* 219–20, 227, 228, 229
Judaism 12
Julebok (demon) 46

Kalends 8, 16, 26, 28
*Katchina* 44, 45, 46
Keens-Douglas, P. 138–9, 141, 146
kinship 13, 14
kitsch 108–13, 118, 128
Kuper, A. 14, 15, 19, 26

laughter 27
lavishness 8, 9, 20, 21, 27
Leach, E. 164, 210
Lenin, V. I. 24
Lévi-Strauss, C. 7, 15, 21, 31, 32, 60,
    151, 169, 209–10
Libanius 7, 9, 12, 18, 20
lights, Christmas 32, 125, 165, 193,
    224
Littré, E. 42
Löfgren, O. 15, 17, 21, 22, 25, 33
London 193
Lord of Misrule 32, 46, 48, 65
Lucia celebrations 218, 220
Luther, Martin 77

McGreevy, P. 89
Malinowski, B. 77
Manchester 177
market analysis 127–8

materialism 6, 9, 18–22, 31, 33, 56,
    62–4, 70, 76–96, 134–52
Mauss, M. 55–6, 168, 196
meal, Christmas 28, 140, 142, 146
men 139, 141, 171
Mexico 60
microcosm 29–32, 33–4
middle class 19, 33, 160
Middletown 57–61, 162
midnight mass 148, 159, 182
Miles, C. 7–8, 9, 23, 27
Miller, D. 19, 21, 211
missionaries 195–8
mistletoe 4, 41, 44, 68, 160
Mithra 10, 25
modernity 22, 25–6, 33–4, 82
Moeran, B., and Skov, L. 17, 22, 24,
    26, 29, 33
money 59, 86, 90, 94, 185
moral economy 167, 168, 172, 217–19
myth 43, 45

Naipaul, V. S. 144, 152
Nast, T. 79, 83
Nativity 38, 47, 49, 179, 199
New Year 6, 9, 26, 50, 89, 121, 122,
    126–7, 166, 218
New Year's Dance 207–8
New Year's Eve (Old Year's Night) 26,
    136, 140, 166
New York 66
North Pole 78
nostalgia 3, 15, 26, 28, 87, 125, 134,
    143, 161, 221, 223

office party 58, 165
orphans 87

paganization 38
pagans 8, 9, 51
pantomime 28, 174
Parang 144
Paris 42
Parry, J. 64–5
party, Christmas 141, 157, 174, 182,
    193, 218
penguins 180
Père Fouettard 44
photographs, Christmas 60
*Pickwick Papers* 160
Pimlott, J. 19, 75, 89, 159, 161, 162
pine 42, 44
play 206

politicians 166
popular culture 11, 22, 24, 27, 28, 146
preparations, Christmas 119
Protestant Church 38, 78, 158–9
pudding, Christmas 150
Pueblo Indians 45, 46
Puritans 3, 65, 68, 76, 89

quarrelling, Christmas 16, 146, 189,
    218, 219
Queen's speech 158

Rabelais, François 27, 32
radio 222
radio phone-in 138
reciprocity 57
Reinach, S. 50–1
reindeer 18, 43, 79–81
relatives 57
respectability 136
Réveillon 48, 49
ritual 4, 6, 14, 21, 22, 32–3, 40, 44–9,
    70, 163, 166, 169–70, 182–3, 186,
    194, 209–10, 220, 231
ritual time 164–70
robins 179
Romans 7, 8, 10, 12, 14, 16, 20, 24, 25,
    27, 32–4
romantic love 114–15, 120, 122
Royal Ontario Museum 75–6

St Francis of Assisi 13
St Nicholas 42, 46, 48, 49, 66, 77
St Nicholas's Eve 45, 79
St Sylvester 48
St Valentine's Day 131, 176
sales, Christmas 62, 138
Salvation Army 40
Samaritans 190
Santa Claus 4, 20, 21, 23, 42, 46, 66,
    76–85, 89, 91, 105, 116, 124–5,
    161, 168, 218, 226
    letter to 85, 135, 176
    *see also* Father Christmas
Saturn 46
Saturnalia 8, 9, 11, 16, 26, 28, 29, 33,
    42, 46, 47, 51, 151
savings, Christmas 138
schools 77, 187
Scrooge 20, 67, 86–9, 134, 146, 160,
    168–9
SCROOGE 95–6
Scullard, H. 8–9

Searle-Chatterjee, M. 14, 15, 22, 30,
    33
sentimentality 14, 28, 33, 146
shamans 197–8
sheaf, Christmas 222, 223
Shinto 122, 126
shopping 21, 61–4, 71, 89–93, 95, 105,
    119, 134, 136, 147–50, 165
shopping mall 91, 93, 95, 136, 147,
    149
Sikhs 159
*Silent Night* 106
Simmel, G. 21
*Sketches by Boz* 170
slaves 16–17, 28, 47
snowmen 135
sociology 128
solstice 10
souls 45
Soviet Christmas 24
'Spanish' 144–6
spirit of Christmas 19, 29, 152
stockings, Christmas 4, 46, 83, 121,
    161, 174, 184, 185, 231
structure of Christmas 26–9
suicide 26
Sundblom, H. 76
sweaters 125
syncretism 4, 11, 22–5, 28, 32, 42

Tanabata festival 112
Taoism 122
television 94–5, 193, 220, 222–3
temporality, Christmas 25
Thanksgiving 69, 71, 159, 165
thrift 9, 20, 21, 32
Tiffany jewellery 118
Times Square 48
toys 48, 50, 81, 138
traditions:
    American 3, 4, 18, 21, 22, 31, 44,
        56–70, 75–96
    Austrian 110–12
    British/English 3, 4, 14, 15, 26, 28,
        42, 44, 46, 66, 67, 157–73, 177–90
    Danish 43
    Dutch 4, 66
    French 38–51
    German 4, 42, 66, 158, 193–4
    Iñupiaq 193–212
    Italian 12–13, 14
    Japanese 105–32
    Scandinavian 49–50

Scottish 47, 48
Swedish 22, 25, 217–33
Swiss 208
Trinidadian 134–52
West Indian 28
tree, Christmas 24, 40, 42, 66, 68, 111, 125, 160, 165, 174, 184, 186, 230
trend-setters 124–8
Trinidad 20, 24, 25, 28, 31, 134–52
tropical snowscapes 135, 150
turkey 158, 160, 170, 174
Twelfth Night 164
twin peaks 6, 26

upper class 160

Van Gennep, A. 164
Victorians 4

Virgin Mary 13, 23
visiting, Christmas 140–2

Warner, M. 13
Weightman, G., and Humphries, S. 4
Winnipeg 57
winter 24, 43, 179
witch 165
Wolf, E. 168
women 43, 60, 116, 139, 141, 171, 190
work 56, 167
working class 15, 33, 160, 228–9
wrapping 60–1, 90, 118, 184–5
wrapping paper, Christmas 40, 41

youth culture 115
yule log 42